Congress Politics in Bengal
1919–1939

Srilata Chatterjee

Congress Politics in Bengal
1919–1939

Srilata Chatterjee

Anthem Press
London

Anthem Press is an imprint of
Wimbledon Publishing Company
PO Box 9779, London SW19 7QA
This edition first published by Wimbledon
Publishing Company 2002

British Library Cataloguing in Publication Data
Data available
Library of Congress in Publication Data
A catalogue record has been applied for

ISBN Hb 1 84331 063 5
Pb 1 84331 035 X

1 3 5 7 9 10 8 6 4 2

Typeset by Mudra Typesetters — Pondicherry, India.

Acknowledgements

This book is an extended and revised version of my doctoral thesis submitted to the University of Calcutta. In the course of my research, encouragement and assistance from my teachers, friends and family helped me to carry on and complete this work. I take this opportunity to acknowledge my debts of gratitude.

I am deeply indebted to my research supervisor Dr. Suranjan Das for his inspiring help with this work in its every stage. He guided me to focus on this specific themes and at the same time inculcated the spirit of historical research upon me. Dr. Arun Dasgupta and Dr. Suprakash Sanyal provided help at the formative stage in my research. I am grateful to Dr. Binay Chaudhuri and Professor Tripti Chaudhuri for their encouragement and advice. I have been enriched by the critical comments and suggestions by Dr. Amalendu Dey, Professor Bhaskar Chakravarti. I thank Dr. Ranjit Roy, Dr. Sujata Mukherjee, Dr. Himadri Banerjee for motivating me. Stimulating discussions with friends have enriched my knowledge and cleared my understanding of the subject. I am grateful especially to Sanjukta Dasgupta and Rajsekhar Basu for not only their comments and suggestions but also for their sustained moral support. I acknowledge my indebtedness to my colleague Dr. Pradeep Ranjan Sengupta for helping me with the translations of the Bengali texts, to professor Suchitra Chakrabarti and my colleagues at the Behala College Kolkata. I deeply appreciate the help rendered by Tias Bagchi and Kanchan Chakrabarti with the computer and printing of the thesis. Lastly I must also thank Dr. Falguni Chakrabarty a close friend for his multifarious help and suggestions during the final stages of this work.

Thanks are also due to the staff of the various Libraries- West Bengal State Archives, National Archives Delhi, The National Library, Nehru Memorial Museum and Library, University of Calcutta History

Department Seminar Library, The Secretariat Library Kolkata, West Bengal Legislative Council Library, Intelligence Branch Record Room, Kolkata.

I am also grateful to M/S Bharabi of Kolkata for kindly permitting me to quote a poem of Jibananda Das.

I am also grateful to the University Grants Commission for the award of Junior and Senior Research Fellowships, which enabled me to carry on with this research work.

Anthem Press has honoured me in a big way by agreeing to publish this work. I am extremely grateful to Kamaljit Sood, Caroline Broughton and Isobel Rorison of the Anthem Press for their support towards the editing and production of the book. I also must convey my thanks to Dr. Crispin Bates for taking such interest in my work and encouraging me to publish it.

My family and friends have always encouraged and supported me in every possible way. My parents both of whom did not live to see the completion of this work had encouraged me to study History and go in for research. My mother-in-law had always insisted that I should continue with my research and took good care of my children so that domestic chores would not hamper my work. My deepest gratitude is to my husband Partha without whose constant support, it would not have been possible for me to complete this work. My children Lagnajita and Somak had also been very cooperative bearing up cheerfully with all kinds of discomfort that they had to face due to my academic preoccupation.

List of Abbreviations

AICC	All India Congress Committee
ABSA	All Bengal Students Association
ABYA	All Bengal Youngman's Association
BCDC	Bengal Civil Disobedience Committee
BPCC	Bengal Provincial Congress Committee
BPSA	Bengal Provincial Students Association
BLCP	Bengal Legislative Council Proceedings
CDM	Civil Disobedience Movement
CONF	Confidential
CPI	Communist Party Of India
CWC	Congress Working Committee
DCC	District Congress Committees
DPI	Director Of Public Instruction
GOB	Government Of Bengal
IB	Intelligence Branch
KPP	Krishak Praja Party
ML	Muslim League
MLC	Member Of the Legislative Council
NCM	Non-Cooperation Movement
PCC	Provincial Congress Committee
POLL	Political
RNP	Report On Native Newspapers
TCDC	Tamluk Civil Disobedience Committee
TSF	Tilak Swaraj Fund

Contents

Introduction

It is generally believed that 'associations brought nineteenth century India across the threshold of modern politics'.[1] The foundation of the Indian National Congress in 1885 was a landmark in the history of associations. Since then the complexities of modern politics have shaped its creed, character and composition both at central and local level.

Until the First World War the nationalist Congress confronted imperialism using techniques ranging from the policy of petitioning favoured by the Moderates to the passive resistance of the Extremists. By the end of the war however, nationalist politics began to reach sections of the populace who had earlier remained outside it. Their potential as active participants in modern politics could not be ignored. A point had been reached where institutional politics could not remain oblivious of the politics of the people. This set the trend for nationalist politics in future years as the two streams interacted, each moulding the other.

This work attempts to identify the links between institutional politics and the politics of the people, exploring its impact on both groups and also on the course of the nationalist movement, especially during the period of Gandhian nationalism. Rather than concentrate on the history of a locality at a specific time when the nationalist struggle was at its height, this study has tried to establish a link between micro and macro studies over a period of 20 years in order to broaden the perspective of nationalist politics. Departing from the conventional historiography, which tends to emphasize either elite leadership or subaltern autonomy, this work seeks primarily to present a viable alternative model of interaction between elite politics and popular politics in Bengal against the backdrop of major developments in nationalist politics between 1919 and 1939.[2]

The years between the two World Wars saw nationalist agitation expand its social base and develop a pattern characteristically different from the earlier period. When Gandhi entered the political arena and began his experiment with mass *satyagraha* from 1919, the mood of political activism changed. The wave of Gandhian Nationalism also reached Bengal and left its mark on the nationalist movement in this part of the subcontinent. Between 1919 and 1939 the involvement of the masses changed the dynamics of the Congress-led nationalist agitation in Bengal. The major shifts in the nationalist struggle during this period foreshadowed the developments in the following decades, which culminated in India's independence in 1947.

II

Cradled between the Bay of Bengal in the South and the Himalayas in the North, Bengal lay in the Eastern periphery of the subcontinent. To its colonial masters it was known as the Bengal Presidency – the commercial, political and financial epicentre of the Empire. The vastness of the Bengal Presidency had always been a cause of concern for British administrators. For administrative convenience, it was arranged into five Divisions comprising the districts which lay within the Divisional boundaries. The Presidency Division was comprised of the districts of 24 Parganas, Nadia, Murshidabad, Jessore and Khulna; the Burdwan Division was made up of Burdwan, Birbhum, Bankura, Midnapur, Hooghly and Howrah; the Dacca Division consisted of Dacca, Mymensingh, Faridpur and Bakarganj; the Chittagong Division was carved out of the districts of Chittagong, Tippera and Noakhali and finally the Rajshahi Division was formed from the districts of Rajshahi, Dinajpur, Jalpaiguri, Rangpur, Bogra, Pabna and Malda. This 'administratively unwieldy province' was the homeland of the Bengalis whose attachment to the province went beyond the comprehension of any administrator's statistical analysis. This was their own land; the most beautiful, the most familiar, the most peaceful and soothing in all the world. It was this *Swadesh* that they were fighting for, and which their leader dreamed of freeing from all crises:

The evening breeze blows through the peepul in the emerald woods of Bengal.
Alone do I loiter among fields; the crisis in Bengal is
As if over; behold the countless Banyan trees – century old –

With verdurous leaves and scarlet fruits on the breasts,
Jingling their branches in wistful songs. Are the peepuls in passion
   too?
The cold corpse of Sati on the lap, for days; he has
Found the simple tale of Uma's love. His matted hair like Shiva's
Is brightened on the seventh lunar day.
On the grassy bank of the sweet Dhaleswari, in Gaurh
No Ballal Sen will ever return; nor will
Raygunakar arrive; Deshbandhu has arrived in the torrential Padma.
Among the fatigued riverine yellow beaked black birds,
Along the eddy, Chandidas has come and Ramprasad too, with his
   Shyama,
Sankhyamalas and Chandramalas; jingling bangles of adolescent girls,
   dead.[3]

III

During its early years, the Indian National Congress functioned mainly
as an annual gathering of the politically conscious elite, and it professed to be 'the most visible outcome of that revolution in the political
life of the Indians, which was slowly transforming their thoughts and
intellects for the last 28 years and which had evoked the nationalist
spirit'.[4] Although its supporters might, in moments of euphoria, have
seen it as India's national party, the early Congress functioned as a
party without a permanent organizational structure.[5]
   The early Congress in Bengal had no separate organized identity.
Leaders of the local associations attended the sessions as Congress delegates. In 1887, Bengali delegates to the Madras session of the Congress
expressed a strong opinion that a provincial conference should be held
every year for the discussion of provincial questions which could not
be covered by the National Congress. This desire bore fruit when provincial delegates convened at the hall of the British Indian Association
during the *Dasserah* vacations in 1888. It was the first of the annual
meetings of the Bengali Congress workers, the Bengal Provincial Conference. The first President of the Bengal Provincial Conference was
Mahendra Lal Sarkar. Within a few years it was felt that periodic conferences in different districts would be more conducive to the dissemination of the political ideas current in Bengal. Accordingly, Rai
Baikuntha Nath Sen Bahadur arranged the first peripatetic conference,

which met in Beharampore in 1895. The Conference continued to be an autonomous institution until the Congress was reorganized after the inauguration of the non-cooperation movement. Its management was then handed over to the provincial Congress committee.[6]

In Bengal the Indian Association had established links with the countryside in the pre-Congress era. After its merger with the Congress in the Calcutta Session of 1886, the Indian Association functioned as a representative of the Congress in Bengal. In 1887 the Indian Association had branches all over Bengal, nearly half of which were village unions, especially in the districts of Pabna and Midnapur. In rural Bengal the Association had sought to create a base among the educated gentry and the occupancy *rayats*. But once the Congress came into being, it stopped the association from frittering away its energies on local issues.

On the other hand, the Congress developed its own base for local political activity, using a number of local political bodies to maintain its provincial links. The district bar associations were highly politicized bodies that often played crucial part in selecting the issues and techniques of agitation. Educational institutions, *Mofussil* newspapers, printing presses, libraries, literary societies and athletic clubs were all semi-political groups. The district associations, people's associations in the subdivisions and municipal rate-payers' association had political objectives, as did municipalities and local and district boards which were the constituent parts of the Bengal Legislative Council.[7] The Congress, represented by the Indian Association, maintained links with all these local bodies, ensuring its monopolistic hold over 'the Congress identity in the province'.[8] Thus in Bengal the politics of nationalism never really lost touch with the hinterland. From the outset these local bases of independent political activity were important levers in the organization of institutional politics. Even in the period dealt with in this book, these centres of politics played a major role in forging links between the Congress and its support base among the masses.

White racial and economic domination had provoked a sharp reaction to British rule among the educated Bengalis, which in turn was reflected in their political activities. From the beginning of the twentieth century, the Bengal Congress leadership resorted to more radical methods of agitation. To the Bengal Extremists, the concept of passive resistance seemed the most comprehensive and forceful. They intended a dual attack on imperialism through their multifaceted mechanism of passive resistance. As well as crippling the British economy through boycott, the Extremists also wanted to eradicate the illusion and euphoria which surrounded the power and mightiness of the British rule. This boycott did not just involve non-consumption of British goods but 'embraced in its purview the whole field of government. It would make administration under the present condition impossible by an organized refusal to do anything which shall help either British commerce in the exploitation of the country or British officialdom in the administration of it'.[9] In their programme of agitation the Extremists had not really excluded the wide mass of the people; 'in this boycott and by this boycott we propose to create in the people consciousness of the *parraj* on one hand and the desire for *Swaraj* on the other'.[10] In *New Lamps For Old*, Aurobindo also regretted the absence of close cooperation between the rich and the poor and talked of revolution from below. But the academic objectivity of the Extremist leaders did not coincide with an appeal for widespread mass uprisings. The *Swadeshi* movement remained confined to Bengal and did not evoke any response from the Congress.

The Bengal Congress was constantly affected by ideological debates among its leaders. They not only aligned themselves either with the Moderates or the Extremists, the two major groups in the Congress, but were organized into further complex groupings centering around personalities. Major players among the Moderates included Surendra Nath Banerjee, N N Ghosh of the *Indian Mirror*, Asutosh Chaudhuri of the Bengal Landholders' Association and Rash Behari Ghosh of the National Council of Education. In the Extremist camp Bipin Chandra Pal and Aurobindo each had his own followers. In Barisal the *Swadeshi* leader Aswini Kumar Dutta had his own group. The bone of contention among all these leaders was the control of the provincial Congress. In spite of their differences they had a sentimental attachment to Bengal, the land of their birth. This shared sense of identity produced a strong alliance between the Bengali leaders against the other dominant regions represented in the Congress. In the Calcutta session of the Congress in 1906 'there came into existence an implicit understanding between the Moderates and the Extremists of Calcutta to push the political demands of Bengal against the conservative Congress high command'. Satyananda Bose had informed Gokhale that '...Bengal is very keen about *Swadeshi*, boycott, partition and national education. The feeling is not confined to the Extremists but is shared by the Moderates also.'[11] In spite of the opposition of Mehta's Bombay clique, four important resolutions were passed by the Calcutta Congress in favour of *Swadeshi*, boycott, national education and *Swaraj*.

Evidently, Bengali politics was not free of friction, but its leaders never allowed this to interfere with questions of national interest. Even after the 1907 incident at Surat, Bengali leaders from both camps met under the presidency of no less a person than Rabindra Nath Tagore in the Bengal Provincial Conference at Pabna and passed a resolution demanding the resummoning of the Congress based on the Calcutta resolutions.

Efforts to reunite the Congress were initiated by the Bengal leaders once again after the outbreak of the First World War. At the momentous Lucknow session of the Congress in 1916 the Extremists returned to their old anchorage in politics. The Banerjee group coalesced with the Extremists and threatened a 'raging and tearing scheme of agitation in connection with our demand for self-government'.[12] These years also saw the initiation into politics of younger men whose new ideas and vigour were to turn the tide of nationalist politics. In the Bengal Provincial Conference of 1917 Banerjee himself proposed that Chitta Ranjan Das should chair the session of the Conference. In the process he paved the way for C R Das to re-enter politics and redefine extremism. Das raised crucial questions in his presidential speech and opened a new vista in the nationalist movement. 'We boast of being educated; but how many are we? What room do we occupy in the country? What is our relation to the vast masses of our countrymen? Do they think our thoughts or speak our speech?'[13] Through his speech he reminded the educated, the wealthy and the high caste that the 'flesh, blood and backbone of the land', the vast mass of the countrymen must not be left out of their endeavours.[14] C R Das also talked of the socio-economic problems of the peasants and the need to restructure the villages so as to provide them with the basic amenities of life. For the first time, an attempt was made to critically evaluate the politics of the elite, who tended to assume that their mode of politics was acceptable to all. Thus by 1917 the elite politicians began to feel the strain of isolation from the general populace and sought to radically restructure the Congress organization.

Bengal had a long tradition of popular protest which pre-dated the politics of associations. Although the Bengali peasants had not taken a directly anti-British stance or posed a threat to British rule between 1858 and 1914, they were still regarded with fear by the colonial government. In nineteenth century Bengal, the chief targets of peasant anger were the European planters and the indigenous landlords.[15] The Congress had always adopted a very cautious attitude as far as the peasant question was concerned. Although individual congressmen had shown concern (for example, Aswini Kumar Dutta in Barisal had spoken for the peasants, as had Surendra Nath Banerjee and Krishna Kumar Mitra for tea-garden labourers), the Congress as an institution had underplayed the question of peasant–landlord relations. In the 1893 and 1894 sessions of the Congress, there were strong attacks on the Bengal government's attempts to ameliorate peasants' rights. Until the First World War there was no attempt to discuss rural issues. Problems such as land redistribution, the causes of rural poverty and debt were attributed to high land-tax demand and the drain of wealth from India. But a radical change was noticed in the 1920s when both the peasant and the working class became important constituent parts of nationalist politics.

Educated professionals had always been a 'great driving force behind the nationalist activities in Bengal'.[16] The *Swadeshi* movement, it has been argued, 'depicted a united Hindu upper caste *bhadralok* agitation; doctors, lawyers, students, journalists, teachers who often had a link with the *rentier* interests in land in the form of *zamindari* or intermediate tenure-holding'.[17] During this period the ideal of mass struggle against foreign rule gained renewed momentum through new organizations such as the *samitis* and national volunteers, although it failed to close the gap between the *bhadralok* and the masses. The *Swadeshi* movement also failed to deal adequately with the Hindu–Muslim question. Notwithstanding these weaknesses, the *Swadeshi* movement had created a base for launching the Gandhian movement in Bengal. The new techniques of mass contact and the novel forms of organization of the *Swadeshi* era were reconstructed in the movement of the 1920s. The press and the platform, which had emerged as effective mediums for spreading a new creed of radical nationalism, continued to be important in the years to come. Other techniques more indigenous in form and character were also adopted to establish contact with the masses. For the upper caste Hindu professionals, the *Swadeshi* movement had already created an experience in mass agitation, with techniques that were to be the main weapons of Gandhian non-cooperation.

IV

Concentrating on the progress of the nationalist struggle in Bengal, this work seeks to examine the nature of the interaction that existed between Congress, representing mainstream political nationalism, and popular social groups and their unorganized politics, emphasizing the impact that this interplay had on the organization of the Congress. An attempt has been made to address the question of how far the provincial Congress was able to orient itself to the aspirations of the people as it transformed itself from a loose organization to a fully-fledged political party.

At the outset the book makes an overall survey of the political, social and economic conditions in Bengal at the dawn of the non-cooperation movement. The leadership in the Bengal Provincial Congress Committee was split into the Home Rule agitators comprising C R Das, Motilal Ghosh, Bipin Pal, Fazlul Huq, Byomkesh Chakrabarti and the hard-core Moderate Surendra Nath Banerjee. Despite their ideological and methodological differences, both sides were perturbed by two major issues – the 1919 Reforms and the control over the Congress in Bengal. As for the domination over the Congress, Das, Byomkesh Chakravarti and Fazlul Huq were trying persistently to control the Indian Association and through it the Bengal Provincial Congress Committee.

In an atmosphere of general political stagnation, Gandhi began his experiments with mass agitation on issues that affected the entire nation. The *satyagraha* against the Rowlatt Act inspired the new generation with something more than just the politics of petitions. At this stage, with the exception of the revolutionaries, most of the politically-minded intelligentsia of Bengal looked upon Gandhi with a degree of tolerance. They acknowledged his leadership in the *satyagraha* and the fact that he possessed a very wide influence over the masses. But he was still 'a nonpolitical leader...who had attained his position of influence through his skillful and persistent championship of the South African Indians'.[18]

Even in Calcutta the general populace remained quite apprehensive about the observance of the 1919 *satyagraha*. They had been asked to observe the Black Sunday (6 April) by fasting. Newspapers, placards handbills and notices had made them aware of the issues behind the *satyagraha*, and its conditions of peace and non-violence. In the districts the response was minimal, with the exception of Dacca where meetings were attended by large audiences that even included the Muslims. But the news of Gandhi's arrest sparked off open violence in the Northern part of Calcutta. It also led to a temporary fraternization of the *Marwaris* and the Muslims of the city.

The *Khilafat* agitation had an important impact on Bengal as the majority of the Presidency's population was Muslim peasantry. They became a willing audience for the new leadership that had emerged among the Bengali Muslims. There was considerable feeling among Muslims regarding the fate of the Caliphate. In the urban centres especially, where the Muslims were influenced by up-country Muslims of UP and Bihar, the government was fearing trouble. While the 'political nation' was simmering with expectations and apprehension, the political leadership was suffering from indecision as to the proposal of non-cooperation. Debates and discussions continued until the Nagpur Session of 1920 resolved the issue in favour of the proposal.

The second chapter highlights the new organizational structure of the Bengal Congress that was built up in the context of the non-cooperation *Khilafat* agitation. This agitation coincided with the organizational changes in the Congress. At national level, a new constitution of the Congress proposed the establishment of a working committee of 15 members, which was to function as a permanent Congress executive.[19] From a loose federation of 200 members, the Congress sought to transform itself into an organized institution. The main object of the organizational machinery developed by the new constitution was to mobilize and control a greater number and range of Indians for political activity. The Bengal Provincial Congress Committee represented the Indian National Congress in the province of Bengal and Surma Valley. The district committees were to carry out the work of the Congress in accordance with rules and instructions framed by the Bengal Provincial Congress Committee.[20] Financially too the Congress was in a much stronger position than in the pre-war years.

The revitalization of the Congress organization in Bengal during the 1920s was facilitated by several factors. Emergence of a new generation of leadership to provide excellent guidance, both at the provincial and district level, was of extreme importance. Organizational support for the non-cooperation movement came from both within and outside the Congress. Volunteer organizations, national educational institutions, Gandhian *Ashrams* and other independent non-educational institutions provided structural support to the movement, acting as centres from which the Congress workers directed their activities. The third chapter is specifically concerned with the involvement of the reorganized Bengal Congress with the non-cooperation *Khilafat* movement. The intensity of the popular upsurge that swept the country in 1921 has often been explained in the context of the economic hardships of the post-war years. Without denying the importance of the economic factor, this monograph also highlights the role played by ideology and consistent vigorous propaganda to draw the discontented masses into open and extended political action against an alien rule. Mass meetings and demonstrations by the leaders proved to be the most effective method of rallying the people – especially the students, labourers and peasants – around the non-cooperation *Khilafat* cause, a movement which saw the participation of various social and occupational groups. This study reveals the constant interaction between radical militarism of the non-institutional movements and organized nationalist opposition to imperialism.

This interplay, which began during the non-cooperation movement, continued on a different scale in the post non-cooperation period as shown in the fourth chapter. After the initial confusion the non-cooperators began to reconstruct a programme on lines that would appeal to the popular imagination. While Gandhi advocated constructive social work, Nehru and Das were in favour of contesting the elections. In the Chittagong Conference of 1922, Chitta Ranjan introduced the concept of obstruction and non-cooperation from within the council. In most of the Bengali districts, organizational reconstruction and constructive social work continued simultaneously as the *Swarajists* dominated Bengali politics.

Disagreement within the Congress was seen as much during Das's lifetime as afterwards. The only difference was that after Chitta Ranjan's death his followers, devoid of leadership, fell prey to clique conflict among themselves. Obviously, this had a negative impact on the Congress organization in Bengal. But whether it stalled the flow of mass mobilization remains to be answered. This book also shows how at various levels, nationalist-minded people took the initiative to organize themselves, both in alliance with the local Congress committee and independently. The network of *Ashrama* and *Sanghas* set up by the revolutionaries to consolidate their scattered organization also sustained the Congress movement. At the same time constructive non-cooperation threw up institutions which were to develop self-reliance through service to the motherland. As events turned out, organizations for constructive programmes and revolutionary organizations merged with the Congress in Bengal. The province was not lacking in political energy. On the other hand, despite factionalism, the Congress had not yet become a redundant element in the nationalist politics of Bengal.

Chapter Five of this book recaptures the Bengal Congress in the context of the civil disobedience movement. The civil disobedience movement brought to light various trends prevailing within the Congress. Unfortunately the movement in Bengal was unable to draw together the divided elements of the Congress leadership. As a result it lacked cohesion and direction, although popular participation was not lacking.

Chapter Six is concerned with the Bengal Congress in the post civil disobedience period. As the civil disobedience movement began to slow down, it became evident that the Congress would have to reorient its programme to ensure that it did not lose its contact with the masses. Mass agitation was called off by Gandhi on 8 May 1933 but individual civil disobedience was retained. Meanwhile, the 1935 Government Of India Act introduced provincial autonomy, which was to come into full force from 1 April 1937. The provisions of the act on franchise particularly enhanced the importance of the rural rich. Moreover, with the announcement of the Communal Award and the distribution of seats in the Legislative Assembly and the Council, the Muslims as a community had already become a major force to be reckoned with in Bengal politics. This work makes an assessment of the 1936 elections and their aftermath with respect to Bengal politics. In the seven provinces where the Congress had accepted ministerial responsibilities it had scope to prove itself as a party of the people and thereby build its political hegemony. In comparison, Bengal restricted the constitutional activities of the Congress. However, as an opposition in the Legislature the Party's credibility was established.

This was also the period when one notes a realignment of political forces within the Bengal Congress. The Socialists were gaining in importance and their influence was responsible for the organization of mass meetings and rallies of workers and peasants. Throughout these years a distinct trend towards *Krishak Praja* and Congress alliance was noticeable, especially in Tippera. With the communal situation becoming more and more complex and the constitutionalists among the Congress becoming engaged in political games within the legislature in Bengal, it was the left within the Congress who were primarily engaged in maintaining links with the people, although differing radically with the political programme of the Congress. Elite politics thus continually interacted with the politics of the people, enriching the forces of nationalism.

The conclusion sums up the main findings; that the nationalist movement actually saw the intermingling of institutional politics, as represented by the Congress, and the politics of the masses. This interplay took place both at the times when there were struggles with clearly defined anti-imperialist aims and when the movement deviated into the constitutional course.

The research has been based on manuscript sources, printed sources, secondary literature and oral interviews collected in India. The manuscript sources include All India Congress Committee papers, Bengal Provincial Congress Committee papers, private papers, home political confidential papers of the government of Bengal and intelligence branch reports. The printed sources include official reports like district gazetteers, settlement reports, official reports from native newspapers and non-official reports such as newspapers and legislative council proceedings. The secondary sources consist of printed books, proscribed books, memoirs and autobiographies. Finally, interviews with some of the political activists of the period have been used to supplement the information gathered from other sources. The source materials, except the oral evidence, were collected from the West Bengal State Archives, National Archives Delhi, the Intelligence Branch Record Room, the West Bengal Secretariat Library, the Jawaharlal Nehru Memorial Library, the National Library and the West Bengal Legislative Council Library.

Chapter 1
Bengal on the Eve of the Non-Cooperation and *Khilafat* Movement (1919–20)

I

In many ways the First World War was a harbinger of change in Indian politics. Economic dislocation, inflated prices and government control on trade increased the hardships of the people, making them increasingly conscious of the oppressive nature of the rule of their imperial government. In Bengal the intellectual element pondered over the cause-and-effect relationship between the political situation and the economic condition.

The Bengali popular press was particularly vocal against colonial indifference to the economic plight of the people. The *Viswamitra* thought that 'subjugation was the real cause of famine because the commercial policy of the government enabled the foreigners to exploit the land'.[1] The *Hitabadi* too was of the opinion that the establishment of mills and factories had not benefited India and the artisan class was growing poorer. *Dainik Bharatmitra* argued that prospect of British capitalists opening more factories would mean further systematic exploitation. *Samyavadi* felt that to eliminate India's poverty it was necessary to ensure not only that the raw materials for manufacture came from India, but also that the manufacturers should themselves be Indians. British policy was held responsible for encouraging foreign exploiters and the *Marwaris*. The *Bengali* pointed out that the monopoly enjoyed by the Railways and the Steamer Company was the cause of high prices. The most insistent cry was against the export of rice. When the restrictions against interprovincial movements of rice crops were removed, it created a great stir. Demand for prohibition of exportation from Bengal was constantly reiterated.[2] The middlemen were deplored for their avaricious attitudes, especially regarding the high prices of coal for which their activities were believed to be responsible.

The demographic curve in Bengal was shifting. The Census Report of 1921 showed that the population in Bengal had risen by 28.6 per cent since 1881. The annual rate of increase was 0.7 per cent. The rural population itself had increased by 27.6 per cent and by 1921 it stood at 44.38 million.[3] But interestingly this trend of population growth was not noticeable in West Bengal, where the growth had been constrained due to malaria epidemics. In a span of 50 years until 1921, the population of rural Central and West Bengal had remained stagnant or even declined by 10 per cent as it had in Nadia and Jessore districts. Frequent attacks of malaria and other tropical diseases had sapped the vigour of the agricultural population. Agricultural production had also been adversely affected by 'the exhaustion of land of the moribund delta and by the mortality and morbidity of labour as a consequence of malarial infection'.[4] In East Bengal the trend was towards a natural increase in population levels. By 1921 Dacca, Tippera, Noakhali and Faridpur had become very densely populated areas, with Bakarganj, Pabna, Bogra and Mymensingh closely following.[5] The Muslim and the *Namasudra* peasants of the region had enterprisingly resorted to extensive cultivation. Labour intensive cash-crop production, especially of jute, had proved a lucrative source of income since 1870. However, this meant that by the 1920s nearly all cultivable land had been exhausted.

Between 1919 and 1921 annual agricultural surveys showed that the general condition of the people was not satisfactory. In 1920 excessive rain caused water-logging damage to low-land paddy in Northern and Eastern Bengal while a spell of dryness clamped over Western Bengal. The continuing high prices of basic necessities materially affected all classes of the population. The situation remained unchanged throughout 1921, as essential goods such as cloth and salt became more and more expensive. The depression in the jute trade meant little financial benefit for its cultivators.[6] Moreover, there was considerable falling off in the area and outrun of the jute crop yielding less income to the farmers. The peasantry, ridden with misfortune, thus became very open to promises of change and better living standards in the days of *Swaraj* which, the leaders pledged, would come within a year.

While rural Bengal was facing the normal problems of natural hazards, demographic ups and downs, rising prices and above all an exceptional temporary crisis created by the war, their industrial compatriots were faring no better. The Bengal delta received the mass of its labouring population from the upper Gangetic plains. These men did not sever their connections with their native homeland. The Indian Factory Labour Commission of 1908 reported that 'the habits of the Indian Factory operatives are determined by the fact that he is primarily an agriculturist or labour on land... His home is in the village from which he comes and not in the city in which he labours.'[7]

It is therefore natural that the labourers would be affected by the political and social upheavals in their villages. The recruits to the mills came from varied regions such as the Telegu speaking districts of Madras, Bihar, Central Provinces, the Uttar Pradesh and Orissa. There was only a small number of Bengali mill workers. Down the river from Calcutta, in the neighbourhood of Budge Budge and Uluberia, local men from the surrounding villages often came to work in the mills.[8] In the mountainous tea estates the work force was mainly of Nepali extraction. In the Dooars tea gardens the labour force was made up of local aboriginals and coolies recruited from the Santhal Pargana. The labour force in the colliery region, especially in the Raniganj area, were aboriginal tribes mainly *Santhals*, or *Kols* or Hindus of inferior castes like the *Baurias, Bhuias* and *Dushads*. They cultivated their own lands and came to the coal fields in search of work only when their own fields did not require their attention and proved less remunerative.

From the middle of 1920 this labouring population of Bengal, simmering with discontent, which had hitherto been expressed in occasional outbursts, began systematic and planned opposition to the authorities. According to the Director of Industries, with a few exceptions, 'the strikes arose from demands for higher wages but the general origin of the demand was the rise in the cost of living which resulted from the Great War. The popular hope that the Armistice would be followed by a substantial fall in prices was grievously disappointed.'[9] The causes of the strikes had been identified as economic. In the context of the pressure of high prices, the increase in wages in the preceding year had been neither sufficient nor uniform. Added to this was the general resentment against profiteering, practised freely by retailers and middlemen and the hatred for capitalist mill-owners who made large profits. The contrast between the affluence and comfort of the masters and the comparative poverty of the mass of workers naturally created ill will. This rancour was further stimulated when the masters justified their unruly behaviour by claiming racial superiority.

The labour strikes of 1920 can also be explained as a manifestation of an epidemic strike fever, which was 'partly engendered by worldwide political unrest, partly fostered by the frequent reports of labour trouble in England and Europe and to some extent also encouraged by political agitators in India'.[10] As to the interaction between these striking labourers and the elite politicians, government reports stated that the non-cooperators recognized the efficacy of strike as a means of creating difficulties for the government. Individual members of the Congress did take an interest and an active part in promoting labour unrest. But even in these cases the politicians came to help the strikers only after an action had begun.[11] As an institution, Congress did not adopt any resolution to support the labourers.

The social situation of Bengal in the early twentieth century, which so influenced the response to nationalist politics, also stemmed from the experiments with the social fabric introduced by the British under the Permanent Settlement. These created a multi-tiered social structure. In the rural areas of Bengal the *zamindars*, by virtue of their rights, headed the rural society. Between them and the lowest tenants stood a number of intermediaries who enjoyed social status and position according to their economic strength and their caste. The villages, although bound by traditional values, were not exactly living in an encapsulated condition. Urban capital and enterprise had been attracted towards land and a considerable section of the upper and middle classes had been making a living from land rents. Kinsmen of the landed gentry invariably migrated to the urban areas for better opportunities and earned their living in the professions. A process of interchange was thus maintained by the professional middle classes in the urban centres having kinship ties with the landed gentry.

The British apparatus of administration, moreover, by linking the entire region in a network, had closely knit the rural with the urban, leaving little scope for isolation. Judicial institutions created a class of lawyers whose close relation with the landed gentry in the country and the trading groups in the city, as well as their professional roles in the political trials, proved to be a useful leverage.[12] Another imperial apparatus was the educational establishments set up at various levels to ensure the spread of education among the masses. The enormous numbers of teachers and students educated in these institutions at various levels, from village schools to the University at Calcutta, along with journalists and other professionals, created a new class of modern intelligentsia. This educated middle class helped to build up links between the city, the district towns and the villages. These links, forged over the course of a century, proved extremely vital in the dissemination of the spirit and message of nationalism in the Gandhian phase. Lastly, the growth of the transport system helped to remove territorial barriers and promote a rapid exchange of sociopolitical ideas.

In the tradition-bound social milieu of India, caste was a vital phenomenon, the influence of which extended into politics. In Bengal in the late nineteenth and twentieth centuries, a considerable number of families of low ritual position increased their power and wealth and a main source of this strength was trade and agriculture. This process of upward economic mobility opened up new opportunities for the lower castes in the shape of Western education and new professions. By the second decade of the twentieth century, their numbers in government service and other professions had greatly increased. These affluent individuals often took part in the Local Board elections and local politics. By the early part of the twentieth century caste associations became a common feature of institutional politics. In general, the 'depressed classes' and their associations remained aloof from the drive for independence. They felt it to be a movement of the high caste Hindu *bhadraloks* with whom they felt no attachment. However, even within such caste groups reactions to the nationalist overtures sometimes varied. While the *Namasudras* of East Bengal openly refused to join and vehemently and actively opposed the movement throughout the colonial period, the *Rajbansis* of North Bengal occasionally got involved in the non-cooperation movement. The *Tilis* who in 1919 were avowed opponents of the anti Rowlatt-Bill agitation changed their attitude by the end of the 1920s.[13] For most of the caste organizations, the anti-imperialist movements presented a dilemma as they now had to reconsider their loyalist stance.[14]

The only caste that merged with mainstream nationalism in Bengal were the *Mahisyas* who constituted the most affluent segment of the agrarian population of Eastern Midnapur. But even among them the difference in the attitude of their caste associations and the general mass of the Mahisya population is noteworthy. While the former professed profound loyalty to British rule, the latter spontaneously participated in the movement for *Swaraj* and created history in Midnapur.

The organized lower-caste movement viewed the Congress as an organization of upper castes and therefore a potential danger in case of transference of power. The Bengal Provincial Congress Committee (BPCC) for their part took little or no initiative to change the character and composition of their organization by drawing the lower castes into their fold. Even in 1924–25, 69.4 per cent of the members belonged to the same social category.[15] Perhaps the sole exception was a social reformer and a Congressite, Digindra Narayan Bhattacharjee who was associated with the Hindu Mahasabha.[16] The Nagpur session of the Congress, however, did adopt a resolution to resolve the problems related to caste hierarchy within the Hindu society, so that no section felt alienated from the struggle against foreign rule. The resolution urged that 'to establish *Swaraj* within one year, settle disputes between *Brahmins and* non-*Brahmins* and make special efforts to rid Hinduism of reproach of untouchability'.[17] As a result, 'the widespread belief was that caste equality was a principle of the non-cooperation movement'.[18] But whether this belief yielded any result in Bengal in the first Gandhian mass movement was yet to be seen.

II

In the arena of institutional politics, the issue with which the Congress leaders were primarily occupied was the proposal for the Chelmsford Reforms. The special Congress session at Bombay (29 August– 1 September 1918) had dismissed the Montagu-Chelmsford proposal as disappointing. But the response of the Bengal Congress leaders to the reforms was not unanimous. The younger generation of Bengal politi- cians including C R Das, Fazlul Huq, Byomkesh Chakravarti and Bipin Chandra Pal, differed with the confirmed Moderates like Surendra Nath Banerjee on the question of the reforms and the demand for full respon- sible government. The other bone of contention among the leaders was securing the control of the Congress. Fazlul Huq, Das and Byomkesh Chakravarti attempted to seize power in the Indian Association and then through it to establish their hold over the Congress. Failing this, they organized an All Bengal Political Conference and captured a majority in the provincial Congress committee when the Moderates failed to attend a meeting. They then cut off the representation of the Indian Association in the BPCC, as a result of which the Indian Association lost the right to send their delegates to sessions of the Congress.

Meanwhile, the Rowlatt Act evoked strong reactions from all sections of nationalists. Gandhi justified the Rowlatt *satyagraha* in opposition to the British Government on the grounds that they had disobeyed the will of God. All governments held authority by virtue of God's will. This government had lost the right to command obedience from its subjects who had the power to revolt. The *satyagraha* against the Rowlatt Act would 'purify the atmosphere and bring in real *swaraj*'.[19]

Moreover he also felt this was the only way to provide the rising generations, who could no longer be satisfied with only petitions and prayers, with an effective means of protest. 'Satyagraha is the only way, it seems to me to stop terrorism', he explained.[20]

The Calcutta disturbances that occurred as an outcome of the Rowlatt satyagraha created a great stir in the popular mind. The day of the satyagraha (6 April) passed off without any trouble. In the afternoon a mass meeting was organized by C R Das and Byomkesh Chakrabarti on the maidan near Octerlony Monument. Although a crowd of 10,000 thronged the meeting, even the chief secretary had to admit that 'the proceedings were orderly'.[21] Those who attended the meetings were chiefly upcountry Hindus, Marwaris, and the Mohammedans. The day of the satyagraha was marked by peaceful demonstration against the Black Act. But reports of Gandhi's arrest in the Punjab sparked off violence. Leaflets and handbills were circulated notifying the people of Gandhi's incarceration. One such leaflet intercepted by the police showed that it urged all communities to join in the protest against the Bill which 'has no need for the innocent Indians'.[22] The northern part of the city observed a hartal as most of the shops as far south as Bow Bazar Street closed. Crowds began to collect on the streets and stopped the trams and other vehicles from doing business. The impact was the greatest in Burrabazar area where the shops were closed and bands of young men and boys chiefly Marwaris and Muslims paraded the streets, stopping tram cars and directing the passengers to alight. The Sikh taxi drivers refused to turn out. In the northern part of the town the tram services were curtailed when the drivers refused to work.[23]

Throughout the day meetings were held and leaflets circulated urging the people to agitate for the release of Gandhi and the repeal of the Rowlatt Bill. According to the report of the Commissioner of Police R Clarke, the direct activists were 'small boys of the Marwari and Bhatia castes with a sprinkle of Mohammedans, but they were incited by others of more mature age who kept in the background'.[24] The striking feature of this incident was the fraternization of the Marwaris, Bhatias and the Muslims. The climax was reached when the Hindus were freely admitted into the Nakhoda Mosque to participate in the meetings held there. 'In the early afternoon, a large crowd collected at the Nakhoda Mosque composed of Marwaris and Bhatias with a sprinkling of Mohammedans who had invited others into the courtyard of the mosque where they were served refreshments. No distinctions of caste were observed'.[25] The assemblage was addressed by Byomkesh Chakrabarti. Another meeting was held at Beadon Square which was attended mainly by *Marwaris*, Bhatias and up-country men. The speakers were Byomkesh Chakravarti, Indu Bhusan Sen, Ambica Prasad Bajpai, Madan Lal Jarojia and Debiprasad Khaitan. They urged the audience to observe mourning and keep their shops closed for four days.

The trouble continued into the next day and the entire zone of Strand Road, Harrison Road, Chitpur Road and Canning Street was filled with tense crowds who had collected on the street from early in the morning and began to pelt the police as soon as they arrived.[26] They even attacked the Deputy Commissioner of Police as he motored down the Chitpur Road from Lalbazar. The crowd swelled as the day proceeded and grew more turbulent especially near the Howrah Bridge end of the Harrison Road. Around midday about 800 people gathered at the Nakhoda Masjid. Most of them were *Marwaris, Bhatias, Jains* and up-country Hindus. The Hindus urged unity among the two communities. A Mohammedan speaker, Syed Ahmed Hossain said that there was no point in closing shops alone, while the Government offices were allowed to continue working. The next two speakers were a high court lawyer who was also a *zamindar* of Khulna district and a *Marwari* priest of the Marawari Dharamsala. A mass meeting was also held at Beadon Square presided over by Byomkesh Chakrabarti. Among the 3,000 men who attended, about 8 per cent were Muslims, 25 per cent were Bengalis and the rest were up-country Hindus of various castes. The speakers instructed the audience to stop agitation since Gandhi had been released. As to the nature of the agitation Amritalal Bose of Star Theatre correctly remarked, 'the authorities pretended so long that the agitation was brought about by a handful of educated persons but what will they say now that, when the dumb had become voiced... It is not easy to persuade people to suspend their business, for it causes loss to both the seller and the purchaser and who has made this demonstration a successful one? it has been done by those whom authorities believed to be unconcerned in all political movements.'[27]

In the districts, the response to the call for *satyagraha* on 6 April was minimal. In the 15 districts of the Presidency, the day was not observed at all. In Bankura there was a demonstration in an outlying village. Only some of the shops were closed and meetings were held in only five districts. Dacca saw the largest meeting, which was attended by about 1,000 people including 30 Mohammedans. Elsewhere, the meetings were small affairs attended chiefly by members of the local bar. The government's inference was that 'the general public in Bengal were not inclined to treat the agitation against the Rowlatt Act very seriously'.[28] However the official report had to admit that 'the outstanding feature of the fortnight was the more serious turn taken by the agitation against the Rowlatt Act, with the receipt of the news of Gandhi's arrest in the Punjab'.[29]

The *Marwari* Association of Calcutta, however, chose to convey their support to the government and vehemently condemned incidents originating out of the *satyagraha* and Gandhi's subsequent arrest. The Bengal National Chamber of Commerce and the Bengal Mahajan Sabha issued manifestos urging the merchant community to have nothing to do with the disturbances of April 1919.

The fate of the Khalifa after Turkey's defeat in the war became a cause of concern for the Muslim leadership in India and in the 1918 session of the League this pro-Turkish sentiment was transformed into 'a deliberate campaign to safeguard the Khalifa's status after his defeat'.[30] The Mahatma, in his usual 'compulsion to right what he saw as a wrong in this instance inflicted by the imperial government on Indian Muslims',[31] supported the movement with his weapon of *satyagraha*. The first step towards this was a decision by the All India *Khilafat* Conference to observe 17 October as '*Khilafat* Day'.

Apprehensive about the effect on the Mahommedans of the announcement of peace in relation to Turkey, the government of India decided to make a survey of the attitude of the Muslims in Bengal to the dismemberment of Turkey. In a letter dated 24 April, the Ali brothers, Shaukat and Muhammad Ali, had stated (in intemperate language) the position of the Mohammedans. They clearly voiced the feeling that they owed no allegiance and professed only hostility to any power that was at war with Turkey. They also stated that their declaration of open enmity to the British government implied that if 'they had the strength to do so they would proclaim and lead a *jihad* and they also go on to say that as their weakness prevent that course they can only perform *hijrat* and advise their co-religionists to do the like'.[32] This letter which was in circulation thus placed before the Mohammedan world a clear issue.

A survey of Mohammedan feeling in the province of Bengal showed that even in the earlier part of the year, the trend was towards a general sympathy with Turkey but with little or no excitement. In some districts the local leaders in collusion with the outsiders were active in stirring up anti-British feeling among the Muslim population on the *Khilafat* issue. In Burdwan for example the Asansol Subdivision had a considerable number of up-country Mohammedans residing in Kulti, Niamatpur, Sitarampur, Asansol, Raniganj and Ondal and the *moulavis* of this region were deeply influenced by the *moulavis* of Uttar Pradesh and Bihar. In the Sadar, Katwa and Kalna subdivision the local Muslim leaders exercised influence. In Hooghly the mill hands in the Sreerampore subdivision were being exhorted to make a common cause with the *Marwaris* by such preachers from Calcutta as Muhammad Azim of Mechua Bazar, Azum-ud-din of Lower Chitpur Road and Muhammad Kudratullah of Joragirja Fulbagan.[33] In Howrah the Muslim community was motivated to join hands with the Hindu agitators both by local Muslim *moulavis* like *Moulavi* Rafiq Ahmed and other influential religious preachers like *Moulavi* Abu Bakr of Furfura. The Muslim mill hands of 24 Parganas were stirred into action by local Muslim leaders such as Khan Bahadur Jahiruddin Ahmed of Bhatpara and *Moulavi* Sayyid Mafakkar Rahman as well as influential nationalist Muslims like *Moulavi* Mujibar Rahaman of Nehalpore, the editor of *The Musalman* and Moulana Akram Khan, the editor of *The Muhammadi*.[34]

In the Cittagong subdivision, Maniruzamman Islamabadi had already began preaching among the Muslims to awaken interest in Turkey. In Noakhali the *moulavis* from outside visited the district occasionally and among them the most frequent visitors were Jaunpuri *moulavis* and Ismail Hussain Siraji from Pabna, delivering lectures on the peace terms. The Hindu press showed deep sympathy with Muslims in the Turkish cause and in their advocacy of the Gandhian programme of non-cooperation. In Rajshahi, religious leaders belonging to the *Faraizi* sect and the *Wahabi* sect were politically influential.

Despite there being a Muslim population in Pabna of 75 per cent, very little interest in Turkey's fate was shown there. In Sirajganj however, some disaffected men gathered round their leader Ismail Hussain Siraji at his residence. *Moulavi* Muhammad Ismail Shiraji along with Moulana Muhammad Abdullahel Banki of village Nurulhuda, Parbatipur in Rangpur district had held several meetings creating some excitement. This man from Burdwan district was an intimate friend of Shiraji and they toured the districts lecturing the people. Besides these districts where some activities were discernible with regard to the *Khilafat* agitation, there were others like Khulna, Bogra, Mymensingh and Dacca where the local population remained unexcited about the fate of the Caliphate, until political and religious leaders from outside the districts influenced them. In Dacca and Bogra for example the leaders from Calcutta greatly influenced the Muslim minds. In Mymensingh town the Muslims were motivated by those from Dacca.

The *Khilafat* Day in October evoked only a mild response from the populace. On that day, shops remained closed in some *mofussil* towns and meetings were held in most districts. In Calcutta most of the Muslim shops remained closed, as did some owned by the Hindus especially the *Marwari* traders. There was no forcible attempt to close shops or prevent the operation of public transport. The apparent calmness of the people caused an official to report that the illiterate masses would not give trouble unless they were invited to do so:

> I have travelled about the villages of Eastern Bengal and they always appeared to me as peace-loving people mainly concerned with their daily occupation.[35]

Contrary to this observation, there was one incident indicative of the intensity of the feelings of the Muslims. This was a meeting presided over by Fazlul Huq and attended by over 10,000, most of whom were illiterate Muslims, thus testifying to the political potential of the *Khilafat* issue.

At the end of December 1919, with the release of the Ali brothers and Maulana Abul Kalam Azad, leadership of the movement gradually passed into the hands of journalists and *Alims* and began to reach the grass root level. Bengal, under the leadership of Azad, was drifting towards a more radical programme so far as the *Khilafat* movement was concerned. This became clear when the Bengal *Khilafat* Conference on 28 February passed a resolution for a second 'Khilafat Day'. Friday, 19 March was fixed as the day on which all 'Muslims should suspend their business and send messages to the Viceroy and the King that in case the question of *Khilafat*, *Jazirat* and other holy places were decided on the contrary to Muslim demands and the *Shariat*, the Muslims would find it difficult to keep their secular loyalty intact'.[36] This conference was important because it testified officially that the trend towards pro-Turkish and anti-British feeling was taking a new turn in the light of a strongly urged fraternization with the Hindu brethren.

The tide of Muslim feeling was so high that *The Amrita Bazar Patrika* reported: 'From the point of view of intense Muslim feeling and fraternity and union that pervaded the atmosphere throughout the course of the deliberations, it can be said that the conference attained remarkable unique success.'[37] The hall was full of Hindu and Muslim delegates but the latter predominated. The Muslim stalwarts along with the *Khilafat* issue also laid special stress on *entente cordiale* between the Hindus and the Muslims.[38]

The Bengal *Khilafat* Committee bulletins reported that meetings were held in most principal cities in support of the *Khilafat* day and the *Hartal* on 19 March. The country was being flooded with *Khilafat* literature. The press was the most vibrant media of propaganda as the *Khilafat* leaders like Shaukat Ali reached the wider mass with their appeal:

> The observance of 19th March as the day of final protest from all Muslims, Government servants, civil and military and the police employees is essential in the interest of *Khilafat* work. The peaceful, earnest and impressive demonstration will clearly show intense feeling of the Indian Musalmaan over this great religious question.[39]

Initially the Muslims leaders did not betray any irreconcilable hostility towards the British government. The text of the resolution, which was to be passed at every meeting, indicated that the Muslims were still pinning faith on the proverbial British sense of justice:

> Respectfully request your excellency to convey to His Majesty the King Emperor that if peace terms with His Majesty Khilafatul Musalmaan, Sultan of Turkey be not in accordance of the dictates of the *Shariat*, then commandments of Islam will force the Muslims to sever loyal connection with the British throne.[40]

But the second bulletin of the Bengal *Khilafat* Committee appeared to be more resolute in its advocacy of non-cooperation with their long-standing ally, the British. The following quote illustrates this:

> The second *Khilafat* Day is to be observed on Friday, the 19th. It has been fully decided to initiate hartal all over India and pass firm resolutions protesting against the British attitude towards Turkey, *Khilafat* and the Holy places of Islam from every town big or small. His Majesty's Musalmaan soldiers and military servants should impress upon their officers, the importance of this religious question and they should inform the government that they would sever all connections with the British Government if Turkey is dismembered and the Holy Places remain in the hands of the non Muslims. Meetings will be held to support the Resolution passed at Calcutta and other places. The mass will be educated with regard to British piece-goods. A subcommittee is being formed in Calcutta under the Bengal Provincial *Khilafat*

Committee for propaganda work so that the second *Khilafat* Day is made more successful.[41]

Accordingly, meetings and demonstrations were organized all over Bengal for the cause of *Khilafat*. Most of these mass meetings were organized by local *Khilafat* committees and meant for all communities. The Howrah *Khilafat* Committee, for example, organized a mass meeting of Hindus and Muslims. A mass meeting was held at Hooghly under the presidency of Pir Hazrat Shah Sufi. This meeting was attended by *Ulema* and common Muslim people from several districts of Bengal. The Pir Sahib described the *Khilafat* movement as not only a political agitation but a religious imperative – a constitutional attempt on the part of the Mohammedans to keep their religious rights intact. The resolutions passed at this meeting clearly indicated how deeply the religious sentiment of the Muslims was hurt by the attitude of the Allies towards Turkey. The meeting clearly expressed the opinion that any sort of interference with the temporal power of the Sultan by the Allies was tantamount to interference with the religious faith of the Musalmaans. The meeting urged the government of India to request the home government to try its level best to give the right of self-determination to the Turks as promised by the premier. Secondly, any sort of interference by any non-Muslim power with the *Jazirat-ul-Arab* was against the cherished religious faith of the Musalmaans. In the case of such interference every Musalmaan should be bound to remove it in a manner sanctioned by Islam. Muslim sentiment was much wounded by the anti-Turkish attitude of the British prelates and the clergy and denounced this as hateful fanaticism that would lead to worldwide strife amongst the Christians and the Musalmaans.

In Barisal a joint Hindu–Muslim mass meeting was held at Raja Bahadur Haveli. Hemyat-ud-din explained the Turkish situation and supported Gandhi. A branch *Khilafat* committee was opened. The meeting urged all Muslim rulers of the Indian states and their subjects to support and put into practice what *Amrita Bazar Patrika* described as 'passive resistance' that was to be initiated by Gandhi. This meeting also passed resolutions on boycott of British piece-goods, citing the apparent hostile attitude of the British public and the clergy against the *Khilafat* as the reason for this action. Anti-British feeling found its expression through boycott of British goods. Several Muslim merchants of Colutolla Street, Canning Street, Murgihata and Zacharia Street stopped placing orders with the canvassers and several canvassers of

British piece-goods went to some leading Muslim merchants with their new samples but returned disappointed. Unless the question of *Khilafat* was decided in favour of the Muslims, they could not expect orders for British piece-goods.[42] The Bengal *Khilafat* Committee was planning to start a regular boycotting campaign once the *hartal* was observed successfully. The committee also endeavoured to open several *Swadeshi* stores in *moffusil* towns and villages with locally raised public subscription.

Throughout 1920 non-cooperation became the major focus of all political questions in the province of Bengal. In February 1920, the Town Hall meetings of the Bengal *Khilafat* Committee, discussing the issue of Muslim grievances regarding the dangers to the *Khilafat*, accepted non-cooperation with the British as a means to fight imperialism. A campaign of the most intemperate kind culminated in a *hartal* on 19 March. But the organizers themselves were apprehensive as to their ability to control the over-exuberant Muslim masses. According to the government reports, 'the *hartal* was practically a failure but this ending of the first round is not without significance'.[43] The storm centre then passed up-country and was characterized by a 'series of meetings of the most outstanding leaders'.[44] Attempts at agitation in Bengal, however, made little progress.

While the established leadership oscillated between acceptance and non-acceptance of non-cooperation, Gandhi launched his programme of non-cooperation on 1 August 1920. When the BPCC met on 15 August to discuss the issue, it had no other option but to accept non-cooperation. In the absence of any defined course of action it felt that the practical details should be worked out by the provinces, according to their particular circumstances. The BPCC did not, however, accept the idea of council boycott and was in favour of non-cooperation from within the council.

In the aftermath of the Calcutta Session of the AICC in September 1920, renewed efforts were undertaken to popularize the non-cooperation movement in Bengal. Twenty-five candidates withdrew from the Council election. Shaukat Ali was engaged in a propaganda campaign for the *Khilafat* Committee of Bengal. A mobilization of the industrial labour force was attempted. During his East Bengal tour, Bipin Chandra Pal made inflammatory speeches that left a deep impact on the young mind. By November much was heard about the 'local agitators, their meetings, pamphlets, efforts to raise subscription and volunteers'.[45] A new era had begun in Indian politics, which saw constant interaction between institutional and popular politics.[46]

Chapter 2

Congress Organization in Bengal 1921–22

Until 1919, the Congress as an organization did not have much connection with the grass roots. However, following the First World War, two broad factors contributed to the change in its structure. The Act of 1919 widened the franchise, which made Congress eager to extend its organizational network to provincial and district levels. This period also saw a considerable section of the Indian people being drawn into nationalist politics. The Congress could not ignore these changes. Therefore, when faced with the problem of adopting a new scheme of agitation in 1920, the Congress had to reform its constitution to gain a broad-based and permanent character.

On the final day of the Congress session at Nagpur in December 1920, delegates approved a new constitution for the Congress committee.[1] The British Committee of Congress was dissolved along with its paper *India*.[2] This marked the end of the politics of petitions. Henceforth, Congress leaders were to concentrate more on their own actions within India than on playing to the British gallery.

The new Congress constitution proposed the establishment of a working committee of 15 members, which was to function as a permanent Congress executive.[3] From a loose federation of 200 members, the Congress became a more active and permanent organization. Congress circles were reorganized on a linguistic basis so as to extend the roots of its organization to the subdivision and *taluka* level.[4] This facilitated the integration into nationalist politics of the peasantry, small town traders and lawyers in the *mufussils*. The number of delegates to the annual sessions of the Congress were fixed in proportion to the population of the province. Membership was made open with a fee of four annas per annum. This ensured a regular income for the organization. The deliberations of the

Congress committee could be carried out either in *Hindusthani* or in the local languages of the linguistically divided provinces.[5] The main object of the machinery constructed by the new constitution was to mobilize and control a wider range of Indians than before, for successful political activity.

In accordance with the Nagpur resolution Bengali leaders engaged themselves in revitalizing the Congress organization in their province, which had fallen into considerable disarray. The Bengal Provincial Congress Committee (BPCC), which was to represent the Indian National Congress in the Province of Bengal and Surma Valley in a meeting held on 12, 15 and 16 February 1921, issued a set of rules for the organization of the Congress committees.[6] The committee was empowered to organize provincial, district and local conferences. District Congress committees were to carry out the work of the Congress in the districts in accordance with the rules and instructions framed by the BPCC.[7]

In the reorganized Congress, each provincial committee was constituted by an elective principle. Every district was a constituency for the purpose of returning members to the provincial Congress committee and the number of members elected by each constituency was based on the population of that district. Election was by single transferable vote. Each member of a district Congress committee who had paid his subscriptions for the current year was entitled to have his name registered in the electoral roll of that constituency within a particular district Congress committee.[8] In 1921 the number of members from each district to be represented in the Bengal provincial committee was as follows:[9]

The BPCC was comprised of one president, two vice-presidents, one secretary, three assistant secretaries, one treasurer and two auditors.[10] The business of the committee was run by a council of 60 members and at least 20 of the elected members were ordinary residents of Calcutta or the suburbs.[11] The newly elected provincial Congress committee met on 12 July 1921.[12] Chittaranjan Das was elected as president.[13] He selected 60 members who would form the council. Birendra Nath Sasmal became the secretary.[14] The BPCC now had a permanent office at 11 Forbes Mansion which was to operate from 12 noon to 6 pm.

Das made arrangements to ensure that Congress workers functioned within a well structured system. While ultimate control remained in the hands of Das as president of the BPCC, the delegation of power and decision-making to important Congress members gave daily operations and procedures a flexible character. This distribution of responsibilities had a psychological impact on the recipients. It gave members a sense of importance and of freedom from restraints within their area of work.

No	District	No of Members
1.	Burdwan	8
2.	Birbhum	5
3.	Bankura	6
4.	Midnapur	14
5.	Hooghly	6
6.	Howrah	5
7.	24 Parganas	12
8.	Calcutta	25
9.	Nadia	8
10.	Murshidabad	7
11.	Jessore	9
12.	Khulna	7
13.	Rajshahi	8
14.	Dinajpur	9
15.	Jalpaiguri	4
16.	Darjeeling	2
17.	Rungpore	12
18.	Bogra	5
19.	Pabna	7
20.	Maldah	5
21.	Dacca	16
22.	Mymensingh	23
23.	Faridpur	11
24.	Backergunge	12
25.	Tippera	12
26.	Noakhali	7
27.	Chittagong	8
28.	Sylhet	12
29.	Cachar	3
Total		268

Jitendra Lal Banerjee, Satyendra Chandra Mitra, Hemanta Kumar Sarkar and Moulavi Shamsuddin Ahmed were to act as personal secretaries to the president of the BPCC. They were required to go now and then to the different *moffusil* centres and ensure that the directions of the provincial committee were carried out to the letter. Das also ensured that the Congress Committees received regular endowments both in cash and kind and appointed the following Congress members to help in the collection of the *Tilak Swaraj* Fund in Calcutta.

1. Moulana Sufi Syed Abu Bakr Sidiqui
2. Moulana Abul Kalam Azad
3. Nirmal Chandra Chunder
4. Nabin Ranjan Sarkar
5. Kumar Krishna Datta
6. Madan Burman
7. Nikhil Chandra Sen
8. Bijoy Krishna Bose
9. Jogesh Chandra Dasgupta

These members were to act in cooperation with Calcutta and district Congress committee councils. They were instructed to organize the collection of funds, ensuring the speedy gathering of as large sums as possible and also soliciting the assistance of influential local men in this work.

C R Das was also anxious to mobilize the support of women for the provincial Congress. He requested the *Nari Karma Mandir* to take all necessary steps to work among the women in Bengal. All correspondence regarding Congress work and the work of the non-cooperation movement that involved women was to be addressed to Urmila Devi. The society also had to give particular attention to the introduction and teaching of *charka* through which, perhaps, non-cooperation could be popularized among women.

Moulavi Mujibar Rahaman, Sasanka Jiban Roy and Anil Kumar Roy were to remain in charge of the office at Forbes Mansion.[15] Gunindra Nath Banerjee would do outdoor work. Motilal Dey was appointed as the second *duftari* (officer). The office staff were to assume charge of all necessary correspondence. In general matters, as in matters of communication, the office was to work under the direction of *Moulavi* Mujibar Rahaman or Sasanka Jiban Roy. Devendra Chandra Sen was appointed as cashier. He would attend the office every day to receive money sent in for *Tilak Swaraj* Fund and deposit it in the Bengal National Bank. The daily account statement was to be signed by Mujibar Rahaman or Sasank Jiban Roy.

A publication committee was also formed with Suresh Chandra Bhattacharjee as the secretary and the following members.

1. Mujibar Rahaman
2. Jogesh Chandra Dasgupta
3. Gunada Charan Sen

4. Makhan Lal Sen
5. Panchkauri Banerjee
6. Sailendra Chandra Chakravarti

This committee was instructed to decide which pamphlets and books should be published for the propagation of the Congress ideal of non-cooperation and also help to write them. If there was any difference of opinion amongst the committee members (and there were at least two dissenters), the matter was to be referred to C R Das. The secretary's role was to supply the press with information about the work of non-cooperation and to ensure that it was published.

A second committee was formed to supply information and to carry out necessary experiments regarding cotton, cotton seed, *Charka* and hand looms. Brahamananda Ghosh and Ananda Prasad Chakrabarty were the secretaries of this committee. The other members were:

1. Basanta Kumar Lahiri
2. Ananda Prasad Chakravarti
3. Tek Chand Aria
4. Ramesh Chandra Chaudhuri
5. Chinta Haran Mukherjee

The process of forming the district Congress committees began from January 1921. The provincial Congress committee deputed its representatives to render help in the formation of district committees. When at least 50 people had signed the agreement to pay four annas each per year, the district Congress committee could begin to function.[16] C R Das wanted the executive council of the district Congress committees to have a representative from each subdivisional Congress committee who would be in charge of his own subdivision. This method of representation ensured active cooperation at all levels of the organization. It created a complete network linking nation with province, province with district, district with subdivision and finally subdivision with the lowest unit, the village. Das did not want the district Congress committee to interfere in the work of the subdivisional committees, preferring that they should take an advisory rather than a dominant role. In case of a dispute, however, the council of the district Congress committee was to settle the matter.[17] All other associations that had existed prior to this reorganization were required to come to an understanding with the Congress committee. If members of the association agreed with the

Congress creed, they had to become members of the Congress and abolish the previous association.

By May 1921 Congress committees had been established in all the districts except Burdwan and Alipore.[18] Calcutta, including the area within its municipal jurisdiction, was treated as a district.[19] Initially Calcutta had four district offices.[20] In some districts like Faridpur and Birbhum the existing Congress committees were reorganized.[21] In Faridpur, Sarat Chandra Choudhury, an ex-pleader (ex-lawyer) of Bhanga, was elected president of the Faridpur district Congress committee while Surendra Nath Biswas, who gave up his practice, was one of the vice-presidents along with Bhabotosh Bose and *Moulavi* Roshan ali Chowdhury. *Moulavi* Tazim ud Din Ahmed, an ex-pleader, was appointed the treasurer and secretary. Jogesh Chandra Dasgupta, assistant secretary of the BPCC, moved the resolution forming the committee. Local people from remote areas of Madaripur, Chikandi, Bhanga, Rajbari and Pangsha registered as members. The model rules framed by the BPCC were adopted with some modifications. The executive council set down a plan of work, according to which two public meetings were held. Surendra Nath Biswas, *Moulavi* Taqub Ali Chowdhuri and others addressed these meetings and exhorted the students and the pleaders to give up their schools and professions to serve the country.

In Birbhum, after the programme of non-cooperation was accepted by the Congress, a number of Congress subcommittees were gradually started in the district. The district Congress committee, which had become non-functional, was reorganized with new people in office. Nabin Chandra Mukherjee, a pleader, was elected president. Jitendra Lal Banerjee, *vakil* (lawyer) of the High Court and Dr Sarat Chandra Mukherji, a private practitioner of *Suri* were elected vice-presidents. The Birbhum district Congress committee enlisted 15,000 members, raised money for the *Tilak Swaraj* Fund and also started several Congress subcommittees and *Swaraj Ashrams* in different parts of the district. The *Suri Swaraj Ashram,* which was situated in a rented house, also functioned as the office of the district Congress committee. In 24 Parganas a new district Congress committee was formed.[22]

By April 1921, Congress committees had been established at the headquarters of 14 districts. Six branch committees had also been formed in various places. *Amrita Bazar Patrika* reported that 28 district Congress committees had affiliated themselves to the provincial Congress committee.[23] The headquarters of the Bengal Non-Cooperation Movement was circulating printed rules and forms for the guidance of the district and branch Congress committees. Even the 4,000 labour organizations were being issued with enrolment forms. In Calcutta the leaders took the initiative to start enrolling for the Congress committees. The Burrabazar Congress Committee had enrolled 1,500 members by May, mostly *Marwari* and up-country members.

Congress committees were also established at local level down to the lowest administrative unit, the village.[24] Local subdivisional Congress committees were formed in important *moffusil* areas like Serajganj, Pabna and Rabari in Faridpur.[25] The Birbhum District Congress Committee established Congress subcommittees in Rampurhat, Bolpur, Dubrajpur and Sainthia. The Rampurhat subcommittee was formed in June 1921 and Jitendra Lal Banerjee was elected as its president. A local cloth merchant was elected as the cashier. The office was situated at the *Swaraj Ashram* in Rampurhat in the residence of Sorodindu Chatterjee, the secretary of the Committee. The subcommittee at Rampurhat was very active. It convened regular meetings in cooperation with the *Swaraj Ashram* at Rampurhat and also collected money for the *Tilak Swaraj* Fund.

In 1921 after the provincial *Khilafat* committee proposed a gradual amalgamation with the provincial Congress committee, many *Khilafat* committees in the districts functioned as Congress committees.[26] At a *Khilafat* conference at Gaibandaha, Rangpur, the representatives of all the branches of the district Congress and *Khilafat* committees decided that henceforth branch Congress committees everywhere would act as *Khilafat* committees.[27] In Noakhali the district *Khilafat* committee also acted as a Congress committee until the end of January 1922.[28] The Congress committee at Murshidabad had one district Congress committee, seven branch Congress committees and about 400 village Congress committees. Sylhet had 700 Congress committees.

Chittaranjan Das formulated a scheme for village organization with the help of Makhan Lal Sen and others. It urged a close cooperation among the local inhabitants and the local committees. The provincial Congress committee was to set up a central board in Calcutta which would direct the work of organization in the villages. The board was to have one representative from each district subcommittee and ten nominees of the provincial Congress committee and it was to be represented in the provincial Congress committees. The district subcommittees were to be in charge of organization in their own districts. A group of experts were to train the workers and the central board would bear their initial expenses but later the local organizations would have to depend on local subscription and donations.[29]

By May 1921, the interior of the Bengal districts had been divided into as many Congress centres as there were *thanas*, each being placed under the charge of a pleader (the term used in primary sources when referring to a lawyer) or a teacher who had resigned from his or her official post. They were usually assisted by student volunteers. Their activities in May 1921 led to a noticeable increase in the number of branch Congress committees and by June there were 49,289 Congress members in 17 districts. The first Gandhian movement had thus been able to reunite the remotest parts of the province with the metropolis through a network of committees. But at same time the local centres did not lose their autonomous role.

II

By the 1920s the Congress was in a much stronger financial position than in the pre-war years. This was largely due to the reorganization of the party with open membership and four anna fees, and collections from other sources providing cash for local work. The *Tilak Swaraj* Fund and the District Fund both provided cash for Congress work. Bengal contributed one lakh 800,000 rupees to the *Tilak Swaraj* Fund between January 1921 and June 1922, which was second only to Bombay's contribution.[30] Hemendra Nath Dasgupta recalled how the people enthusiastically contributed to the nationalist fund as *Deshbandhu* toured around east Bengal spreading nationalist propaganda.[31] At a ladies' meeting in Comilla about 2,000 rupees worth of gold jewellery was collected.[32] In response to Basanti Devi's call the women of Jalpaiguri collected gold ornaments and also 2,000 gold coins.[33] Munshi Mohammed Sonaullah gave large sums to the Congress and *Khilafat* funds and also helped to establish spinning schools.[34]

Contributions to the Congress fund came from a wide cross section of society. In Barisal, Chitta Ranjan Das and his wife collected 7,000 rupees in cash and ornaments, a large proportion of which was donated by the Kalashakti family and other important families of the district.[35] On the other hand, in Jalpaiguri, the 'fallen women' persuaded by *Deshbandhu* had contributed 20 rupees and one guinea by selling rice which they had earned by begging.[36] Two blind beggars had given *Deshbandhu* four annas each for the *Tilak Swaraj* Fund.[37] Suprava Devi recalled that in Midnapur a sweeper had contributed one rupee to the *Tilak Swaraj* Fund.[38] About 20,000 rupees were collected during a public meeting in Jalpaiguri. In Dacca, Joy Datta, an immigrant to Burma, gave 5,000 rupees for the *Tilak Swaraj* Fund.[39] At Suri, in Birbhum, Deshbandhu and his wife collected as subscription for the *Tilak Swaraj* Fund a sum of 6,000 rupees in cash and ornaments. In Asansol subdivision of Burdwan C R Das collected 34,000 rupees. Many leaders sold off their personal property to finance the Congress organization and the movement. Jatindra Mohan Sengupta sold his house at Chittagong to provide for the stranded coolies of Chandpur.[40]

G D Birla, Kesoram Poddar and Sukhlal Karnani were among the Calcutta *Marwari* businessmen who were the principal sponsors of the Bengal Congress.[41] This becomes clear from G D Birla's book, *In the Shadow of the Mahatma*, where he admitted that he had given financial help to Gandhi for the nationalist cause:

> I was doing my best to support him with money – the commodity which he lacked the most – in his struggle to help the depressed class.[42]

In the districts too the *Marwaris* played an important role in raising funds for Congress work. In Bankura the rich *Marwari* community, which included the Rathira, Goenka, Kanailal Marwari and Fulchand Marwari and also the Bengali merchants and rice mill owners, the Nandis, Sahana and Samanta families shouldered the burden of providing money, rice, oil, flour and other edibles to the Congress workers, helping to keep the organization running. They were also associated with the *Khaddar*-selling programme of the Congress.[43]

The money collected for the Congress within a particular district was remitted to the district office. This included the four-anna subscription and the doles of rice that were collected by the volunteers as '*Musti Bhiksha*'.[44] All other contributions were deposited in the *Tilak Swaraj* Fund. But all contributions made by the *Tilak Swaraj* Fund, either for initial or any other expenditure, became a part of the district fund as soon as the district committee or local committees received them. Such financial arrangements ensured a close cooperation between the different levels of Congress committees.[45] District funds were administered by the treasurer of the Congress committee. In some of the districts like Rangpur the amount required for each subdivision was specified.[46] A regular budget totalling about 4,500 rupees per month had been prepared, including 1,500 rupees for the volunteer uniforms. The members of the district volunteer corps were entrusted with the collection of funds.[47] The district Congress committee in Birbhum raised about 8,000 rupees for the *Tilak Swaraj* Fund.[48] In Birbhum the newly formed Congress subcommittees contributed to the *Swaraj* Fund.[49]

The BPCC directed the district Congress committees to submit weekly reports in prescribed forms showing the amount of money raised every week for the *Tilak Swaraj* Fund. In February the amount raised in Comilla was 16,500 rupees and in Chittagong the total was 11,000 rupees. Two kinds of receipt forms were issued, one for donation to the *Tilak Swaraj* Fund and the other for subscription to the provincial Congress committee fund. C R Das even contemplated the printing of official receipts for a sum of 10 lakhs for the *Tilak Swaraj* Fund. The receipts were to be smaller than government currency notes and slightly larger than *Khilafat* notes. The forms were to contain a serial number, a portrait of Gandhi and signature of C R Das. A flow of funds through the district Congress committees ensured an even balance in the power relationship among the various committees as far as monetary matters were concerned. Ultimately this ensured that the entire organization was well equipped financially.

The *Tilak Swaraj* Fund was actually a reserve fund which served two purposes. It paid the initial expenses to every district Congress committee in order to enable it to begin functioning. If the district Congress committees had insufficient funds to cope with the work, the *Tilak Swaraj* Fund made additional contributions.[50] The funds were administered by the BPCC and the local Congress committees had no power to spend any portion of the money.[51] In Bengal Chitta Ranjan Das himself controlled the administration of the *Tilak Swaraj* Fund.[52] The money raised for the fund was remitted to him except where accounts at the local banks had been opened in his name.[53] Those who were in charge of collection for the *Tilak Swaraj* Fund were given receipt books and they worked under the guidance of the district or subdivisional Congress committees, depositing their collections with the committee secretaries.[54] The *Tilak Swaraj* Fund made contributions only through the district Congress committees. Local Congress committees were obliged to provide detailed information regarding their demands to the district committees in order to draw aid from the Swaraj Fund.[55]

III

During the years under consideration Congress leadership saw the rise of a new generation of leaders. Revitalization of the Congress organization in Bengal in the 1920s could largely be achieved because of this new generation of leaders who provided excellent leadership both at the provincial and district level.

Organizational leadership for the non-cooperation movement primarily came from those who enjoyed a degree of economic independence from the government and had acquired a degree of political sophistication. Independent professionals were particularly prominent throughout 1920 and 1921.

Chitta Ranjan Das was himself a striking example of the role of professionals in the non-cooperation movement. He was born in a *Vaidya* family at Telirbag village in the Vikrampur district of Dacca.[56] His family had been in the legal profession for three generations and was well known in the Brahmo Samaj.[57] *Deshbandhu*'s grandfather practised law in Barisal. His father, Bhuban Mohan Das, who had settled in Calcutta, edited a weekly paper which was the voice of Brahmo public opinion and slowly developed it into a political newspaper.[58]

Chitta Ranjan went to London to qualify for the Indian Civil Service Examination.[59] While he was there he played a leading role in the political campaign of the Indian students who were protesting against the derogatory remarks of some of the opponents of home rule.[60] Chitta Ranjan failed the Civil Service Examination. Instead he joined the Inner Temple and was called to Bar in 1893.[61] By 1907 he had established himself as a successful lawyer for both civil and criminal cases.[62]

Chitta Ranjan's involvement with the nationalist movement began in 1904 through the establishment of *Swadeshi Mandali* for propagating the ideas of self help and *Swadeshi*.[63] He developed a political alliance with Bipin Chandra Pal in opposition to the Moderates within the Indian National Congress.[64] In 1906 at the Bengal Provincial Conference in Barisal he drafted the main resolution on a new nationalist line of self reliance.[65] He was also associated with the National Council of Education and at his request Aurobindo joined as the first principal of the institution.[66]

Chitta Ranjan's legal defence of such extremist leaders as Bipin Pal, Aurobindo Ghose, Barindra Kumar Ghose and Ullas Kar Datta made him well known. He undertook several other political cases, including the Dacca Conspiracy case in 1900, the Delhi Conspiracy case in 1914, the Alipore Trunk murder case of 1918 and the Kutubdia Detenu case.[67] In his presidential address to the Bengal Provincial Conference at Calcutta he expressed regret that the elite had lost touch with the masses and prepared a plan for the reorganization of villages which could provide the city-based elite with grass roots support.[68] Following this conference, Das steadily rose in importance in the political stage of Bengal.

As a delegate from Bengal to the All-India Congress Seminar at Calcutta in 1917, Das had supported Annie Besant and her Home Rule League. With Besant's Home Rule League controlling the Congress, the influence of the Moderates led by Surendra Nath Banerjee began to wane.[69] Das successfully isolated the Moderates to finally establish his control of the BPCC.[70] Once in power, Chitta Ranjan and his group refused representation of the Indian Association in the BPCC.[71] Surendra Nath left Congress and started the Liberal League. The other group which exercised considerable influence in the provincial Congress was the Gandhites represented by Jitendra Lal Banerjee and Shyam Sundar Chakrabarti.[72] The former, an inhabitant of Rampurhat in the Birbhum district, was a pleader at the High Court.[73] Shyam Sundar Chakrabarti was the former associate editor of *Bande Mataram* and a member of Aurobindo's group, but later he became a staunch follower of Gandhi. Thus both the factions had their political roots reaching down to the extremist faction of the *Swadeshi* era. Das' faction, however, included a rising generation of extremist politicians who, through their active participation in Home Rule agitation, came to dominate the Congress.

Other notable examples of leadership by independent professionals were that of Jatindra Mohan Sengupta of Chittagong and Birendra Nath Sasmal of Midnapur. Jatindra Mohan's father, Jatra Mohan Sengupta, was a leading lawyer of Chittagong. He invested his income in land and became the *zamindar* of Barama Village. He was also a member of the Bengal Legislative Council.[74] The family of Jatra Mohan was well known and respected by his subjects for his developmental works in his *zamindari*.[75] Jatindra Mohan went to England after graduating from Presidency College and then returned to join the Calcutta High Court.[76] He began his political career in 1911 as a delegate to the Bengal Provincial Conference at Faridpur. In 1920 at the special session of the Congress, he was elected secretary of the reception committee. In 1921 he left his legal practice, mainly at the insistence of Das, to organize the movement in Chittagong.[77]

Birendra Nath Sasmal was yet another representative of the new Congress leadership. He came from a well known, established, affluent and enlightened *Mahisya* family of Midnapur.[78] The members of the family received western education in the nineteenth century and were associated with the Brahmo movement.[79] Although they were landowners, family members also joined the legal profession.[80] Birendra

Nath Sasmal became a barrister and practiced law after his return from England. Initially he had joined the Calcutta High Court but later practiced in the Midnapur District Court. Birendra Nath became involved in politics immediately after his return from England. In 1905 he participated in the anti-partition agitation. His political activities were centered mainly around Midnapur town and Calcutta.[81] In the 1920 Calcutta Congress session he was a member of the reception committee. He supported Gandhi's resolution on non-cooperation.[82] In 1921 he left his legal practice and joined Chittaranjan Das. Birendra Nath was well known in his district for his social service work especially at the time of floods.[83] Akhil Chandra Das was a well known lawyer of Comilla and a leading Congressman of the district. In 1916 he became a member of the *Bangiya Babastha Parishad*. In almost all the districts lawyers provided the lead in the movement.

Members of the teaching profession constituted another source of social support for the Bengal Congress. Anil Baran Roy, a professor of philosophy at the Bankura Missionary College, was one of those non-cooperators who left his teaching post, influenced by Gandhian ideals.[84] Nripendra Chandra Banerjee had been a college teacher and only a fringe participant in nationalist politics for years.[85] Persuaded by Chittaranjan Das he joined the movement and became second in command to J M Sengupta in the Chittagong District Congress Committee.[86] He started the *Saraswat Ashram* for constructive work.[87] Ananta Kumar Sen of Barisal was a close associate of Aswini Kumar Datta. He refused a government job and chose instead to impart education through nationalist schools. *Amrita Samaj*, Barisal National School and *Barisal Seba Samiti*, were established by him. He also edited the daily, *Kesari*, and a collection, *Swarajgita*, which became immensely popular among the nationalist workers. Bijay Modak was a headmaster of a local school in Srirampur. During the non-cooperation movement, he left his job to join the Congress.

Among the students who became prominent in the Congress in the wake of the non-cooperation movement were Pravash Chandra Lahiri and Someswar Prasad Chaudhuri. The former became the secretary of the Rajsahi District Congress Committee and also joined the *Anushilan Samiti*. The latter was a young medical student who organized the peasantry of Rajsahi and Pabna into a revolt against the excesses of the Midnapore Zamindari Company. Prafulla Chandra Sen had passed his BSc and had been appointed as an 'article' in an audit office when the non-cooperation movement began. Setting aside his plan of going to

England and becoming a chartered accountant, he joined the movement. His friend Rabi Palit was appointed the secretary of the Hooghly District Congress Committee and Prafulla Chandra accompanied him to Hooghly and began his work there.[88]

Mainstream Congress nationalism also attracted the attention of other successful young men. For example, Subhas Chandra Bose resigned his civil service job in May 1921 because he found it 'impossible to serve both masters at the same time – namely the British Government and my country'.[89] He hurried back to India from England to join the struggle that was then in full swing. His prolonged discussion with Chitta Ranjan Das impressed him so much that he felt that he had found 'a leader and meant to follow him'.[90]

Congress leadership in the days of the non-cooperation movement was reinforced by revolutionaries joining the organization. The introduction of revolutionaries into the Congress, especially those belonging to the *Jugantar* group, was largely due to the persuasion of Chitta Ranjan Das.[91] Since it was becoming increasingly difficult to work underground, the *Jugantar* group decided to embark on open political activity through the Congress and planned in the process to rebuild their shattered organization.[92] The revolutionaries who joined the Congress felt that they could now accept the Congress programme, because under Gandhi's leadership the Congress was no longer an elite organization.[93] Moreover, the members of the revolutionary groups had realized that terrorist activities by small groups could not in itself lead to freedom, and that it must instead begin with the awakening of a desire for freedom in the Indian people. Hence they agreed to experiment for one year with the policy of non-violent non-cooperation advocated by Gandhi.[94]

Bhupendra Kumar Datta had been sent by his co-workers in the *Jugantar* group to discuss with Gandhi the possibilities of revolution. He personally disagreed with Gandhi that the country would become independent at the end of one year of non-cooperation.[95] However, the *Jugantar* group undertook to accept Gandhi's leadership for one year after which if *Swaraj* was not attained they threatened to revert to their old revolutionary methods.[96] They were convinced that the Congress movement would awaken the country but not that it would lead to full independence. The revolutionaries joined the Congress movement with this awareness and were not totally divorced from terrorism.[97]

At district level the revolutionaries did more than any other group to organize the Congress movement. Many of them had begun to work for the Congress at the insistence of the non-cooperating students, lawyers and teachers that they knew. Once the non-cooperation resolution was accepted in the Calcutta Congress session, the revolutionaries of Rangpur began to take keen interest in the movement. In November 1920 a meeting of the North Bengal Party was held, organized through the efforts of Dhiren Ghatak and Suresh Bhattacharjee, at which it was decided that the members would join the movement.[98] Manoranjan Gupta, Satin Sen and Aswini Ganguly were among the members of the *Jugantar* faction in Barisal who took the lead.[99] In Mymensingh district Surendra Nath Ghosh organized the Mymensingh District Congress Committee and became its secretary.[100] Suren Ghosh belonged to an upper middle class family. His father was a *talukdar* who had associations with secret political parties. In 1920, he attended the Calcutta session of the Indian National Congress. The following year he met Gandhi and was converted to his ideal.[101] Purna Das in Faridpur had built up a strong organization.[102] He came from a poor family of lower rank *Kayastha* from Samaj Ishibpur village in Madaripur subdivision. His involvement with the revolutionaries developed in 1910 when he organized his own revolutionary cell in Madaripur along with his friends. After his release in 1920 he joined Das and accompanied him to the Nagpur session.[103] Atul Chandra Sengupta from Chattogram had been associated with the *Jugantar* group since 1908. In 1921 he joined the Congress and organized the non-cooperation movement in Chattogram.

Basanta Majumdar and Lalit Barman were active workers for the Congress in Tippera.[104] The former belonged to a *zamindar* family in the district of Comilla. He joined politics during the anti-partition agitation. While in Calcutta he came into contact with the *Jugantar* group and organized the party in Comilla, Chittagong and Sylhet.[105] Kshitish Chowdhury in Noakhali, Jatin Roy in North Bengal, Kalipada Bagchi in Rangpur, Bijoy Roy Chowdhury in Gaibandha, Kshitish Sarkar in Serajgang, Bijoy Roy in Jessore, Bhupen Datta in Khulna, Asutosh Das and Bhupati Majumdar in Hooghly, Jiten Mitra in Burdwan and Harikumar Chakrabarti in 24 Parganas all joined the Congress and built up its base in their respective districts.[106]

Harikumar Chakrabarti joined the revolutionaries at an early age. Along with Naren Bhattacharjee (M N Roy) he organized a revolutionary group at Changripota. In 1906 he joined the *Anushilan Samiti* and in 1907 he came into contact with Bagha Jatin. He built up a strong following for Bagha Jatin in Changripota. In 1911 he organized the Young Men's Cooperative Credit and *Zamindary* Society in Gosaba. In

1915 he was arrested at Harry and Sons, which was a business house that secretly harboured revolutionary activities and maintained contact with Batavia. Through this organization the revolutionaries were trying to get arms aid from Germany when Harikumar was arrested. After his release he joined the Congress.[107]

Dr Asutosh Das had been initiated into the struggle for nationalism by his mentor Satish Sengupta. He joined the Anushilan Samiti and organized the revolutionary movement in the Hooghly district. In 1914, after completing his medical studies, he joined the army as a medical officer. Once the First World War ended he resigned from his post and became engaged in social work in Haripal. In this malaria- and kalajar-infested area, he developed a medical centre and trained a group of young men in healthcare and nursing. With their help he was able to eradicate kalajar from the area.[108]

The *Jugantar* group gained control over young people too. In Faridpur, Birbhum and Hooghly they secured a number of members, many whom came into contact with them through the Congress organization.[109]

Members of the Dacca Anushilan Samiti also cooperated with C R Das. Among them were Sris Chandra Chatterjee and Pulin Behari Das.[110] They had secured for Das the support of 300 ex-convicts, mostly members of the Dacca *Anushilan Samity* in the Nagpur session.[111] Sris Chandra entered politics in 1905 as an active leader. As a student he had participated in the activities of the *Anushilan Samiti*. He had defended the nationalists in the Dacca Conspiracy and Barisal Conspiracy cases. He was a close associate of C R Das. Pulin Behari Das, a revolutionary from Faridpur opened an *Akhra* in Tiklatuli following Sarala Devi in Calcutta. In 1906 he was initiated into revolutionary ideals by P Mitra and opened the *Anushilan Samiti* of Dacca to train young men in the art of *lathi* and dagger play. Between 1907 and 1910 he became the leader and *Sarbadhinayak* of the *Samiti* and by 1908 had build up 600 branches all over Bengal and outside the province.[112] In 1920 he organized the *Bharat Sevak Sangha*.

Purnananda Dasgupta a young BA student and a member of the *Anushilan Samiti* became an active Congress worker and started the Dacca District Congress Committee. He was appointed its secretary.[113] Members of the Barisal *Anushilan Samiti* resolved, in a meeting held at Jubbalpore in the house of Jnan Barman, that political sufferers would exert their utmost to assist with the non-cooperation propaganda.[114]

Apart from the *Jugantar* or *Anushilan Samiti*, members of other revolutionary groups also participated actively in the non-cooperation movement. Khagendra Nath Chattopadhyay of Dakshineshwar was a member of the *Atmaonnati Samiti* and joined the non-cooperation movement in 1920. A strong revolutionary centre was built up in Baranagar under his leadership.[115] Through their organizational network the revolutionaries could reach out to the masses and they were instrumental in carrying the Congress organization down to the grass roots.

Influenced by Gandhian ideals, many Congressmen in Bengal became involved with constructive social work which also broadened the social base of the Congress organization. Mention may be made of Prafulla Chandra Ghosh who began his career as a member of the Dacca *Anushilan Samiti*.[116] The method of violent revolution left him unsatisfied so he left the *Samiti*. At the special session of the Calcutta Congress in 1920 he met Gandhi and joined the movement. Dedicating himself to constructive work he organized the *Abhoy Ashram* at Dacca.[117] Initiated into the Gandhian ideal of constructive social work, Satis Chandra Dasgupta engaged himself in social work to spread the ideal of non-cooperation. Influenced by Gandhian ideals from his student days Anath Nath Basu participated in the non-cooperation movement and involved himself in constructive work in the villages. He also joined the Hooghly *Vidyamandir* and later Pathabhavan and Santiniketan.

In the villages of Bankura the local people, inspired by the philosophy of social service, engaged themselves in constructive work. Their activities and support helped local leaders to organize the Congress movement. In Bankura district the headmaster of a local middle school, Govinda Prasad Sinha, had transformed his school into a national institution in 1921.[118] At Brindabanpur in Bankura Kishorimohan Chatterjee, a retired engineer, constructed with his sons a work shop with a spinning wheel, looms and other farming implements to give his village an economic boost.[119] In Faridpur, enthusiasm for *charka* spinning had stirred the subdivisional towns. Rajendra Nath Ganguly, a doctor in Kulpatty, was trying to invent an automatic spinning machine. In Gaurchar and Kistopur villages of P S Sadarpur, the Ghosh, the Mitra and the Biswas families had arranged for *charka* spinning and cotton sowing in their respective villages.[120] Narendra Nath Das of Sankrail, Comilla set up a weaving centre at his house and accepted apprentices.[121]

The non-cooperation movement was able to motivate the women to actively participate in nationalist politics. In Bengal, women had taken active part in revolutionary activities, but the participation had remained confined to few individuals only. A more widespread participation of women from all sections of the society in a collective anti-British agitation began from the period of the non-cooperation movement. Among the leading women activists was Basanti Devi who actively participated in picketing and the boycott of foreign clothes. Along with her husband C R Das she was actively associated with nationalist politics until 1927.

The daughter of illustrious parents Dwaraka Nath Ganguly and Kadambini Devi, Jyotirmoyee Ganguly completed her Masters degree and taught in different schools and colleges all over India, sometimes in the capacity of a principal, and she remained closely connected with the movement for female education. She helped in the organization of the *Vidyasagar Vani Bhaban* established by Lady Abala Basu. Her association with the social and educational movements had already made her prominent, so when she joined politics in 1920 her intelligent personality and organizing capability immediately placed her in the position of leadership. She organized a womens volunteer corps in the Congress. Throughout 1921 and 1922, she participated actively in the agitation; it was only after the movement that she became a member of the Congress. Urmila Devi, sister of Chittaranjan Das, also joined the non-cooperation movement and was one of the first three ladies to court arrest. She was also a member of the BPCC and the All-India Congress Committee.

In the districts too, the women joined the movement along with their male compatriots. Ashalata Sen inspired political, nationalist consciousness among the women of East Bengal through social and constructive work. In 1904, at the age of ten, she published a nationalist poem in *Antapur*, a monthly magazine. She took part in spreading the message of *Swadeshi* at the insistence of her grandmother, Nabasasi Devi. In 1921 she joined the Gandhian movement and with the help of her father-in-law established the *Silpasram*, a weaving centre for women, in her own home at Gandaria, Dacca. She became an active member of the Congress and the representative of the Gaya Congress in 1922.

The connection between the *Khilafat* cause and the non-cooperation movement drew a considerable section of Muslims to the Congress. A new group of Muslim leaders emerged during this period. They were the products of the movement for educational reforms that was launched in the nineteenth century among the Indian Muslims. One stream of the movement was led by the *Ulema* who sought to strengthen the Islamic culture in India from within through the founding of the *Madrassah*.[122] The other movement centering around *Aligarh*, advocated western education for the Muslims.[123] In the years preceding the First World War two religio-political orientations became clear for this new breed of Muslim leaders. Firstly, emphasis on religious issues brought about an alliance between westernized Muslims and *Ulema* and secondly an anti-British sentiment paved the way for a Muslim *entente* with the nationalist movement.[124]

In Bengal, the leadership of the *Khilafat* non-cooperation movement devolved to the *Ulema* and the English-educated Bengali Muslim professionals like Fazlul Huq receded into the background. The *Ulema* who were in command of the majority of the Muslim population were products of either the Deoband School, followers of Pir Sahib of Furfura, or belonged to the Faraizi sect.[125] Many of them were *Madrassah* educated and had early revolutionary connections.

An *Alim* who became prominent in the field of Congress politics in the 1920s was Maulana Abul Kalam Azad. He had rebelled against his scholarly heritage to follow a career in journalism. Born into a Sufi family of the *Qadiri* and *Naqsbandi* orders, he was initially educated at home. But the writings of Sir Sayyid Ahmed led him to question the value of traditional education. His career as a journalist began at an early age when he wrote articles for Urdu newspapers. In 1912 he started the journal *Al Hilal*.[126] This was also the period when as an *Alim* and a *Pir* he began to follow his hereditary profession as a religious leader. A professional journalist and an *Alim*, Azad was able to influence a large section of the Muslim population. He believed in rationalism and also that religion was a matter of heart and could only be felt. His opposition to the *Aligarh* movement also dates back from this period.[127] Through *Al Hilal* Azad mingled political and religious issues. He advocated that it was the religious obligation of the Muslims to struggle for the country's freedom, as equal partners with their Hindu compatriots.[128] Azad was an outspoken champion of Turkey's cause. He was an individual who sought to revitalize Muslim cultural and social life and give them a new orientation that would be a combination of the East and the West.[129]

Mujibar Rahaman the editor of *The Musalman* was a pro-nationalist Muslim who gave up his studies to join the anti-partition agitation.[130] Pir Badsha Mia of Faridpur belonging to the Faraizi Sect was the religious head of the Muslims in Bengal and was one of the vice-presidents of the provincial *Khilafat* committee. Badsha Mia was associated with the New Mohammedan Revolutionary Party of Bengal organized by Maulana Azad after his release from jail in 1920.[131] The party was corresponding secretly with the provincial government of India, then supposed to have been founded at Kabul.[132] Maniruzzaman Islamabadi was the organizer of the Islam Mission and the *Anjuman-i-Ulema-i Bangla*. He, too, was associated with the New Mohammedan Revolutionary Party.[133] Muhammad Akram Khan was an *Alim* educated at the *Alia Madrassah* Calcutta, who played a prominent role in the movement of 1920. He began his political career by actively participating in the anti-partition agitation of 1905. He was also the first president of the *Anjuman-i-Ulema-i Bangla*.

Another *Alim* prominent during the *Khilafat* movement was Maulana Abu Baqr Sidqqi, the *Pir Sahib* of Furfura, Hooghly. He was not originally on good terms with the Bengal *Khilafat* leaders, especially Azad and Akram Khan,[134] but he joined the movement as a result of a campaign by the up-country Mohammedan leaders Shaukat Ali, Dr Kitchlew and Rafi Ud Din Ahmed Qidwai in February and March 1920.[135] However, he made it clear at the annual *urs* gathering at Furfura that he aimed only to preserve Muslim religious rights and had no connection with politics.[136] In North Bengal, especially Rangpur, the *Wahabis* provided Muslim leadership for the movement. Abdullahel Banqui of Dinajpur provided the leadership.

In September 1920 the special session of the Congress and the all-India Muslim league held in Calcutta endorsed the non-cooperation programme.[137] The All-India *Khilafat* Committee also accepted the resolution.[138] In Bengal an office was started by the provincial *Khilafat* committee for registering the names of volunteers.[139] In October 1920 *Anjuman-i-Wazin-i Bangla* and the *Anjuman-i-Ulema-i Bangla*, the two rival organizations, met in a Conference to approve the programme of non-cooperation.[140] The Bengali Muslim press strongly advocated the forging of links between the *Khilafat* and the *Swaraj* movement. The *Saptahik Mohammadi* wrote 'without free India, Islam cannot be saved'.[141] To secure the establishment of self-government in India, *The Mohammadi* commented, may be a political task to others but to the Muslims it is like a great *Jehad* in the defence of religion and race.[142] The Muslims were also urged to join the Congress, which was representative of all sections of the people and could work most satisfactorily for the attainment of *Swaraj*. The *Zamana*, a nationalist Muslim paper, wrote: 'if *Swaraj* is regarded as essential to the solution of the *Khilafat* problem, Muslims should try their best to increase their influence in the National Congress and to make the Non-Cooperation Movement a complete success.'[143] On 4 June 1921 Maulana Mujibar Rahaman and Maulana Akram Khan, as editors of *The Musalman* and *The Mohammadi* respectively, issued a joint statement urging Muslims to rally round the Congress for a satisfactory solution of the *Khilafat* question.[144] Nationalist newspapers like *The Musalman* reported mass meetings in Calcutta, Chittagong and Goalundo.[145] Throughout 1920 *Khilafat* meetings were organized in the Muslim-dominated areas of Bengal. Such means of mass contact drew the Muslim population, especially the youth and the religious leaders, the *Ulema*, into the nationalist movement. They in their turn acted as political mobilizers at grass root level.

However, the incorporation of the *Khilafat* agitation into the mainstream nationalist movement had a negative aspect. The cause of *Khilafat* in many cases determined Muslim participation in the non-cooperation movement. The Turkish peace terms were published in May 1920 and in June at the Allahabad Conference the central *Khilafat* committee accepted Gandhi's policy on non-cooperation because it was in every detail in keeping with the *Shariat*.[146] Moulana Abdul Kadir Azad Shobhani of Cawnpore stated that the movement was in clear accordance with the injunctions of Islam, which allowed three stages of defence, *Jehad*, *Hijarat*, and *Hayat-i-Azadi* or non-cooperation. It was the religious duty of every Mohammedan to follow non-cooperation with the British.

Not unnaturally, even the Muslim nationalist newspapers urged their readers to join the non-cooperation movement as a religious duty. *The Mohammadi* argued, citing from the *Koran*, against friendship with those who had warred with the Musalmans and tried to turn them out of the country.

In the process of mobilizing the people, the Muslim leaders also maintained in their speeches the Islamic nature of the *Khilafat* cause. Even leaders like Maulana Azad, in the course of his address to a predominantly Muslim audience of merchants and labouring classes at the Tantibagan *Khilafat* meet on 10 March 1921, stated that it was an Islamic duty to adopt non-cooperation, to hold aloof from lending assistance to the hostile party or entertaining a feeling of love towards them.[147] Mohammed Ali at the Halliday Park meeting on 8 September 1921 urged the Muslims to boycott British cloth 'which [has] extinguished the light of faith and caused the bloodshed of your brothers, their women and children'. *Khilafat* could be restored only if *Swaraj* was attained. For the Muslims, non-cooperation always remained a religious-cum-political movement. Humayun Kabir in *Moslem Rajniti* indicated clearly that during the phase of the non-cooperation movement many Muslims had joined politics at the call of religion.[148] This was especially true for the more conservative *Ulema* leaders like Pir Sahib of

Furfura. The leadership of the *Ulema* in the *Khilafat* non-cooperation movement strengthened the hold of these religious leaders on society, and orthodoxy and sectarianism began to get the upper hand. The *Ulema* from the very beginning of the *Khilafat* movement demanded strict observation of traditional religious rites.

The Indian Muslims considered themselves to be part of the worldwide Islamic nationalism. Maulana Akarm Khan in his address to the Third Bengali Muslim Literary Conference in 1919 stated that the nationality of the Muslims was based on religion alone. Although non-cooperation leaders were constantly insisting on the need for Hindu—Muslim unity, the religious connection of the *Khilafat* non-cooperation movement was kept alive. So once the non-cooperation movement ended, communal unity also disintegrated.

The involvement of Hindu religious preachers in the non-cooperation movement was also noted by official sources. A meeting was held in Nagpur on the 28 December 1920, attended by 106 *Sadhus*, at which it was decided to form an association to be known as '*Sadhu Sangha*'.[149] The association was to be affiliated to the Congress and would work for the attainment of *Swaraj*. It was also intended to hold a mass meeting at Ayodhya or at Ujjaini in the middle of January to select the delegates who would set out to influence the *Sanyasis* in the Himalayas. According to a report of the Intelligence Branch, Gandhi was 'reported to have thanked the *Sadhus* for supporting the non-cooperation movement and to have advised them to visit the cantonments and military centres to explain to the native soldiers the advisability of relinquishing their employment. He also advised them to move about recruiting areas in order to hamper enlistment for the Army'.[150]

This report was further corroborated by a statement made to the Bihar and Orissa Police by one Krishna Ram Bhatt in January 1921. He was an employee of the Tata Iron and Steel Company who attended the session of the Indian National Congress at Nagpur in December 1920. According to him, a meeting of the *Naga Sadhus* had been held in the Congress Camp and they had decided to undertake the non-cooperation propaganda. The *Naga Sadhus* were held in high esteem by the masses who attached importance to their instructions. They roamed around the villages and towns and through their religious identity captivated the simple minded, God-fearing masses. One could already discern a note of appreciation and conviction in the power of these *Sadhus* from the confessions of Krishna Ram Bhatt: 'When these Nagas took up Non-Cooperation, the scheme would spread like wild fire among the masses of India and eventually the government would be unable to control the 33 crores of people and would have to give *Swaraj*.[151]

From the beginning of 1921 the activities of the *Sadhus* and *Fakirs* in Bengal also increased. But only in a few cases have they been definitely identified in district reports with the non-cooperation movement. Among the individuals who styled themselves as *Swamis* and participated actively in the non-cooperation movement was Swami Biswananda (real name Rasal Singh). He worked to create unrest among the workers in the collieries. In the Chandpur and Chittagong areas Swami Dinananda played an important role in activating the masses. He was a professor of the Shibpur Engineering College. In Chittagong he organized processions and meetings with J M Sengupta in the strikes and *hartals* in the town. The mill areas of the 24 Parganas had been visited by several *Swamis* including Iswar Das of Chapra, Bihar and Orissa. Assam Special Branch Records reported that in March a *Sanyasi* named Surja Das preached non-cooperation in the Garo Hills and visited Mymensingh. Swami Shambhu Giri of the Duttatroy *Akhra*, Chittagong, also had full sympathy with the non-cooperation movement and attended several meetings in the district. He had considerable influence with the up-country men of the locality.

Swami Shajananda arrived at Kurseong from Bhagalpur. Initially he travelled around lecturing on religious subjects and explaining the *Vedas*, the *Gita* and the *Ramayana* at the Hindu temple Serai. He would commence his lectures with illustrations on the lives of Pandavas and Srikrishna from *Mahabharat* and *Gita*. Then gradually he would shift to politics of the recent times and advocate the use of *Swadeshi* goods, the boycott of foreign articles and establishment of the *Panchayat* system to settle disputes, justifying them on the ground that they were ancient religious practices.

Other active participants of the non-cooperation movement were Khagendra Nath Goswami, a *sebak* of the Ram Krishna Mission, Mymensingh. He presided over a non-cooperation meeting in Bogra, where he was actively connected with the movement. He talked of Hindu–Muslim unity and the effectiveness of willpower and also urged withholding from cooperation with the police. Sadhu Kripal Das Udashi of the Sikh *Gurdwara* of Chittagong was an active agitator. He participated in all the political meetings, delivering exciting speeches. He had some influence over the Punjabi workforce. During the Assam Bengal Railway strikes, he deterred the Punjabi workers from resuming work. The officer in charge of the Santipur police station, Nadia, reported that a *sadhu* named Kripa Nath Das, belonging to the

Ramanandi sect, visited Santipur recently on his way from Puri via Krishnanagar. He preached boycott of foreign cloth. What was important about him was that he was a member of the local Congress committee and paid a monthly subscription of one rupee. On the other hand the *sadhus* from Bengal were also politically active in other provinces. Sadhu Kumarananda of Calcutta, for example, delivered three lectures in Chanda, Central Provinces. Muslim *Fakirs* like Abdul Rahman arrived in Darjeeling and preached sedition and Kundalia Sha *Fakir* of Khaja Ajmeer Sharif in Ajmer town, a supporter of non-cooperation, preached in different parts of Bengal inciting anti-British sentiments. The participation of Hindu religious preachers in the non-cooperation movement thus prepared the ground for the rise of Hindu extremism in the post non-cooperation period.

I V

The volunteer organization which had begun to spread rapidly in Bengal since November 1920 was linked with the *Khilafat* and Congress movement of the 1920s. They developed both within and outside the framework of the Congress institution.

In Calcutta the Muslim leaders took the initiative in forming the volunteer corps. After the Muslim leaders Muhammad Akram Khan, Maniruzzaman Islamabadi and others returned at the end of the Amritsar Congress in January 1920, a *Khilafat* committee was organized by the extremist Mohammedan leaders including Nazimuddin Ahmed and Hakim Abdur Rauf.[152] This committee arranged for the reception of Shaukat Ali and other ex-internees of the Punjab. The committee that was entrusted with arrangements for the reception organized a volunteer corps consisting of 907 foot, mounted and cyclist volunteers under the captaincy of Golam Hossain Mal, Abul Hussain and Azim Khan. Both Muslims and Hindus were enlisted as volunteers and they belonged mainly to the merchant class. They were honorary workers, who had already served as volunteers in the special setting of the All-India *Khilafat* and Muslim League Conference in September 1920. When, at the special session of the Congress in 1920, these organizations accepted the non-cooperation resolution, the volunteers withdrew from the organizations. Those that remained formed the Central Mohammedan Volunteer Corps with their office in Seraj Building at 31 Lower Chitpur Road.[153]

In the next phase of the volunteer movement the students played an important role. Once again the Muslim students took the lead. The boys of the Calcutta *Madrassah*, after they boycotted their schools in response to the non-cooperation resolution on 29 October 1920, started a National *Madrassah* under the name *Madrassah Islamia*. The services of the students of this institution were utilized as volunteers in both Calcutta and the *mufassil*.[154] Two groups of six students each were sent to East Bengal and Assam.

The volunteer organization received a fresh impetus during the special session of the Congress in Calcutta. Bengali and Bhatia volunteers thronged the session.[155] A large number of Mohammedan volunteers had also been active in connection with the special session of the Muslim League. The Central Mohammedan volunteer corps under Golam Hossain Mal was formed during this time.[156]

The Hindu leaders only took an interest in the formation of volunteer corps for spreading the message of non-cooperation after the Nagpur session of the Congress in December 1920. The Bengal Non-Cooperation Volunteer Corps was formed under the guidance of Shyam Sundar Chakrabarti, Bhola Nath Barman, Padam Raj Jain, Bama Charan Majumdar and others.[157] The Corps consisted of 50 Bhatias, Muhammadans and Bengalis, many of whom had worked as volunteers on the occasion of the reception of the ex-internees and at the Congress special session at Calcutta. Their office was at 83 Lower Chitpur Road and they were engaged in non-cooperation propaganda work, distributing leaflets and organizing meetings in connection with the non-cooperation movement.

Through the volunteer movement members of the labouring class were also brought within the non-cooperation movement. Muhammad Osman of Monghyr, a teacher in Abul Kalam Azad's *Madrassah* in Ranchi came to Calcutta in April 1921 and joined the *Khilafat* office as head preacher on a salary of 50 rupees per month.[158] He travelled around the mill areas in the vicinity of Calcutta, striking up friendships with the *sardars* and other labourers and exhorting them to attend the meetings in Calcutta.[159] He trained the young labourers as volunteers and under his instruction batches of volunteer groups were formed under different captains at Kidderpore, Tantibagan, Chore Bagan, Entally, Sahib Bagan, Patwar Bagan and Shyambazar. Such groups were composed of between 800 and 1,000 men drawn mainly from low caste Muhammadans and mill hands. They were paid a wage of eight annas per day when at work.[160] The captains attended the *Khilafat* office daily and received orders from Osman. These volunteers were utilized for non-cooperation and *Khilafat* demonstrations whenever the occasion demanded.

In September 1921 the BPCC started a new volunteer corps, the National Service Worker's Union under the guidance of National Service Board.[161] The members were mostly ex-*detenus* like Satyendra Nath Mitra, Pulin Behari Das, Pravash Lahiri, Shamsuddin Ahmed and Subhas Bose. The National Service Board undertook to organize volunteer corps in Bengal. In every district and subdivision a volunteer corps would constitute a captain and a vice-captain on a salary of 50 to 75 rupees per month. Volunteers were to be registered at a wage of 15 rupees per month. Thus, throughout Bengal, a well-knit organization was established.

In the districts the Congress Committees also took the initiative to organize volunteer corps, although only after the Bezwada Conference. Four district volunteer corps were started. The North District Volunteer Corps consisted of 40 members including Shyam Sundar Chakrabarti, Jitendra Lal Banerjee, Ramesh Sen and Makhan Sen. The others were the Central District Volunteer Corps led by Bipin Behari Ganguly, Provash De and Satyendra Mitra, the South District Volunteer Corps headed by Hemendra Nath Dasgupta, Jogesh Das Gupta and Radha Shyam Singh and the Barabazar District Volunteer Corps under the leadership of Padam Raj Jain, Bhola Nath Barman, Nagendra Lal Modi and Madhav Prasad Shukla.[162] The volunteers of these organizations were sent out to the *mufussils* for village propaganda work.

The Madaripur *Swarajya Santi Sena* was formed under the leadership of Purna Das after the Nagpur Congress session in December 1920.[163] The *Santi Senas* were distributed in 16 centres called *Nebashes* and were trained in ordinary drill regularly.[164] The *Santi Senas* from Madaripur went to Rangpur and established a volunteer corps in July 1921.[165] This corps was also drilled regularly. Later it was led by Birendra Chandra Mukherjee, an ex-professor of Rangpur College.[166] He changed the designation of the corps to *Bangiya Swaraj Sebak Samiti*.[167] He engaged himself in an extensive recruitment campaign with the object of enlisting 600,000 volunteers.[168] The district was divided into four subdivisions and 29 *thanas*. Biren Mukherjee himself was the captain, with vice-captains or subdivisional officers under him for the four subdivisions of Sadar, Kurigram, Gaibandaha and Nilphamari.[169] Each *thana* was to have two *thana* officers, *nayaks*, each with a fixed number of volunteers under their charge. The volunteers were called *habildars*.[170] They wore regulation badges bearing the inscription *Bangiya Swaraj Sebak Samiti*, Rangpur. A budget of 4,500 rupees per month had been prepared which included 1,500 rupees for clothing.[171] The volunteers were responsible for collection of funds, formation of village Congress committees, enforcement of the Congress committee's programmes of progressive constructive social work, supervision of *Chakra*, formation of village volunteer corps at the rate of 2,000 rupees per *thana*, picketing of wine and ganja shops, and holding public meetings.[172]

At Fulchari in Rangpur a Congress *thana* had been running since November 1921. Harihar Majumdar of Galna police station, Fulchari, was appointed its *nayak*. There were three *habildars* and 2,000 volunteers under him for the purpose of organizing the Fulchari *thana*. In Rangpur the *Santi Sena* movement had spread very rapidly and by August 1921 the commission of Rajshahi Division reported that about 125 such groups had been enlisted.[173]

Besides the existing volunteer organizations at Pabna town and Serajganj, the *Santi Sena* of Madaripur established a corps in Pabna.[174] At Natore in Rajshahi District a youth organization was formed of boys between eight and twelve years old who regularly practiced archery.[175] The *Swaraj Sevak Sangha* under Provash Lahiri, secretary of the district Congress committee, was the central volunteer organization in Rajsahi.[176] In the Tamluk subdivision of Midnapur *Tamralipta Santi Sena* and *Moyna Santi Sena* were formed as volunteer bodies.[177] The *Sevak Samiti* under Swami Darsanananda at Raniganj Burdwan was also active. At Noakhali, Howrah and Kurigram the volunteers were regularly drilled.[178]

In Birbhum there was no regular volunteer corps. But the *Swaraj Ashram,* which was controlled and financed by the district Congress committee, had between 10 and 15 volunteers who were employed to spread the creed of non-cooperation in the interior of the districts. Non-*ashram*-ite local people also enlisted themselves as volunteers to work in villages.[179] Independent organizations also sprang up in several areas. The *Jatiya Sechha Sebak Samiti* was started by Mokhada Samadhya and Jayanta Bose. Systematic recruiting for membership of these organizations began in April 1921, with students being the major enlistees.

After December 1920 when the Nagpur Congress suggested the raising of a national service corps, enlistment under the new scheme was fairly rapid. By 19 May 1921, regular corps of volunteers were established in many parts of the province. Almost all the corps were built up along a definite organizational scheme which improved with time. At Faridpur, in Eastern Bengal, at Pabna in North Bengal and in Rangpur the movement gained strength. But it reached its zenith of efficiency at Rangpur where by the end of the year the whole district was organized into subdivisions and *thanas*.

The government declared the volunteer organizations as unlawful associations, but this merely served to increase the pace of recruitment. In the districts of Mymensingh, Barisal and Bankura, 700, 360 and 200 new volunteers respectively were enrolled. In Bankura and Dinajpur the proclamation gave a strong impetus to the recruitment process. But the weakness of the volunteer organization lay in the fact that it was built up at a time when nationalist fervour was at its peak and many of its institutions and features were created for launching a nationwide movement which was unsustainable once that fervour subsided.

V

The non-cooperation movement saw attempts to establish national institutions as alternatives to the British or British-aided institutions. This also helped to strengthen the Congress organization. In 1919 there were four national schools with a combined total of 326 pupils, a marked decrease from the 369 that there had been in 1918. The four existing national schools were the Bengal Technical Institute with 173 pupils, the Bengal National Reading with 58 pupils, Santipur National School with 32 students and Chandpur National School with 63 students. Regarding these schools the Director of Public Instruction (DPI) of Bengal reported that; 'the present attitude of the authorities of the existing national schools towards the government is reported to be friendly and no unfavourable report has been received during the year against any teacher or pupil for complicity in political crime...'.[180]

In 1920 the number of national schools was reduced to three but the number of students increased to 500. Until then, the the DPI reports presented a picture of friendly attitude towards the government.[181] Only the inspector of schools in the Chittagong division reported that Chandpur National School occasionally allowed its boys to take part in Congress propaganda work in the neighbourhood.[182]

But the non-cooperation movement had given the national institutions a new lease of life 'which arose in the earlier days of unrest in Bengal and which never entirely disappeared'.[183] The movement also saw the establishment of new national institutions. There were no national institutions in Burdwan, Dacca and Rajsahi Division even in 1920. But by 1921, 32 schools had sprung up in the Burdwan Division with a student population of 2,184. There were 94 new schools in Dacca Division with 9,046 pupils, and 13 in Rajsahi Division with 760 students. Within one year 139 national schools with 11,990 students appeared. The Presidency Division, which had only two schools in 1920, reported that this had increased to 16 in 1921. The Bengal Technical Institute, which was the only institution to provide vocational training, also attracted new students and about 468 were admitted in 1921. In Chittagong Division the Chandpur National School, a solitary relic from the *Swadeshi* period, thrived along with 15 more new creations. Eleven of them had 1,010 students attending them. Among these national schools 16 schools were already existing and recognized by the University of Calcutta. In the Burdwan Division there were three such schools, four in the Presidency Division, two in the Chittagong Division, and seven in the Dacca Division. According to the inspector of schools, no uniform curriculum was followed in these schools except with regard to recognition of vernacular as the first language and English as the second language. The divisional inspector reported:

> ...the phenomenal rise in the number of national schools in the province was to be attributed to the result of the preaching of non-cooperation doctrines which denounced the purely literary character of the present system education. Naturally the attitude of these schools are reported to be unfriendly to the government This is corroborated by the fact that some of the teachers and students of these institutions are reported to have been convicted of political offences.[184]

These schools were maintained by locally generated funds and contributions from the Congress funds. The government felt that the main aim of these schools was to give 'general with technical education and to free themselves from departmental control' and expected that since the schools were 'maintained amid deplorable conditions, they will collapse sooner or later chiefly for want of funds'.[185]

The Tilak National School was opened by Gandhi near Mechuabazar in Calcutta. Teaching was in Hindusthani and the school curriculum included instruction in spinning, tailoring, carpentry, typewriting and commercial training. The school was to be under the supervision of Professor Sambas Vaswani. About 250 students had enrolled.

Among these educational institutions the most important were the revitalized national institutions of the *Swadeshi* period that had perished. New national institutions were also opened. They often provided the Congress committees with workers and the much necessary space for office work. In Hooghly, for example, the Hooghly *Vidya Mandir* was set up which acted as the office of the district Congress committee.[186] At Patiya the Gandhi *Vidyapith* was established with 100 students.

Among the non-educational organizations that helped to sustain the nationalist movement were such institutions as *Abhoy Ashram, Kalyan Sangha* at Hooghly and *Swaraj Ashram* in Birbhum. The *Abhoy Ashram* came into existence during the days of the non-cooperation movement at Gandaria Dacca under the initiative of Dr Prafulla Chandra Ghosh, Suresh Banerjee and others.[187] The *Ashram* aimed to attain *Swaraj* by developing all the activities of the people. The *Ashram* ran national schools at Nawabganj and Furshali in Dacca and also undertook to spread the use of *Khaddar* among the masses.[188]

The *Bangiya Swaraj Sevak Sangha* was formed during these years and set up branches in different areas at the initiative of the local gentry. In Chikandi the local pleader Narendra Nath Chakrabarty started the Chikandi *Swarajya Samity*. The local centre of the *Sangha* was at Chikandi because the pleaders of the area were extending their support to the scheme. Several branches were opened in the more backward areas of Faridpur like Panditshar, Palong, Idilpur, Bhojeswar and Rajbari. The members roamed the villages organizing meetings, selecting *panchaits* to settle disputes. They also set up arbitration courts and Bhabatosh Basu, the pleader of Chikandi Bar who had suspended his practice, settled all undecided disputes. The district magistrate of Faridpur reported that; 'the members were winning the sympathy of the public by their special good work like when a servant in a hostel died but nobody else came forward to burn the dead boy, while they did'.[189] Such philanthropic deeds readily won them the support of the common people. The reports described them as 'students in Calcutta, specially trained for this purpose and sent out to work in their home districts'.

The Chikandi centre was working so efficiently that the officials feared that 'within a few months the masses will be organized'.[190] *Swaraj Sevak Samitis* were also established at Kurigram and Ulipur in Rangpur, Shazadpur in Pabna and Bhanga in Faridpur. In Goila Bakarganj, a *Swaraj Sampradaya* was started by Jyotish Chandra Gupta and Kesu

Chandra Sen. The *Sampradaya* was a branch of the *Barisal Swaraj Sangha* intended to carry on non-cooperation and *Swadeshi* propaganda in the area.[191]

Kalyan Sangha, an *Ashram* in Hooghly, sheltered Congress workers.[192] The *Satyashrams* of Daulatpore Jessore, Baherak and Chattogram were centres from which the revolutionaries who had joined the Congress carried on propaganda work.[193] A similar *Ashram* in Mymensingh called *Srigauranga Ashram* was set up in the house of Kulada Shankar Rai. Its object was ostensibly to help the poor and give them medical treatment but in fact the *Ashram* worked as a recruiting ground for volunteers. The members moved about collecting supporters and money.[194] These institutions were not a constituent part of the Congress organization but were meant to provide it with structural support by acting as centres from which the Congress workers could direct their activities.

The most important long-term contribution of the non-cooperation movement was the evolution of a strong hierarchical Congress organization. Bengal was no exception to this rule. The BPCC, it has been seen, was linked to districts and villages through a network of lower level Congress committees. The Congress also established links with a number of other organizations that lent their support during this period. The charismatic leadership of Das and his associates contributed to the force of nationalism in Bengal. During this period there also emerged a new leadership from the districts and villages. In the wake of the non-cooperation movement the Congress organization was restructured in such a way that the local institutions and the local leaders became important links in the entire edifice.

Chapter 3

Congress and the Masses: The Non-Cooperation and *Khilafat* Movement in Bengal 1920–22.

I

The reorganized Congress that emerged in Bengal in the 1920s adopted diverse methods of mobilization to build up its support base during the non-cooperation *Khilafat* movement. This chapter examines the nature of Congress interaction with popular politics between 1920 and 1922 when nationalist fervour acquired a great momentum.

The remodelled Congress, which developed strong village links in the wake of non-cooperation agitation, was sustained by ideological and political propaganda. While this initiative went a long way towards guiding the disparate economic grievances and a general anti-British feeling into a non-violent anti-imperialist struggle, equally important was the spontaneous self-mobilization of the masses and their conscious acceptance of the nationalist message of their leaders. The relationship between nationalist propaganda from above and the self-initiative of the people is therefore an interesting area of study.

The Congress leadership adopted various methods to mobilize different social groups and draw them into the non-cooperation movement. In the city of Calcutta, as well as in the countryside, mass meetings emerged as rallying points for a wide cross-section of people. The preliminary agitation among the Muslim masses was conducted by up-country Mohammedan leaders Sahukat Ali, Dr Kitchlew and Rafi-Ud-din Ahmed Qidwai who toured the province and held meetings at the *mufassil* centres to propagate anti-Turkish Peace Treaty campaigns.[1] During this period several meetings were held to impart the message of boycott and *Jehad* against the foreigners even in such remote areas as Gunbati in the district of Tippera.[2] After the special session of the National Congress at Calcutta in September 1920, extremist leaders like Sarala Bala Devi, Jitendra Lal Banerjee and Shyam Sundar Chakrabarti, who had earlier remained aloof, began to address meetings instead of merely attending them. Bipin Chandra Pal presided over a Muslim Conference at Sylhet.[3] Religious preachers often addressed the masses in the meetings as well. In Faridpur, Moulana Immad-ud-din Nuri of Tipperah was identified as the 'most striking speaker who received invitations from leading men of the villages in the interior to give lectures'.[4] He held meetings in different places in the Kalkini and Madaripur police stations. He was a religious preacher but he introduced such secular topics as Khilafat and non-cooperation agitation, reduction in the area of jute cultivation and the need for technical institutes.

To mobilize the student community, the Congress leadership organized meetings immediately following the Calcutta Session in 1920 specifically to discuss the role of students in the movement. Initially, Bengali leaders like C R Das and B C Pal, supported by congressmen from other provinces, vehemently opposed the boycott of schools and colleges. Chitta Ranjan Das wanted to make the boycott of educational institutions consistent with economic boycott and urged non-withdrawal of students from schools and colleges until the full programme of non-cooperation could be put into force. But after the Nagpur Congress the leaders changed their stance. They exhorted the students to give up all thoughts of education until Swaraj had been attained. Regular meetings were held at which nationalist leaders decried the government institutions as having a demoralizing and dehumanizing atmosphere from which the students should be weaned away. The students were to join national schools and colleges, not in the hope of continuing their education as before, but to devote themselves to the service of the nation.

At a crowded student meeting in Mirzapore Park Bipin Chandra Pal remarked that, this being a fight for national freedom, the problem of education must take a subordinate place to the problem of Swaraj. The main aim of national schools and colleges would be to maintain some sort of moral and intellectual discipline among the youth who were leaving the government institutions.[5] Maulana Ahmed Ali, in his address to the students at College Square in January 1921, advised them to go back to their villages and educate the masses by training them in different industries and the improvement of village sanitation and to keep up village spirits in order to make non-violent non-cooperation a success.[6] On 10 and 11 January 1921, the Bengal Provincial Khilafat Committee organized a public meeting at Wellington Square and Beadon Square to explain the the duty of students concerning the Congress resolution of

Nagpur.[7] The speakers were Shyam Sundar Chakrabarti, Sris Chandra Chatterjee, Nirmal Chandra Chunder, Ambica Ukil, Ahmed Ali, Ambica Prasad Bajpayee, Padam Raj Jain, S P Roy, *Moulavi* Ahmed Ali and others. In Faridpur, non-cooperation meetings were held by the *bhadralok* to rouse the student community and to keep them in a state of agitation.

Daily reports on non-cooperation in *The Musalman* refer to regular rallies held in the districts to motivate popular participation. Besides the specific agenda of the non-cooperation resolution, general matters like Hindu–Muslim unity and village reconstruction were also discussed. Most of these meetings were held in busy areas, meeting places where different types of people could gather in an open space. The Faridpur District Congress Committee, for example, held what an official report called 'a monster mass meeting in Goalundo Ghat, obviously a very busy riverway'.[8] People of all classes and professions attended these meetings and audience numbers swelled in some cases to more than 30,000. *Moulavi* Muhammad Rowshan Ali Chowdhury was voted to the chair. Choudhuri Muhammad Takubali and Pandit Namrupji Sharma delivered the speeches. They explained *Swaraj*, non-cooperation and the Congress organization. The audience were urged to become members of the Congress and those who enrolled were invited to attend the subdivisional Congress committee at Rabari in April. In Malda, five successive meetings were held between 20 and 24 April at Shibganj, Nawabganj, Gomastpur and Chowdala and this brought to a successful close the tour of *Moulavi* Ahmed Ali Saheb. Immediately afterwards, the boys of Nawabganj school went on strike. At Nehalpur in the Basirhat subdivision of 24 Parganas, a non-cooperation meeting of the Hindus and the Muslims was held. Prafulla Chandra Banerjee, a renowned pleader of Basirhat, renounced his practice on the same day that he was voted to the chair. *Moulavi* Akram Khan urged the students to boycott government institutions and the lawyers to suspend practice. All people were advised to take to spinning, the litigants were exhorted to boycott courts and take recourse to arbitration and the farmers asked to concentrate the cultivation of rice and cotton and stop the cultivation of jute.

Rallies were also organized to spread anti-British sentiment among the working class and the peasantry. The labouring class, through *Khilafat* non-cooperation meetings in the industrial areas of the metropolis and the suburbs, were introduced to the concept of non-violent *satyagraha*. In April 1920 at Garden Reach a meeting was held which was attended by 3,000 workers.[9] During the National Week subscriptions were collected throughout the mill area. In the coal fields of Raniganj, Jamuria and Barakar mass meetings were held to stir up labour agitation. At Ballarpur, a meeting was organized presided over by a local Bengali *zamindar* and colliery owner. Darsanananda addressed a gathering of 300 up-country workers, whipping up racial ill feeling against the Europeans.[10] At Jamuria, a speech by Darsanananda propagated the 'Bolshevik principle' of equality between the rich and the poor.[11] Darsanananda explained to a gathering of 5,000 labourers on his second visit to Jamuria that the real objective of the meetings was to hinder the work of the European-owned collieries and to strengthen and enrich the collieries belonging to Indians. To foment trouble he instructed the labourers to cease work and join the collieries owned by Indians unless Andrew Yule, which was preventing other companies from increasing wages, granted a wage increase of 100 per cent.[12]

Non-cooperation propaganda was directly responsible for precipitating the strike at Ichapur Rifle Factory. The chief organizer of the strike, Sudhansu Kumar Bose, an apprentice at the Kanchrapara Railway Workshop, was a member of the party of Purna Das.[13] With the help of local wealthy and influential personalities like Rudal Singh he exerted influence over the factory employees and built up a strong organization at Kanchrapara.[14] A non-cooperation meeting was organized for the workers and Sudhansu Kumar Bose addressed the audience, advising them to give up drinking and to form a *panch* to act as arbitrators in settling disputes. The decision was also taken at this meeting to stop work if demands for a higher wage was not met.

Once systematic recruitment of volunteers started in April 1921, the mill *sardars* were invited to attend the non-cooperation meetings in Calcutta by Muhammad Osman of Monghyr, the head preacher of the *Khilafat* office who had been deputed to train labourers as volunteers. In Darjeeling non-cooperators spread their message among the tea-garden labourers. Khagendra Kishore Ball and Debendra Nath Das arrived at Kurseong and delivered several lectures on the boycott of foreign goods. Debendra Nath Das also spoke in a meeting in the market place of Darjeeling town. He talked about the predicament of the tea-garden coolies who received a meagre daily wage and suggested that if they stopped work for a time their wages might be increased. This meeting was attended by about 500 men.[15]

In rural areas too, the most popular method of reaching the people was the organization of meetings and *sabhas* where local leaders and often Congress and *Khilafat* leaders from Calcutta tried to explain to the peasants the meaning of *Swaraj*, relating the atrocities committed by the British in the Punjab and explaining the economic exploitation by the colonial rulers. These meetings were held all over the province from September 1920. At these assemblies, thronged by the rural multitude, the leaders always emphasized the need to spin cloth, set up arbitration courts, reduce the area of jute cultivation and switch over to rice cultivation.

From 1920 onwards, *Khilafat* leaders in Eastern Bengal preached non-cooperation to the Muslim cultivators on account of the wrong done to the *Khalifa*. As will be seen later, the jute boycott programme was popularized among the peasants mainly through meetings where the volunteers discussed the need for reducing the acreage under jute cultivation. Thus along with the industrial centres, the agrarian sector provided much potential support for the non-cooperationists. Throughout the non-cooperation *Khilafat* movement, mass meetings and demonstrations proved to be the most effective method of rallying the people, especially the students, labourers and rural peasants. Even in early 1922 the volunteers were enlisted chiefly from districts like Burdwan, Chittagong, Dacca, Jessore, Midnapur and Mymensingh.[16] They were mainly students, labourers and peasants but also included grocers, shopkeepers and other such men from the districts. Thus, as the intensity of the movement grew, all sections of society united in anti-British opposition.

The press was a strong medium of Congress propaganda in Bengal. A rich variety of nationalist newspapers already existed, both in English and in Indian languages. The most widely circulated extremist English daily was the *Amrita Bazar Patrika*. Representing the liberal nationalist school of thinking, it supported the Indian National Congress and its programmes, but not uncritically. The paper used to be published from Calcutta and edited by Motilal Ghosh. The *Amrita Bazar Patrika* supported Gandhi's non-cooperation programme, especially constructive non-cooperation. The *Patrika*, however, disapproved of the Calcutta resolution which 'touched only a very small section of the nation'.[17] The students and legal professions could help to popularize the idea of non-cooperation and prepare the country for national strike. But the real strength of the movement lay in the masses whose enthusiasm could be roused only by *Swadeshi* and boycott. The *Patrika* editorial of 25 December 1921 strongly advocated economic boycott; 'the economic condition which the combination of administration and exploitation has brought about if properly explained to the masses will rouse enthusiasm for Swaraj far more than the Punjab and Khilafat wrongs'.[18]

The Servant, published in Calcutta and edited by the pro-Gandhian Congressman Shyam Sundar Chakrabarti, became the major voice of non-violent non-cooperation. It supported and encouraged boycott of British educational institutions. In its editorial of 17 January 1921 it wrote that 'towards the fulfillment of the movement the first step has been taken. At a splendid rally, worthy of the traditions of Bengal, the students of Calcutta Colleges have come out in their thousands'. It argued that the 'intent underlying the boycott of schools and colleges had been misunderstood. The students were to boycott educational institutions so that they have no association with the bureaucracy. Though the leaders have the duty to make provision for the future training and education of the students, that cannot be interpreted either as a consideration or an inducement for boycott. Their sense of self respect must prompt them to avoid the existing educational system'.[19]

Vernacular newspapers in Bengali and Hindi also gained circulation during the non-cooperation and *Khilafat* movement. The *Dainik Basumati*, a Bengali daily paper, was published from Calcutta and edited by Hemendra Prasad Ghosh and Satish Chandra Mukherjee. It was a nationalist newspaper which was severe in its criticism of some aspects of the non-cooperation movement, especially the burning of foreign cloth to stir up popular feeling.

The most popular Hindi daily was *Bharat Mitra*, published from Calcutta. It was edited by Lakshman Narain Garde, a Marathi Hindu Brahmin and its interest centred mainly around the home rule agitation.[20] The *Dainik Bharat Mitra* was the extremist daily edition of *Bharat Mitra*. It urged the nationalist leaders to unite under the banner of the Indian National Congress to make 'non-cooperation a complete success'. The other extremist Hindu daily was *Biswamitra* edited and owned by Mul Chand Agarwal of United Provinces, the headmaster of Mahasaya Vidyalaya.[21] Cultivators and traders, it urged, should be brought within the ambit of non-cooperation. The advantages of boycotting foreign goods should be preached to them in order to give impetus to *Swadeshi* industries. The paper urged Congress to announce that no cultivator should sell wheat to a trader who intended to export. The Indian traders were also urged not to buy wheat for export.

A large number of weekly newspapers published from the districts acted as a link between Calcutta and the *mofussils*. Most of them were published in Bengali. *Barisal Hitaishi*, was edited by Asutosh Bagchi, Durga Mohan Sen and Baidya Chandra Har.[22] The former was a revolutionary from Betpor police station, Ganrandi. He joined the press after his release from jail in 1908. The other two were graduates of Calcutta University.

Another Bengali weekly, *Charu Mihir*, was published from Mymensingh by Baikuntha Nath Shome, a Hindu *Kayastha* and the manager of the Patia Estate District Rajshahi. Durga Das Roy, a pleader from Mymensingh was a co-publisher of the paper with Baikuntha Nath Shome. This weekly was the mouthpiece of the People's Association of Mymensingh. The tone of the paper was extremist. It supported non-cooperation with the British. 'The method of non-cooperation is easy and natural and is sure to attain the desired end. The movement has a strong hold over the popular mind', a *Charu Mihir* editorial observed on 19 April 1921.[23]

The non-cooperation movement in Midnapur was covered by *Midnapur Hitaishi* and *Nihar*. The former was a local Bengali extremist weekly published from Midnapur town.[24] *Nihar*, a weekly from Contai, was edited by a local *Mahisya* Madhusudan Jana. It was the organ of the local Congress and connected with *Brahmo Samaj*. The paper supported non-cooperation.[25]

The Herald was published from Dacca. It welcomed the Congress decision to 'work among the masses and introduce *charka*'.[26] The *Rarh Dipika* was published from Rampurhat in Birbhum.[27] *The Musalman*, an English weekly, was published from 24 Parganas, edited by *Moulavi* Mujibar Rahaman. It was an organ of the pro-Congress extremist Muhammadans, supporting non-cooperation, especially through the boycott of educational institutions.[28] It urged students to give up their studies in 'government-controlled institutions where slaves are only manufactured' and suggested they 'should even go without any education if national schools and colleges are not forthcoming'.[29]

Another influential Muslim newspaper was *The Mohammadi* edited by Muhammad Akram Khan. He also published another Urdu daily, *Zamana*. Through these organs, hostility to government action was preached. The Muslim population was exhorted to oppose the British, especially to destroy the English cloth trade; as the English had done the greatest harm to Turkey, Muslims were bound to strike more ardently than Hindus to bring *swadeshi*. *The Mohammadi* also promoted the cause of unity between Hindus and Muslims.[30]

However, the press could reach only a limited section of the population, namely the literate and those who had the money to buy newspapers. It could also be circulated only within a limited area and remote villages remained outside the sphere of the press. To propagate the ideas of Gandhian nationalism among such sections of the population in the rural and urban areas numerous leaflets and pamphlets in English, Hindi and Bengali were published at local level. They proved to be the most popular means of promoting nationalist ideas. The Hindi leaflets advocating non-cooperation that particularly gained in circulation included *Bideshia, Firingia* and *Ashajog Jhankar.*

In the countryside folk art and songs were used to pass on the nationalist message. *Jatra* and *Kirtan* processions were extremely popular forms of art which attracted a huge gathering. *Swadeshi Jatra* on patriotic themes became popular in the rural areas. Patriotic songs and music had a particular appeal to popular consciousness. The trend which started in the late nineteenth century from the time of the *Hindu Mela* continued into the twentieth century, with even greater vigour. The songs that became popular during the *Swadeshi Andolan* continued to inspire the populace. Not only in Barisal but throughout Bengal the songs of *Charan Kabi* Mukunda Das, for example, reinvigorated popular consciousness of the national cause. Mukunda Das also formed his own group for performing the art of *Jatra* and wrote *palas* (stories) on patriotic themes. During the non-cooperation movement he wrote and enacted pieces on themes like *Karmakshetra, Path* and *Palliseva.* Some of his songs sung during this period were 'A Manai Bharat Galo' ('False Pride is the Bane of India'), 'Amon Sonar Deshe Asiare' ('The Devil Has Come to This Golden Land'), a song sung in the villages by the tillers of the soil, 'Jagare Bhai Sabe Smaria Keshabe' ('Wake Up in the Name of Lord Krishna') and 'Babu Bujbe Ki Aar Male' ('Babu, What Would it Take You to Realise?'). Songs of Rajani Kanta Sen, Kamini Kumar Bhattacharya, Dwijendra Lal Roy, Atul Prasad Sen and Aswini Kumar Dutta were equally popular. 'Chere Dao Kacher Churi, Banga Nari Kobhu Hate Aar Poro Na' ('O Women of Bengal, Get Rid of Your Foreign Glass Bangles, Never Wear Them Again') by Monmohan Chakravarti remained popular because of its theme of boycott and its appeal to the women of Bengal to rise in conscious protest against British rule. Commonly known as the battle song, 'Othre Bhai Hindu Musalman Sakale Bhai' ('Wake Up All the Hindu and Muslim Brothers') by Satish Chandra Banerjee was also reminiscent of communal harmony. The songs of Rabindra Nath Tagore of course always had a special appeal to the Bengali mind. Equally forceful were the songs of Kaji Najrul Islam. Bankim Chandra's 'Bande Mataram' ('I Worship Thee, Oh My Motherland...') also continued to retain its popularity among the common people.[31]

Constructive non-cooperation was yet another dimension of the movement for *Swaraj*. It imparted a spirit of self help, reducing the people's dependence on the institutions of the *Raj*. For instance, in Calcutta alcoholic drinks were prohibited and people were persuaded to give up drinking. Among the educated classes *Khadi* grew more and more popular. Two weaving institutions were opened by the North Calcutta Congress Committee at Sonagachi Lane in the house of a prostitute and the government suspected that the motive was to 'influence the woman to make a will in favour of the national movement'.[32] Several new shops were opened which sold country-made cloth. A handloom business was also started. Arbitration courts were set up all over the province whose number increased to 534 in August and continued to increase every week. In addition, 231 arbitration boards were set up in Rangpur and Barisal.

Gandhian leaders sought to win the support of the working class by organizing the workers and improving the quality of their life. A group of young Bengalis led by Nagendra Nath Gangopadhyay (a son-in-law of Rabindra Nath Tagore and a non-cooperator who had left Grace Bros so as not to serve a foreign capitalist firm drawing money out of India) accompanied C F Andrews to organize trade unions in Calcutta.[33] Pandit Krishna Kumar Shastri, a disciple of Gandhi from the Arrah district of Bihar, was engaged in similar constructive work in the vicinity of Titagarh. He preached Hindu–Muslim unity, formed arbitration courts and persuaded the mill hands to give up toddy and liquor. Both Hindu and Muslim mill workers regarded him with respect and followed his instructions in social and religious matters. His constructive programme was immensely successful in Titagarh.

In South West Bengal the Congress built up a strong base, mainly through providing welfare support at times of distress. To the penniless peasants and artisans, the Congress workers brought hope, suggesting alternative sources of income by spinning and weaving. In Bankura the non-cooperating Congressmen directed their efforts towards revitalizing the economy through constructive work. In Brindabanpur village a workshop was set up in Barajora police station for teaching spinning and weaving and also improving agricultural techniques. Peasants and artisans of Barajola and Gangajaghati attended the workshop.[34] They received payments in cash according to their output. In the subdivisional towns, there was great enthusiasm among the townsfolk for learning spinning and weaving and even inventing new techniques. In the Kulpaddy police station of Faridpur, a local doctor called Rajendra

Nath Ganguly was trying to develop an automatic spinning machine. The local affluent high caste families Mitra, Ghosh and Roy in Gaurchar police station, Sadarpur, and the Biswas family in Kestopur village arranged to provide facilities for spinning *charka* and also encouraged the sowing of cotton seeds in their respective villages.[35] At the sadar subdivision of Faridpur, a meeting of the *Bhadralok* of the town was held, presided over by Govinda Ram Marwari, a Faridpur town cloth merchant. The audience proposed to start a national weaving institute, towards which people were urged to subscribe.[36]

Indu Bhusan Guha, a matriculate student of Fanindra Deb Institution, opened a small shop in the local market and along with 88 of his friends he sold *khadi*.[37] In Howrah district a cloth shop at Grand Trunk Road that sold *swadeshi* cloth appointed a man to give public demonstrations of the *charka* method of spinning. In Khulna district at Tala, Sayyid Jalaluddin of Tentulia organized the local peasants. Spinning became extremely popular and the sale of British cloth almost ceased as *swadeshi* cloth was much cheaper. In the city of Calcutta a spinning school, *Abaitanik Charka Vidyalaya*, was set up to give free instruction on spinning and weaving.[38] Here too, the creation of a national weaving institute was proposed, towards which people were urged to contribute.[39]

In addition to encouraging village handicrafts, the Congress also set up courts of arbitration as part of its constructive programme. The number of these courts kept on increasing. By the middle of the year 1921 the provincial total for such judicial bodies reached 598. In Rangpur the members of the *Swarajya Samiti* at Chikandi moved around selecting *Panchayats* to settle disputes. If the *Panchayats* failed to arrive at a solution the dispute was referred to Bhabatosh Basu, a lawyer who had left his practice.

At Dalsakandi in Pabna a branch of the *Swaraj Sebak Sangha* was formed. Courts of arbitration and a night weaving school were set up.[40] In the Suja Nagar police station of Pabna District 250 villagers from Kohalilpur, Sagar Kandi and Govindapur enlisted as Congress members. In Rangpur, especially at the Chikandi Centre, organizational work was spreading very fast and official reports claimed that within a few months the masses would be organized.

In Birbhum after the initial propaganda drive by upcountry men the movement gained in popularity among the people. Most of the poorer people gave up drinking *pachai*. The local liquor shops were destroyed.[41] Several meetings were also organized in the Rampurhat circle principally to prohibit the drinking of liquor in the locality. The up-country men of Rampurhat also organized a meeting where they vowed not to consume liquor. Anyone found drinking would be fined and would have to pay the fine to the person who discovered the transgression. In Shibtala village the people themselves took the vow not to drink and fixed a much higher fine than usual, 2-8-0 (2 rupees, 8 annas, 0 pai), to be deposited in the temple of Shiva. Already most of the people in Fatipur village in the jurisdiction of Moureswar police station had given up drinking. In Nalhati police station, there was a campaign against the consumption of liquor and cigarette smoking. The town held a meeting, led by the local *zamindar* Rajeswar Bhakat, to awaken an understanding among the people of the harmful effects of drinking.[42]

The method of mobilization which was most effective in popularizing the Congress among villagers was the programme of village organization and welfare work. In the interior of the province the districts were generally divided into centres corresponding with the *thanas* or police stations. Each centre was placed under a non-cooperating pleader or teacher, assisted by a group of volunteers who formed Congress committees, collected funds, distributed spinning wheels to the villagers and stood by them at times of distress. Their activities led to an increase in the number of branch Congress committees and by the end of May 1921 about 49,289 members had enrolled as Congress members in 17 districts.[43]

Official records contend that the non-cooperation *Khilafat* movement was introduced into Bengal from outside and that it was not a movement indigenous to Bengal.[44] The movement in Bengal definitely originated from within the province and bore distinct characteristics but in some of the districts the initial attempts at mobilization were made by unknown up-country men. For example, a Hindusthani *sadhu* named Peari Bhai arrived in Bankura town. During his ten-day sojourn there he visited the schools, colleges and Bar libraries exhorting the students, lawyers and other professionals to leave their institutions and join Ghandi's movement.[45] He arranged public meetings to explain the meaning of non-cooperation. In Birbhum too the movement was popularized among the people by two up-country lads, Deo Narayan Prasad and Saraju Prasad, who came from Calcutta to Mollarpur.[46] They called themselves disciples of Gandhi and toured the villages with paper flags shouting slogans 'Mahatma Gandhi Chi Jai, Shaukat Ali Ki Jai, Hindu Musalman Ki Jai'. They urged the people to give up liquor and resolved in a meeting that whoever broke this law would have to pay a fine of 14 rupees and also be given a shoe beating. Thus in the wake of the non-cooperation movement, consistent efforts were made by the leaders to reach the masses through various means and draw them into the movement.

II

There is no doubt that the initiative towards non-cooperation with the British came first from the Muslims. In February 1920 at the conference of the provincial *Khilafat* committee held in Calcutta, resolutions were moved by Fazlul Huq and Maulana Abul Kalam Azad requesting His Majesty's forces to sever connections with the British government and also urging the Mohammedan members of the council and title holders to surrender their offices and titles.[47] Boycott of British goods was added to the two former resolutions. Resolutions were to come into effect if the Turkish peace terms failed to satisfy the Muslims.

Bengal was described by the Viceroy as 'the storm centre of the *Khilafat* agitation'.[48] The new Muslim leadership under A K Azad, backed up by the work of Muslim leaders like Abdul Bari and Shaukat Ali who visited the province, was able to mobilize the Muslim masses into anti-British agitation. As discussed in Chapter One, throughout 1920 there was unceasing effort to raise awareness of the *Khilafat* cause among the Muslim masses. Even during the *Khilafat* committee conference in April and May 1920 and at the sessions of the Indian National Congress, Shaukat Ali issued orders to keep the agitation alive. But 'the Calcutta men alone could not keep the agitation alive. The Provincial leaders deliberately established links with the Muslims who wielded local influence and through them carried on an intensive propaganda campaign'.[49]

The non-cooperation movement saw widespread participation of Bengali students who protested against government institutions through boycott. Students of the *Madrassah* College, Calcutta, boycotted their institution and resolved to establish a national school.[50] In the districts, institutions like Chittagong *Madrassah*, Moslem English High School and Jatra Mohan School were also boycotted by the students. Their lead was followed in Comilla, Dacca and Hooghly.[51] But the student strike of November and December 1920 was only partial. Teachers, parents and guardians opposed the student movement in all the schools except for one *Madrassah* at Comilla. While the countryside was in ferment, the atmosphere remained calm in Calcutta throughout December, the only incident being at the Scottish Church School and

City College – the polling stations for council election – where students left in a body after being insulted by the police within the college premises.[52] The student community proved to be the most susceptible to the propaganda of the non-cooperators.

Even during the interlude between the September and December sessions of the National Congress, the leaders advocated student strikes to protest against the existing education system and take the first step towards an improved national education. At the Congress session in Nagpur in December 1920, the resolution of non-cooperation incorporated the boycott of educational institutions and stressed the importance of opening national institutions. Parents were to decide whether children below the age of sixteen should be withdrawn from school, while older boys and girls were asked to make the decision according to their own conscience.[53] The student conference that was held at Nagpur at the same time as the Congress session also accepted non-cooperation in an unconditional, wholesale and immediate form.

On 13 January 1921 the students of Bangabasi College came out and processed to Ripon College where they were joined by its students. It was reported that 700 students from Ripon College, 1,300 from Bangabasi College and 500 from City College joined the procession.[54] About 500 postgraduate students and university law students also joined the strike. The students of Vidyasagar College, Scottish Church, St Xavier's College and Sanskrit College boycotted their classes. Several students of the Oriental Seminary and other schools also boycotted their Schools.[55]

The demonstrators from Ripon College, Bangabasi College and City College assembled at College Square. In a meeting at Mirzapore Park held under the presidency of Mujibar Rahaman (editor of *The Musalman*), the students undertook for the first time to address the audience. S N Bari, a student of the Bangabasi College, condemned the present system of education which engendered slave mentality and created only clerks and public servants.[56] The students of the *mofussils* were also urged to take up the national cause. The students pledged to support non-violence. The leaders, meanwhile, promised to start a National University and also arrange for medical education if medical students joined the movement.[57]

In another public meeting at Mirzapore Park the female students were entreated to leave their institutions and join the nationalist movement.[58] Gandhi himself, at a meeting at Mirzapore Park, appealed to students to leave their studies. The Calcutta Medical College students who had been immune to propaganda by the leaders were overwhelmed by his appeal.[59] Someswar Prasad Chaudhuri recalled how as a young medical student he was greatly move by Deshbandhu's speech in a meeting at Hedua and, disregarding all the attractions of further studies in Europe, responded to his call. He joined the newly opened National Medical College.[60]

Once the process of student mobilization began, it generated a momentum of its own as a result of which the movement spread spontaneously. Then the students themselves acted as the mobilizers.

The excitement that gripped the Calcutta students also spread to the *mofussils*. The districts, especially in East Bengal, had already been astir with student unrest in November 1920. Students of Carmichael College, Rangpur, joined the non-cooperation movement. By 21 January 1921 the Carmichael College strike had developed to such an extent that obstacles had been set up to prevent the students from attending classes. An ultimatum to nationalize the college within seven days was presented to the magistrate collector. The governing body decided to close the college until 5 February 1921.[61] In Dacca, Jagannath College was closed and the students of the Dacca Medical School also joined the movement. The non-cooperating students of Rangpur College were so organized that they had divided themselves into two parties. The leader of the first group was to hold meetings in the different villages to instruct the villagers to grow less jute and more paddy and cotton, to use *charka* and to abandon foreign-made commodities for country-made goods. The other group was to preach general non-cooperation through boycott of the present system of education, government courts and foreign goods.[62]

Young boys of classes X, IX and VIII of the Zilla School in Rangpur also adopted non-cooperation. In East Bengal Institution, some of the non-cooperating students rushed onto school premises and the scholars left the classes as a body.[63] Demonstrations were held before the Dacca *Madrassah* and seven boys, five of whom were in the junior section, joined the demonstrators. The principal closed the *Madrassah*. In Bogra, about 50 boys of the three upper classes of the Bogra Zilla School left their classes without permission in sympathy with the non-cooperation movement. The students of the government-aided Coronation High School boycotted their institution demanding that it be converted to a national school.[64]

In Faridpur town the agitation in early February 1921 centred around the student movement. Attendance at most of the government educational institutions was falling. The Bhanga HE school, the biggest in the town, was closed down and reopened on 15 February 1921 attended by only 150 of its students. The Islamia and the Mustafapur HE school had been closed. The schools at Sibchar and Palong were functioning but poorly attended. Student strikers demanded that these schools should be nationalized. In Tulashar HE school most of the students stopped paying fees. In Mymensingh the non-cooperation movement, which had been doing badly, received a stimulus when prohibitory orders were issued to prevent Deshbandhu from entering the town. Most of the candidates for matriculation boycotted their examination. Pleaders suspended their practice and a *hartal* was observed from the afternoon of 2 March 1921.[65]

The movement to start national schools continued alongside the boycott of government educational institutions. At Bhanga, Sarat Chandra Roy Choudhuri and Pran Shankar Das Gupta, pleaders of the locality, opened a national school which was to have additional classes for technical training, spinning and weaving. The Bhanga *Kalibari* was selected as the premises and the students were educated by teachers from Calcutta and local pleaders while they sat on mats on the floor. Another national school was opened by Shyama Kanta Choudhury, a pleader of Madaripur, in a hired house belonging to one Jnan Chandra Majumdar. Between 75 and 125 students of the Madaripur HE School joined the institution, although the HE school was still open. Pratap Chandra Guha Roy, a leading Congressman of Faridpur opened a national school at Kendua, his native village. Another national school was started at Gosairhat in a hired warehouse in the market. The students paraded through the streets collecting subscriptions.

In Faridpur and in other districts the boycott of schools and colleges became an important topic of discussion among the *bhadralok*. There was a strong belief that some sort of technical training needed to be introduced in the schools to benefit the students. In the Sirajganj subdivision of Pabna, national schools were opened at Shazadpur by a leading *mukhtear*. A national university was also opened at Sirajganj and 40 non-cooperating students submitted their fees through this centre for the *Adya* examination. The popularity of the national university was evident from the number of candidates who appeared for the first university examinations; 3,793 for the *Adya*, 242 for the Intermediate, and 137 for the degree-level exams. Moreover, 460 students applied for permission to attend the *Madhya* Intermediate Arts (IA) and Intermediate

Science (ISc) examination and 160 students wished to take the *Upadhi* or BA examination.[66]

In Faridpur town, where the gentry was led by Ambica Charan Majumdar, non-cooperation agitation had not taken root immediately. But the town was disturbed by students strikes. The observation of the district magistrate was that 'the student agitation had aroused immense sympathy in the mass of the people and the spirit of non-cooperation was slowly penetrating the interior villages'.[67]

Thus the period from January to March 1921 saw student strikes, boycott of government schools, the search for alternative means of education through national institutions and the enlisting of students as volunteers. This resulted in considerable reduction in the number of students in all the districts of the province.[68]

District	July, 1920	July, 1921
Calcutta	29,565	18,001
24 Parganas	9,383	9,110
Hooghly	9,046	8,936
Howrah	8,403	8,280
Noakhali	5,138	3,626
Assam Pradesh	12,976	10,997
Jessore	6,247	5,541
Khulna	6,186	5,804
Nadia	6,743	6,529
Mymensingh	8,958	5,277
Bogra	3,538	2,668
Burdwan	7,291	6,745
Bakura	2,702	2,258
Barisal	10,419	6,767
Pabna	6,562	5,687
Murshidabad	5,358	4,507
Midnapur	6,484	5,543
Dinajpur	1,996	1,522
Tippera	13,382	8,503
Dacca	15,818	10,529
Rangpur	4,088	3,409
Rajshahi	2,793	2,642
Faridpur	12,014	7,749
Jalpaiguri	960	894
Birbhum	2,956	3,000
Chattogram	8,149	6,202
Malda	1,813	1,490

A survey of the educational institutions also shows that in most of the government educational institutions there was a decrease in attendance in 1921.[69]

College	No. of Students	
	1920	1921
Mymensingh, Anandamohan College	679	627
Bagerhat College	234	143
Bangabasi College	1,730	1,244
Bethune	113	120
Barisal Brajamohan	762	667
Burdwan Raj College	144	123
Rangpur Carmichael	631	422
Central College	466	152
Chattogram	449	402
City College	1,839	1,612
Guwahati Cotton College	483	413
Daulatpur Hindu	601	524
Diocesan	90	84
Pabna Edward	347	354
Hooghly	264	247
Hetampur Krishnachandra	59	53
Krishnanagar College	295	209
Baharampur Krishnanath	1,193	987
Loreto	12	14
Midnapur	239	182
Sylhet Murarichand	526	426
Presidency	684	770
Faridpur Rajendra	376	258
Rajsahi College	853	818
Ripon College	1,715	1,207
Sanskrit College	194	79
Scottish Church	1,103	985
Sreerampur College	295	256
South Suburban	762	438
St. Pauls College	243	225
St. Xaviers	791	759
Uttarpara	179	88
Comilla Victoria College	809	565
Coochbihar College	440	332
Narail	130	106
Vidyasagar College	1,623	1,330
Bankura Wesasleyan	449	358
Dacca	783	...
Jagannath College	402	...
Indian Science Congress	518	...
Total	23,887	17,579

During the last phase of the movement, in the city of Calcutta, the students provided the support required for organization and mobilization. They picketed shops dealing in foreign cloth in the Burrabazar area and organized *hartal* on the day the Duke of Connaught arrived to inaugurate the reformed council.[70] Events like these provided the non-cooperators with an excellent opportunity to mobilize support against all actions of the whites. Prior to the Duke's arrival the volunteers used leaflets, meetings and even door-to-door campaigning to urge the people to boycott all the events and ceremonies arranged for his visit. Another such occasion came with the visit of the Prince of Wales later in 1921. The Congress called for a boycott of the occasion. Volunteers, led by Subhas Chandra Bose, campaigned extensively to boycott the entertainment to be held in connection with the visit. *Hartal* as a form of protest was declared on 24 December 1921. A large number of students of different colleges (especially the city colleges) were reported to have left their respective colleges on that morning, and most of them went to Forbes Mansion to enrol as volunteers.

Under the influence of Gandhian ideals, many teachers and lawyers also left their professions. In Bankura, Professor Anil Baran Roy organized the non-cooperating students and teachers to form volunteer associations, Congress offices and other organizations. Anil Baran Roy, along with fellow non-cooperators like Kamal Krishna Ray and Kalikinkar Karmakar, would move around from village to village explaining the meaning of non-cooperation to the local inhabitants.[71] In each area local Congress workers explained to the people the main reasons for their poverty, holding the British and colonial state of the country responsible. They told the people that government policies had ruined indigenous industries and agriculture and the only remedy for the situation was *Swaraj*. They read *Desher Dak* by Sakharam Ganesh Deuskar to the villagers and also held musical performances where the singers tried to reach the people through *kirtan* or patriotic songs.[72]

The professional class responded to the call for the boycott of law courts and other government institutions. Boycott of law courts began in February 1921.[73] Nine pleaders resigned in February and 68 in March. Chitta Ranjan Das provided the lead by leaving his practice. In many districts, local lawyers gave up their practices to organize the movement. In Chittagong, Jatindra Mohan Sengupta left his practice to join the movement and in Midnapur Birendra Nath Sasmal did the same.

Birbhum is another district where the movement was organized by independent professional groups, especially lawyers, who left their professions to work for the non-cooperation movement. According to official reports Birbhum was a quiet district which never witnessed any organized political movement or agitation against the government before the non-cooperation movement began.[74] Then in January 1921, Jitendralal Banerjee, a prominent Rampurhat congressman, organized a meeting in his town.[75] Following this, the non-cooperation movement in Birbhum began to spread through the district in the form of public meetings in some places, and elsewhere with student strikes, *hartal*, and above all the picketing of liquor shops.

A complete *hartal* was observed in the town of Suri on the day of the opening of the Industrial and Agricultural Exhibition. The fair was so poorly attended that the authorities decided to close it down two days early. On 20 and 21 February 1921, meetings were held in Dubrajpur,[76] attended by the local leading *Marwaris* and Bengalis. Darsanananda Swami was invited to speak at the meeting. By April, about 109 lawyers including 11 in Sylhet district and one in Cachar had suspended practice.[77] After Deshbandhu Das visited Bogra, nearly all the pleaders and *mukhtears* of the town had suspended practice.[78] The Bogra Bar also resolved that all the pleaders should suspend practice for a month to protest against the maltreatment of the tea-garden coolies.[79]

In Sirajganj Abaninath Lahiri, Jogendralal Roy and Nagendranath Mojumdar gave up their extensive practice in obedience to the Barisal conference resolution. Kunja Behari Dey and Akshay Chandra Lahiri, leaders of the local Bar, *Moulavi* Abdul Majid and Girish Chandra Bhowmik suspended their practice. Their actions inspired others to follow. Some non-cooperating pleaders went to Uttarpara to advance the cause of non-cooperation. A huge meeting was held that attracted about 10,000 people. The 70-strong Munsiganj Bar Association voted to suspend their practice for three months. *The Musalman* reported 'in course of a month or so, a considerable number of lawyers have suspended their practice'. In Comilla alone about 35 pleaders and four *Mukhtears* gave up their profession. Many of them, especially Akhil Chandra Dutt, had large practices.

The educated section of eastern Midnapur responded enthusiastically to the call of non-cooperation. Birendra Nath Sasmal, who had begun his political career in Calcutta as a member of the provincial Congress, returned to his village to build up the organization there. Chittagong, Noakhali and Sylhet also saw their pleaders sacrifice their practices for the cause of independence.

Not all districts, however, saw the same degree of professional sacrifice. In Dacca, Howrah, Mymensingh and Rajshahi, the proposed suspension of practice by the lawyers was rejected by the members of the Bar association.[80] In Chittagong the members of the local civil and criminal court Bar association met informally to discuss the duty of the lawyers in the present movement. Suspension of practice was not considered economically viable or absolutely necessary until an all-India general strike was decided upon by the leaders. But several lawyers expressed their willingness to take up village organizational work.[81]

A significant feature of the non-cooperation movement was the enrolment of women volunteers. They picketed liquor shops and held demonstrations. The involvement of Basanti Devi and other ladies in the *khaddar*-selling programme and their subsequent arrest created an immense public stir. After the arrests of Chitta Ranjan Das on 6 December 1921 and his wife and sister three days later, the student community responded by enlisting as volunteers at 169 Forbes Mansion in Wellington Square, the centre of activities.[82] From there, batches of volunteers proceeded directly to Burrabazar. On 8 December, the situation reached such a climax that the whole of Harrison Road was blocked by a shouting mass of humanity and the traffic was completely blocked. Later Forbes Mansion was abandoned and the national school at Amherst Street became the recruiting centre.[83] Between 13 and 18 December 1,732 arrests were made. After 24 December the volunteers were still active. Carrying Congress and *Khilafat* placards, the volunteers urged the public to boycott foreign cloth.[84] *The Musalman* gives a report of the 'Volunteers on Duty' on the day Basanti Devi and other ladies courted arrest trying to sell *khaddar*:

> Of the Congress and Khilafat Volunteers sent out on Duty on Monday last, six were arrested. Of these, two were Khilafat volunteers and the rest were Congress volunteers. All of them were arrested in Burrabazar. They had khaddar with them which they were trying to sell. When they were arrested stocks of khaddar which they possessed were taken away by the police. Of the batches sent out on Tuesday, the first batch was led by Chitta Ranjan Das. On receipt of the news of arrest several more batches were dispatched to the places where the arrests were made.
>
> Batches of Congress volunteers were out again on Wednesday to Burrabazar for selling khaddar. At about 1.30 p.m. Basanti Devi, Urmila Devi, Suniti Devi organizers of the Nari Karma

Mandir in company with six volunteers went to sell khaddar in Burrabazar. They were later arrested.

A large number of volunteers were sent out yesterday in batches of five each to popularize khaddar. The three ladies were seen picketing on Chirrup Road and Nimtollah Ghat street followed by a crowd of men. The ladies were asking the shopkeepers to close their shops on the 24th instant. At Burrabazar some Sikh ladies were seen carrying on propaganda work helped by some volunteers.[85]

On 15 January women volunteers attempted to hold meetings at Mirzapore Park and College Street in defiance of civil law to inaugurate civil disobedience.[86] In Bhowanipore, at a meeting organized by the South Calcutta Congress Committee, the women took a leading role. On 7 February the members of the *Nari Karmi Mandir* organized a procession which increased in size as more and more women, especially Sikh women around Shambhu Nath Pandit Street, came out to support the march. The procession included Nepali, Sikh and up-country people.[87]

Among other occupational groups joining the non-cooperation movement, the working class and peasantry were the most prominent. Official reports indicate that the industrial centres were fertile ground for the non-cooperators.[88] In the large industrial centres, conditions had already been created for the elite politicians to rally the working class behind them. Labourers in the plantations, mines and industries were growing more and more conscious of their predicament. Since the pre-war years, both in Calcutta and in the suburbs, workers had heard anti-British sentiment being preached:

> In 1913 in the context of the Balkan wars, Pan-Islamic agitators like Ismail Hossain Sivaji, Mujibar Rahman and Maniruzzaman Islamabadi (all from a *Swadeshi* background) and Muhammad Akram Khan were cooperating actively with veteran *Swadeshi* leaders like Krishna Kumar Mitra and Shyam Sundar Chakravarti. Some radical Hindus of Telenipara, it was alleged, had employed an agent named Hyder to preach *Jehad* against the British...among all the mill hands belonging to the mills on both sides of the river between Hooghly and Calcutta.[89]

In September 1918 a large crowd of coolies made incessant attempts to break through from Garden Reach and obtain entry into Calcutta. The non-Bengali agitators like Fazlur Rahman eulogized the actions of Khudiram Bose and other revolutionaries while propagating anti-British sentiments.[90]

The industrial sector was restless with agitation through out the year 1920 as the workers organized a number of strikes to improve their working conditions. In the latter half of 1920, no less than 89 strikes occurred in the Calcutta industrial area.[91] The last six weeks saw an outburst of 12 strikes in the Burdwan district affecting both coal fields and some of the industrial undertakings at Raniganj.[92] The director of industries reported that 'by the end of the year there was practically no group of employment in the Hooghly river and the Asansol areas in which strike had not occurred'.[93] Jute mills, engineering foundry and metal works, transport, storage of merchandise in the port and city of Calcutta, public utility services, printing presses, cotton mills, railways and collieries were affected by labour unrest.

The initiative for strikes during this period came mostly from the workers themselves, although in some cases outsiders also intervened and guided the strikers. When Atlas Construction Company workers went on strike demanding a rise in wages the firm believed that this was the result of outside interference, as several workers admitted that they had been instructed to strike.[94] The workers of the Oriental Gas Company were addressed by politicians several times. On 18 October, workmen of Messieurs Stuart and Company, coach builders, refused to work demanding a wage increase and holidays on all Hindu and Muslim festivals. The management was convinced that the strike was 'engineered' by outsiders. In the Shalimar Works Limited, Shibpur, external influences caused prolongation of the strike. Pleaders intervened and meetings were held at Howrah and Garden Reach, which were addressed by the outsiders.[95]

Moreover, by the 1920s, with the emergence of a new Congress leadership inspired by Socialist ideals, trade union politics gained a new dynamism. The All India Trade Union Congress was founded in Bombay on 31 October 1920. Barristers S N Halder and Indu Bhusan Sen had been elected to organize labour associations in Bengal. Nationalist leaders like Chitta Ranjan Das and Jatindra Mohan Sengupta also came forward to organize the working class. Congress leaders had entered the trade union movement aiming not only to improve the condition of the workers but also to strengthen the movement for *Swaraj*. The Bengal Central Labour Federation initiated an effort to extend and consolidate its organization. Its meeting of April 1921 to adopt a new constitution was presided over by J N Ray and attended by nationalists like

Chitta Ranjan Das, Nisith Chandra Sen, S N Halder, Bhola Nath Barman and Padam Raj Jain. A large number of mill *sardars* and Bengal labour union secretaries were also present on the occasion. Chitta Ranjan Das emphasized that the affiliated unions should be purely Indian in composition.[96] A permanent body of office bearers was created which included leading nationalists.[97]

The involvement of nationalist leaders in the trade union movement is revealed through Gourlay's analysis that 'among the outsiders Non-Cooperator nationalists formed the single largest group holding about 15 per cent of union leadership position analysed'.[98] In Calcutta the Government Press Employees Association was formed on 21 January 1921 of which Mrinal Kanti Basu (the sub-editor of The *Amrita Bazar Patrika*) was the president, Indu Bhusan Sen and Ambica Prasad Bajpai vice-presidents and S N Halder was the treasurer.[99] The *Jamadars* Association organized on 28 April 1920 had up-country agitators like Sriram Bari of Amritsar in the important posts. An extremist agitator, Bari was also the secretary of the *Punjab Sava*, a political association of Calcutta Punjabis.[100] The vice-president, Bholanath Barman of Lucknow was also the secretary of the *Hindi Natya Parishad*, an organization of the Extremist *Marwaris* of Calcutta. Its Secretary Purushottam Rai, was also a nationalist having taken active part in the *Khilafat* agitation, and was also the secretary of the Upper India Association, an organization of the *Marwari* and other up-country extremist agitators. Among others connected with that body were Pandit Neki Ram Sarma, Ambica Prasad Bajpai, Metha Jamini a pleader of Lyalpur, Padam Raj Jain and Mahadeo Prasad Sukul, all of whom were active Congress and *Khilafat* workers.[101]

During the same period the Indian Seamens' Union developed a connection with and was affiliated to the provincial Congress. The secretary of the Seamen's Union, Muhammad Daud, who was a member of the Muslim League, wanted to bring the seamen under the influence of leaders like Maulana Azad and Chittaranjan Das.[102] Similarly, the Calcutta Motor Drivers Association formed on 23 May 1920 enjoyed the patronage of such personalities as Byomkesh Chakrabarti, Indu Bhusan Sen and S N Halder. The Punjabi taxi drivers belonging to this association became Congress volunteers and provided transport for the delegates of the all-India Congress session at Calcutta in 1920.[103] The *Lohar's* association situated in the Forbes Mansion compelled its members to follow Gandhi's advice by forming *panchayats*, boycotting foreign goods and abstaining from liquor.[104] Purna Chandra Basu, a non-cooperator and a close associate of Gop Bandhu Das of Cuttack organized labour unions, especially among the Uriya and the up-country labourers of Calcutta. He himself became the secretary of the *Central Uriya Labour Association* founded on October 1921.[105]

In the districts too, the non-cooperators played an important role in forming labour unions. In Burdwan the Raniganj Paper Mill staff association was formed in February 1921 at the initiative of Swami Darsanananda. The members were selected by him from among the *sardars* of the coolies and labourers of the paper mill.[106] Swami Darsanananda also organized the Raniganj Central Labour Association. In Chittagong, employees of the Burma Oil Company formed a union under the leadership of Jatindra Mohan Sengupta. The Burma Oil Company's installation centre at Maheshkhali became the centre of agitation. Company employees boycotted the company's agent, Bullock Brothers. Even the crew of a mail boat was urged to join the strike by the non-cooperators and the employees.[107]

The Chittagong Central Labour Union was formed on 24 April 1921 with its office in the Jatra Mohan hall. Its president was *Maulavi* Abdul Bari Chaudhuri of Fatikchari. He was an affluent merchant of Rangoon, where he had organized labour unions but April 1921 marked the beginning of his non-cooperation political activities. Jatindra Mohan Sengupta served as the secretary of the union which was formed during the Burma Oil Company's strike in 1921.[108] Ex-detenue and non-cooperator Purna Chandra Das was the president of the Madaripur Labour Association at Charmaguria, Faridpur district. The vice-president Subhendra Mohan Basu Majumdar, secretary Sudama Pande, assistant Secretary Kalipada Roy Chowdhuri and treasurer Kularanjan Mukherjee were all revolutionaries. The members included the coolie *sardars*. In Dinajpur, Sashi Bhusan Vidya Binode, a local non-cooperator was the secretary of a labour union of cooks, servants, cartmen and coolies established in 1921.[109] Swami Darsanananda declared in a meeting his intention to start a new labour union, organizing the different scattered casual labourers like cooks, *khansamas, dhobis*, sweepers, barbers, *darwans* and clerks to stir up a general strike. The meeting was attended by J L Banerjee and Brindaban Sarma among others.

The other labour organizations were comprised of non-cooperators, non-political outsiders, nationalists, and men from the professional and business communities. The Tram Workers Association formed on October 1920 had both non-cooperators like Nirmal Chandra Chunder and nationalists like N C Sen associated with it.[110]

Nationalist inspiration played an important role in the formation of the railway worker's associations in October 1920. The move to spilt the Railway Workmen's Association had been continuing for some time. The Bengal Nagpur Railway Indian Labour Union was formed at Kharagpur in November 1920. On 25 April 1921, in a meeting of the East Indian Railway Employees, N C Sen, while presiding over the gathering, urged them to form an Indian union separate from the Railway Workmen's Association.[111] The East Indian Railway Labour Union and the Assam Bengal Railway Employees Union came into existence in May 1921. Nationalists and non-cooperators joined the union committees.

In September 1920 Gandhi, on his way to the special congress session, stopped at Kharagpur and advised the railwaymen to form a separate union for Indian workers. During a non-cooperation meeting one N S Marathe (probably sent to Kharagpur by Gandhi immediately after the Congress session), continued to encourage this action. Consequently some representatives of the Indian railwaymen at Kharagpur reached Calcutta and asked the Congress leaders to help them form a union. On 14 November 1920 in Kharagpur, Bipin Chandra Pal, Sris Chatterjee, Surendra Nath Haldar and N C Sen addressed a meeting. It was decided to form a branch of the Indian Railway Labour Union at Kharagpur. An all India Railway Labour Union Advisory Board was set up under the chairmanship of Chitta Ranjan Das, with Surendra Nath Halder, Indu Bhusan Sen, Bipin Chandra Pal and Abdul Jabbar as members. The Indian Railway Labour Union Kharagpur later came to be known as Bengal Nagpur Railway Indian Labour Union.[112]

The coal fields in Raniganj, Jamuria and Barakar were seized by labour discontent when Swami Darsanananda and Biswanand, with the help of the *Marwari* coal traders and Bengali colliery owners, began to form labour unions.[113] The clash of interest between the Indian colliery owners and the European managing agencies over the control of the coal trade and mining meant that the former were keen to tender their support to the union movement. Deputed to the coal fields by the Trade Union Congress at Nagpur Swami Biswananda along with Dip Narayan Singh and Chandra Banshi Lal Sahay formed two labour unions at Raniganj and Barakar.

The Andrew Yule and Company's Sibpur Power House was paralysed by a labour strike. The labourers were addressed by Swami Darsanananda who instructed them that unless Andrew Yule, which was preventing other companies from increasing wages, granted a 100 per cent wage increase, workers should leave their employ and join the Indian-owned collieries.[114] To the low caste and tribals Darsanananda became God personified and they earnestly believed that if they did not follow him, he could bring blindness and barrenness of women. Strikes began at six collieries owned by Andrew Yule, four collieries belonging to Equitable Coal and one managed by the Bird company, involving a total of 5,300 miners. Jograj Marwari, Dip Narayan Singh and Swami Biswananda and Darsanananda directed the strikers at Burn and Company's Kulti Iron Works. In July when Chitta Ranjan Das visited Raniganj, Asansol and Barakar, he urged the inhabitants of the mining area not to support the European businesses in any way. Continuous propaganda of this type by non-cooperation leaders created serious disturbance in the mining area.[115]

At the Ichapur Rifle Factory, in response to propaganda by prominent non-cooperators like Sudhansu Kumar Bose, an apprentice of the Kanchrapara Railway Workshop, about 5,000 rifle factory workers went on strike. They demanded an increase of 35 per cent in their wages. Once the strike began Sudhansu Bose was dismissed from work and the nationalist labour leaders N C Sen and S N Haldar intervened on behalf of the agitators. S N Haldar was appointed by the workers as their representative.[116] The strikers received support from other labour organizations like the Bengal Central Labour Federation whose secretaries Mohammed Mohasin and Said Rahman Hakim Saheb of Kalutola frequently visited the strikers and urged them to remain firm.

Official records show that the strikers at Kanchrapara maintained links with their colleagues in the Ichapur Rifle Factory. Sudhansu Bose knew Jaharldi Mistry of Dumdum Cantonment, one of the leaders of the rifle factory agitation, who acted as the connecting link between the two places. In both Kanchrapara and its neighbour, Sodepur, the prime movers of the agitation were employees of the factory who had contacts among the non-cooperators. The workers attended meetings which were addressed by labour agitators from Calcutta. Bama Charan Majumdar visited Kanchrapara and instigated the workers not to resume work until their demands were granted. The Ichapur Rifle Factory labourers even held secret meetings. Rahat Hussain of the Calcutta *Khilafat* Committee addressed one such secret meeting at Palta. At Monirampur, barrister J N Roy, president of the Central Labour Federation, presided over a meeting where a labour association was formed and a labourer's union bank was opened.[117] Volunteer groups for picketing were formed. The agitation also spread to the Shell Factory at Ichapur and Cossipore.

In a meeting of employees of these three factories at Agarpara, a *panchayat* was appointed to settle disputes. The labourers collected 10,000 rupees from among themselves.[118]

In Calcutta and in other industrial suburbs of the province, labourers were enlisted as Congress and *Khilafat* volunteers. Muhammad Osman of Monghyr, head preacher of the *Khilafat* office, established cordial relations with the *sardars* and other labourers and enrolled workers as volunteers. Several batches of volunteers were organized by him under different captains at Kidderpore, Tanti Bagan, Chore Bagan, Entally, Sahib Bagan, Patwar Bagan, Shyambazar and Chitpur.[119] These groups together involved between 800 and 1,000 men, mostly Muhammadans and mill hands. They were paid eight annas per day. The captains received orders from the *Khilafat* office. Osman and Muhammad Mohim also trained *Khilafat* volunteers from other labour associations with which they were closely associated, for example the *Manjhis* and *Dandis* associations and *Khansama*'s association. These volunteers worked in cooperation with the *Khilafat* workers.

In the tea gardens of Himalayan Bengal, the coolies suffered from such extreme poverty due to low wages and severe working conditions that they responded spontaneously to non-cooperation propaganda.[120] In Darjeeling the non-cooperators instigated unrest among the tea-garden labourers. Khagendra Kishore Ball and Debendra Nath Das arrived at Kurseong and delivered several lectures on the boycott of foreign goods. Debendra Nath Das also spoke in a meeting in the marketplace of Darjeeling town. He talked about the predicament of the tea-garden coolies and suggested that if they stopped work for sometime, their wages might be increased. This meeting was attended by about 500 men.[121]

In July 1921, there occurred several spontaneous and unorganized strikes. A special officer was deputed by the government for propaganda work in the affected area. The Indian Tea Association was also asked to impress upon the planters the need to keep in touch with the workers especially in view of the reports that, 'for many months past, agitators connected with the non-cooperation movement have been at work among the coolies on estates both at Assam and Surma Valley. They have stirred up a general spirit of unrest among labour. The religious susceptibilities of the coolies have been exploited to the full even to the extent of leading the coolies to believe that if they failed to leave their work under the alleged orders of Gandhi, their families and herds would be turned to mud or stone'.[122] The tea-producing areas of Jalpaiguri district, known as *Dooars,* remained comparatively unaffected by the national movement, partly because of poor communication but more importantly because the district Congress was dominated by Indian tea planters who refused to allow Congress to preach the anti-imperialist message to their workers.

What the message of non-cooperation and the Gandhian ideal of *satyagraha* did was provide an opportunity for the lower classes to express their acute sense of economic exploitation and racial abasement under foreign rule. The Chandpur coolie uprising was one such spontaneous protest by those who toiled in the tea gardens in Assam – an event which also showed the importance of rumour in spreading the impetus for protest. In the Chargola valley of Assam the tea garden labourers, most of them inhabitants of Bihar and UP, began to leave the tea gardens rejoicing in the rumour that Mahatma Gandhi had ushered in a millennium. The propaganda work of the non-cooperators in Assam and Surma valley had created a strange unrest among the labourers. The representatives of the agency houses who interviewed the coolies in the Chargola Valley found them in a state where rationality had no influence over them. They believed Gandhi was the prophet, a source of authority higher than any established. Such was the charismatic appeal of the Mahatma that the labourers earnestly believed that by leaving the tea gardens they were obeying his orders, and that he had made complete arrangements for transit to their districts even including a special steamer which was to await them at Karimganj.[123] The CID report stated that 'the exodus was without doubt due to propaganda spread among the coolies by *sadhus* and other agents of the non-cooperation movement'.[124] Gandhi however expressed his disapproval of the entire episode and described it as a manifestation of labour unrest, purely a labour strike.

The East Bengal steamer and railway strike that followed in protest against the Gurkha military outrage on the helpless coolies stranded at Chandpur on 20 May had been described as a sympathetic strike.[125] On 21 and 22 May the local non-cooperators called for a *hartal* which was observed in Chandpur, Comilla and Chattogram.[126] That the situation demanded a *hartal* and that the local Congress workers were contemplating a strike was evident from an intercepted telegram dated 21 May sent by Akhil Chandra Datta to Sengupta in Chittagong that read '*Hartal* absolutely necessary'.[127]

On 24 May the Assam Bengal Railway staff also went on strike. The president of the Assam Bengal Employees Union, J M Sengupta, declared that the strike was a protest against the treatment of the plantation coolies and that it would continue until arrangements were made for their repatriation. On 25 May at Chattogram town the union held a meeting where the decision to continue the strike was accepted.[128] Once the strike began, Sengupta, as president of the Assam Bengal Railway Employees Union informed a representative of the Assam Bengal Railway that the strike was caused by the dissatisfaction of the employees and was in no way connected with the political situation. The employees would resume work only after there was settlement between the agent and the union. In a joint manifesto C R Das and J M Sengupta declared that unless the railway employers considered the grievances of the strikers in a 'sympathetic spirit', the agitation would continue. The manifesto also recommended that each member of railway station staff should apply to the nearest Congress committee for advice and financial help. Similar directions were issued to the Congress committees by Das, to help any Assam Bengal railway striker who might ask for help.[129] C R Das on several occasions declared the railway strike as 'a religious war' and that 'the railway employees were truly non-cooperating and their cessation of work cannot be styled as a strike'.[130]

From 27 May, the workers of the East Bengal steamer service also ceased work. The strike spread to Goalundo, Barisal and Khulna. The local Congress workers, led by Hardayal Nag who had been working at Chandpur, contemplated the strike of the railway and steamer service in support of the coolies.[131] Nag wired to Nurul Huq Chaudhury, president of the Inland Steamship and Flat Employees Association, that Abdul Majid Garoali the president of the Serang Union had been forcibly sent to Chittagong. The next day the steamer staff at Chandpur went on strike. Nurul Huq Chaudhury also announced the opening of an Indian Steamer Service between Calcutta and Barisal. The advertisement claimed the support of the Indian mercantile community and the public, describing the service as necessary to the 'constructive programme of the non-cooperation movement and also in order that the national commerce and industry may survive against the mighty British capitalists'.[132] The Calcutta merchants paid 50 lakhs of rupees for starting the company.

At the end of 1921 the labourers actively participated in the *hartal* organized by Bose to boycott the visit of the Prince of Wales. During that week about 349 arrests were made, of which 48 were Bengalis, 39 students and 123 mill hands from Telenipara, Metiabruz, Shyamnagore, Khurda, Kamarhatty, Gondalpara and Bhadreswar.[133] The remaining were boatmen or *majhis* and 'low class Muhammadans' from suburbs.[134] Since 5 December, scores of young men, Bengalis, Hindusthani,

Muhammadans and Sikhs, roamed about in the Burrabazar area carrying pieces of *khaddar* and urging the shopkeepers to observe *hartal* on 24 December.[135] They courted arrest without any protest. On the first few days, the volunteers arrested were mainly mill hands but afterwards they were joined by the student community.

The non-cooperation resolution did not include a programme specifically for the agricultural population of India. However, in a continuation of Gandhi's draft proposal of non-cooperation, the Congress resolution incorporated a proposal for an organization down to village level.[136] The organization of rural life and population so as to bring the 'masses in line with the classes' in the fight for national autonomy or *Swaraj* was a concern of the leaders reiterated often in the press, in public meetings and also in the Congress conferences after September 1920.[137] Gandhi himself told the merchants of Calcutta in 1920 '*Swaraj* depends on the agriculturists and if they cooperated with the government then all your virtues will not help in winning *Swaraj*'.[138] *Deshbandhu*, as a member of the working committee in charge of Bengal, drew up a scheme for rural organization which aimed at making every village self-sufficient, through the introduction of *charka* in every home, establishment of *panchayeti* to solve the problems of litigation and introduction of free primary education.[139] Thus it can be seen that the leaders had constructive non-cooperation in mind as they considered how to extend peasant participation in the movement.

Khilafat and Congress volunteers were employed to spread the message of non-cooperation among the farmers but the leaders did not have plans for large-scale agrarian upheaval; the peasants were expected to limit their activities to the constructive programme. However, the agrarian population of Bengal in 1921 did not confine their activities within the limitations set down by Congress. Their fury often took its own form and official documents reported that events in the latter part of the year proved that the movement had gone beyond the control of its leaders.[140]

Most of the existing literature on the peasant movement has explained this large-scale peasant participation in terms of economic factors. The economic crisis of the post-war years, they argue, was responsible for a growing discontent among the agrarian class which the leadership exploited to incite them to anti-British agitation. Of course, the economic pressure of the war years, the long term crisis in agriculture and mobilization by the political leaders from above were important. But one must also weigh the importance of other conditions which were an integral part of the peasant environment; their society, their culture and above all their conscious receptivity to the nationalist ideas that reached them. Rural village life in Bengal was firmly in the grip of religious and social codes which influenced their norms of thought and behaviour and therefore cannot be ignored when considering their political involvements.

The First World War has been held responsible by many scholars for the growing discontent among the people and their overwhelming response to the call of their leaders. Rising prices, scarcity of consumer products and unemployment among the middle class youths are believed to have combined to create a volatile situation.

The season and crop report of the year 1920–21 showed that the weather had been favourable for rice crops. With continuing high prices for basic necessities materially affecting all classes of population, the only redeeming feature was the satisfactory harvest of the autumn, winter and summer rice crops. This was the observation of G Evans, the director of agriculture in Bengal, in his report.[141] The prices of grain and other articles of daily use remained high and the jute trade was facing a depression. But the situation had begun to improve by the end of 1921 and the beginning of 1922. The wholesale price of grain fell by two per cent and in Bengal the price of rice also fell by two per cent. Even the statistical abstract for British India 1917–18 to 1926–27 shows that the prices rose to the highest point in 1920 and from 1921 recorded a continuous fall.[142]

Prices in India 1913–23

YEAR	PRICE*
1913	143
1914	147
1915	152
1916	184
1917	196
1918	225
1919	276
1920	281
1921	236
1922	232
1923	215
1873	*100*

*Price index where 1873 is considered the base year with a price index of 100

'Statistical Abstract for British India, 1917–18 to 1926–27' quoted in Judith M Brown's *Gandhi's Rise to Power, Indian Politics 1915–22*.

Agricultural Department Crops Reports of 1922–23 showed that jute prices had been recovering and the prices of imported foreign goods and rice were falling, causing an improvement in the general condition of the people, especially in the bigger jute-producing districts.[143] The picture portrayed in the post-war years was one of immense economic distress in the immediate aftermath of the war with conditions picking up slowly from 1921 onwards. The non-cooperation movement however, although it began against the background of economic crisis, reached its height when conditions began to improve.

Mobilization in the rural areas began with meetings, constructive social work, organization of the Congress committees and boycott of schools and colleges. In eastern Midnapur, for example, Birendra Nath Sasmal and his co-workers popularized non-cooperation by spreading Gandhian ideas of village reconstruction. They explained to the villagers how colonial rule had economically crippled India. They also taught the villagers the means to self-sufficiency through spinning and weaving. Midnapur was one of the regions that had fallen victim to the destruction of handicraft industries like salt manufacture and weaving. The bitter memory of the slow decline of a once prosperous region was still alive in the minds of the inhabitants and therefore they were easily drawn to the propaganda of the non-cooperators.[144] In *Dhorai Charit Manas*, the *tatmas* (low castes) came to know about Gandhi when the non-cooperating volunteers called a *sabha* (gathering) in front of the district board clock tower and master *sahib* who had resigned his job had abused the government, and the *Laat* Sahib in the *sabha*. Master Sahib had become a *Chela* or follower of Gandhi Baba, the greatest magician even greater than Siridas Bawa. The message was brought to *tatma tuli* (the neighbourhood of the *tatmas*) by Babulal, one of the *tatmas* who worked in the district board as *chaprasi* (personal attendant) to the vice-chairman.[145] Thus when the Gandhian message was received by the common people it was coloured by their own imaginations. It has been shown by Shahid Amin regarding the peasants of eastern UP and north Bihar that 'their ideas about Gandhi's orders and powers were often at variance with those of the local Congress *Khilafat* leaders and clashed with the basic tenets of Gandhism itself'.[146]

After the leaders had begun to organize the villagers by teaching them self-sufficiency, it was suggested in December 1920 that national unions should be formed for the purchase and sale of local produce without middlemen.[147] But nothing came out of the plan. Official reports show that the first move towards mobilizing the masses in opposition to the rulers came with the launching of the jute boycott programme in February.[148] In the northern and eastern districts of Bengal, jute was adopted as the principal commercial crop in the small peasant economy, to reduce dependence on rice. But the war had created a crisis which resulted in steep decline in the price of jute. When the government of Bengal, hoping to improve the situation, proposed steps for the restoration of the prices of raw jute, the European jute interests reacted fiercely. The initial setback of 1914 was overcome by 1917 when production in the jute mills increased due to wartime requirements.

But the exploitation of the jute cultivators by the mills continued. The peasants were forced to part with raw jute at an abnormally low price. By 1917 the mills had purchased raw jute in such excessive quantity that the storage areas were full to capacity. By 1920–21 a deep recession was created in the raw jute market, supply becoming greater than demand. The need for restricting the acreage under jute cultivation and increasing the area for cultivation of paddy was becoming increasingly obvious. Questions were raised in the Bengal Legislative Council on the subject. One member, Tarit Bhusan Roy, asked the council to recommend to the government that immediate steps be taken to impress upon the cultivators the need to restrict jute cultivation.[149]

Cultivation of commercial crops was associated in the middle class sentiment with economic and racial domination by the colonial rulers. Commercial crops had been introduced to increase colonial appropriation from the agrarian sector. It led to extensive rent exploitation and usury. Such concepts of agriculture for the sake of commercial purpose and for profit did not appeal to the Bengali sentiment. On the other hand rice, a symbol of Lakshmi the goddess of wealth, meant prosperity. It removed all ills and ensured food for everyone. Even wealth acquired through the cultivation of rice was morally justified in the minds of the Bengali people.

It was not only the rural middle class but the peasantry who distrusted the jute traders and moneylenders. The local literature, mostly written in verse, was emphatic in its expression of their protest against jute cultivation and the slump of 1920. A F M Abdul Hai in *Adarsha Krishak*, published in Mymensingh in 1921, ridiculed the ignorant peasants of Bengal who, tempted to make money the easy way, took to jute cultivation and found themselves in grave distress in the clutches of moneylenders.

In the jute-growing districts of Bengal, peasant anger in 1921 was directed against commercial exploitation by the jute traders and moneylenders. So when the Congress approached the *rayats* with their jute boycott programme in February, the cultivators of Mymensingh, Dacca and Barisal districts vowed to restrict cultivation.[150] Throughout February and March 1921 in all Congress and *Khilafat* meetings held in the rural areas, reduction of jute cultivation was a major topic of instruction by the leaders. In the Nehalpur subdivision of Basirhat, 24 Parganas, at a well-attended non-cooperation meeting of Hindus and Muslims, *Moulavi* Akram Khan asked the agriculturists to take to the cultivation of rice and cotton and reduce the acreage under jute.[151]

At Gaibandha, Rangpur district, the *Krishi Unnati Sabha* organized a meeting where the cultivators vowed to reduce the area under jute cultivation. At Karatia Hat the non-cooperating students persuaded the buyers not to buy jute seedlings and the sellers had to return home with their products as no customer came to buy them.[152] In Harirampur Dacca district the area for the cultivation of jute was restricted to little more than half an acre.[153] In Mymensingh the district Congress committee issued a pamphlet exhorting the cultivators to grow cotton in place of jute. At Noakhali the student non-cooperators ploughed up a field sown with the crop and played football there.[154]

Throughout April similar destructive methods of protest continued to be used. Surprisingly, not a single complaint was lodged against the non-cooperators. However, the movement could not be sustained because, quite simply, the price of raw jute was higher than that of paddy. The cultivators found it more profitable to grow jute, which sold at 6 to 12 rupees per *maund* (a unit of weight which had different values in different localities, but was commonly 37 kilos) rather than rice, which sold at at 5 to 7 rupees per *maund*.[155] It was also probable that jute cultivators found it difficult to change overnight to the cultivation of paddy. For a century they had been toiling to cultivate jute and it had become such a habit with them that deviation was impossible. As Rabindra Nath Tagore observed about the peasants of Bengal:

> The peasant who cultivates jute is not by nature indolent. But he is so bound by his habits that he will not agree to cultivate other crops even if it is profitable.[156]

Despite this, the campaign yielded significant results which even the officials could not ignore. 'The cultivators consciously began to think of other methods to improve their position and this prepared the way for the no tax and no rent movement which later appeared in Eastern Bengal'.[157]

As non-cooperation gathered momentum, rural areas became scenes of intense peasant agitation. Peasant movement against landlords was first launched in north Bengal, in the Midnapore Zamindari Company's lands. During the First World War, when Germany stopped the export of indigo, the price of this cash crop rose tremendously. Consequently after 1914 extensive cultivation of barley and indigo was reintroduced by the Midnapore Zamindari Company in north Bengal and with it began the inhuman oppression of the cultivators. Even in the twentieth century large tracts of land in north Bengal continued to be given over to the cultivation of indigo. During the First World War the system of tenancy that prevailed in this part of Bengal was the *utbandi* system, where lands were settled with tenants for a short period during which they enjoyed no rights over them.[158] This arrangement made it even easier to oppress those who worked on the land. The landlords also did not grant any receipt to their tenants for the rents collected from them.

The Midnapore Zamindari Company which held lands in Rajshahi, Pabna, Nadia and Murshidabad found the *utbandi* system useful for growing indigo and barley. Lands which had earlier produced indigo were let out on *utbandi* and bore other crops till they were wanted again for indigo. In the sand bars of Padma for example, the company entered into contract with the tenants that after paddy had been reaped, they would sow a crop in this land on *begar,* with seeds to be provided by the company. This land was rent free and only half the share of the produce was payable to the company. If the tenants defaulted the terms of the contract, the company would confiscate the land.[159] This system appeared very convenient to the farmers as the sand bars of Padma were extremely fertile and it needed little labour to grow anything there. But in reality the company forced the farmers to grow indigo or barley. Thus the nature of the *utbandi* tenancy always created tension between the landlords and the tenants.

Oppression by the landlords took various forms. In this system the company took a share of half the crops produced instead of rent. The company generally selected the best portion of the crop as its share and put it up for auction. The company's men frequently employed the practice of fraudulent calling at these auctions. Once the price was fixed it formed the basis on which to settle the rent for the rest of the land.

The cultivators also had to pay *abwabs* or payments in excess of rent, not only to the company's *sahibs* but also to the *Amlas, Naib* and *Dewan* in the company's service. Other illegal exactions included compensation for destroying the grass on the companies lands on which animals grazed. This was called *Khur Jalani*. The company also claimed a share of the fruits that grew in the homesteads of the tenants. In the floodwater-logged company lands, the cultivators had no right to catch fish. Oppression and even torture of the womenfolk was common if the tenants disobeyed a company order. Thus the peasants lived a life of humiliation and complete subordination, bearing everything in silence.[160]

The initiative to organize protests against this inhuman treatment came from the local people. Ghanashyam Agarwal, a local merchant of Dhapari in Pabna district, had been repeatedly urging the Congress volunteers at Calcutta to send a good speaker to inspire and organize the peasants.[161] Someswar Prasad Chaudhuri, a young medical student, decided on his own initiative to visit the region. Since the Congress was not in favour of striking up tension between landlords and tenants, C R Das warned him that he should not expect their organizational support. However *Deshbandhu*, on finding him adamant, permitted him to work among the peasants and report to him personally.[162] Someswar Prasad and Prasanna Kumar reached Dhapari where they were received by Ghyanashyam Agarwal. The latter took them to Gangabazar in Rajshahi district from where they began their campaign.

The *zamindari* of the Midnapore Zamindari Company began from Gangabazar. This tract of borderland between Pabna and Rajshahi district was an extremely fertile region. The inhabitants, 90 per cent Muslims, were landless labourers earning their living through tending cattle and selling vegetables. Someswar Prasad was forbidden to hold meetings in the *zamindari* of Majpara Gangabazar. So he began to approach the cultivators personally though the *Paramanik* or the head men of the local villages who exercised a strong influence over the cultivators. Hussain Mollah of Bairagi Char was one such head man who helped him to organize a meeting at Bathan Bari village.

At social, cultural and religious gatherings the message of Congress was preached. Since the majority of the population was Muslim, Someswar visited the local mosques every Friday during evening prayers to talk about the country's subordination and how the people should remove the fetters of dependence. As the message of the Congress spread, local people voluntarily took the oath to resist oppression. Jafaruddin Mollah, a student of IA class joined the Congress. In the Gangabazar area between 10 and 12 villages became organized with the help of the local people.[163]

As the reaping season approached, the *Nagdis* of the company would hire farmers by throwing a copper penny, and if the men took the coin they were obliged to go and work. The system was known as *begar* and that coin as *dadan*. Someswar, along with his co-workers, decided to rouse the peasants to cease work. He held a meeting with the *mandals* of the villages. Many of them disagreed with strike action. Finally after prolonged discussion it was settled that strike would be called in only one village, far from the *Kuthi* and only for a day. The *hartal* was to be called at the *mauja Bathanbari* which was situated at the heart of the *Kuthi*.

The next day when the *Nagdis* arrived to collect the workers, the head man informed them of the decision not to work. Even in face of unendurable torture the farmers stood their ground and refused to work. Soon the strike spread to other *maujas* of the Midnapur Zamindari Company in the Pabna and Rajsahi *Sadar*.[164] Since the Congress was against peasant agitation, Someswar Prasad was criticized severely for causing tension among the farmers. Bijaylal Chattopadhyay, a Congress volunteer who was visiting Nadia at the time, opposed Someswar's move in a meeting but the strike continued. The indigo factories at Sonal Kundi, Mahiskundi and Harishankara stopped functioning. Even after the arrest of the Congress leaders the movement did not abate and continued under the leadership of Jafaruddin Mollah until the Bilmaria *Kuthi* was totally ruined and the company's white employers were forced to leave the place.[165]

In Nadia too, the tenants of *Zamindar* Surendra Nath Acharya stopped working in protest against their overlord's oppressive treatment. Someswar Prasad had been invited by Bilasram Rai, son of Baktarmal Agarwal of *Haludbari* and a congress worker of Nadia to lead the peasant agitators of Refaitpur. All the efforts of the Congress volunteers to prevent the strike failed.[166]

Peasant fury during the days of non-cooperation was often directed against native *zamindars*, moneylenders and traders. Along the Assam border of Rangpur district, the non-cooperators encouraged agitation by local tenants against *Sahas* and *Marwaris*. The tenants of Baharbund and Bhetarbund Pargana within the Kurigram subdivision in Rangpur withheld their rent. Maharaja Manindra Chandra Nandi of Kassembazar who was the *zamindar* of Baharbund Pargana was warned by his tenants that if he paid revenue to the government, they would stop paying their rents.[167] In other parts of the district too the tenants were rather refractory and rents fell below the expected level. The tenants always blamed economic distress as the main cause for non-payment of rent. But official reports say that non-cooperation had fanned the flames of civil disobedience.[168] In Santhal Pargana of Rangpur the *Batasha Rayat's Samiti* which had joined the non-cooperation movement preached violence against the *Marwari zamindars*.[169]

Towards the end of the year, as non-cooperation propaganda began to spread into rural interiors, and the peasants continued to agitate against taxes and settlement operations, British officials began to be very concerned. From as early as September 1921 *chaukidari* tax collectors were facing great difficulties in collecting tax in certain parts of Rangpur. Social boycott was implemented against those who paid *chaukidari* tax. Mohiuddin Bepari was socially boycotted when he paid one year's *chaukidari* tax in contradiction of an order passed by the *Damer hat* Congress committee.[170] In November 1921, agitation started up against the settlement operations in Pabna, Rangpur, Bogra and Birbhum. Settlement officers found that the villagers had made up their minds to postpone the operations until the rice crop had been reaped.[171]

In districts like Rangpur, non-cooperators regularly sent volunteers to the village *mandals* to appraise them of the danger of dragging chains through fields of ripe paddy.[172] As a result the cultivators did not allow the *annuirs* to do their work. The wave of non-cooperation also reached Bogra where for sometime *Khilafat* meetings were held in market fairs. There was continuing talk of *Swaraj* and toppling of the *Sirkar*.[173] Itinerant *maulavis* were spreading tales of outrage on the Muslim holy cities and dismemberment of Turkey. The cultivators talked of Kamal Pasha, king of Hediaz and political trials. 'The coming of the settlement operations united the people in an immediate and understandable grievance against the government and opposition to settlement operations became the test of *Swaraj*.'[174]

In Bogra, the centre of agitation against settlement was Mokamtola in Shibganj police station, six miles from the Rangpur border. The settlement officer Macpherson wrote that even before the harvest there was already tension among the cultivators over the commencement of the settlement operation.[175] The headman played a key role in igniting the apprehensions of the peasants to the point where they were ready to revolt against authority. Householders were forbidden to provide food and shelter to the *amins* or to sell anything to the settlement officers in the markets.[176] Official reports held the volunteers responsible for this widespread tension. They had been preaching the boycott of foreign goods at various places in Bogra, including Mokamtola.[177]

From Mokamtala the disturbance spread to Buriganj Khetlal where Suresh Chandra Dasgupta had been working incessantly since the beginning of the new movement. He held meetings in the neighbourhood of Buriganj advising the peasants to throw all sorts of obstacles in the way of the *amins*, to refuse them shelter and food and to be as uncooperative as possible with their land-surveying work.[178] An important feature of this opposition to survey and settlement operations was violent assault on the settlement officers. At Biroli village police station in Joypur *hat* an *amin* was attacked and his chain snatched away.[179] In some areas, like Panchbibi and Joypur *hat* at Khetlal, resentment among the cultivators cropped up in spite of the comparative freedom of these *thanas* from volunteer activities. Survey and settlement work in Bogra and Rangpur could not be resumed until the volunteer organizations were proclaimed illegal.[180]

In Birbhum, too, villagers prevented settlement operations from being carried out. The farmers had a poor crop in 1920 and were hoping for a bumper harvest in 1921 and 1922. Jitendra Lal Banerjee had been preaching non-cooperation with the rulers and when settlement operations began the peasants were more than ready to resist them. Tarashankar Bandhyopadhyay in *Ganadevata* showed how the arrival of the settlement operators created apprehension among the village folk. Rumours regarding survey and settlement operations created tension in the village and petitions for their postponement poured in. The *amins* were driven out; their shelters were burnt down and many were escorted to the nearest railway station and given their fares home. The settlement officer and his assistant were publicly insulted and narrowly escaped assault.[181] Even after vigorous disciplinarian measures and the arrest of J L Banerjee, a certain amount of passive resistance still remained. In Jessore the *amins* themselves, returning from Bogra, told the villagers of Jhenida subdivision to take advantage of the non-cooperation movement and refused to attend the camps.

Eastern Midnapur became a scene of acute peasant unrest when Birendra Nath Sasmal, a local lawyer and one of the lieutenants of *Deshbandhu*, launched a campaign against the newly founded union boards.[182] The Bengal Village Self Government Act of 1919 had recommended the establishment of union boards for the better administration of the villages.[183] In July 1919 the Contai Local Board whose chairman was Rai Bhupendra Nath Gupta advised the introduction of the act in Contai *thana* as an experimental measure. But later at a special meeting convened on 31 August 1919 there was a unanimous resolution to introduce the act throughout the subdivision.

In January 1921 when the nation responded to Gandhi's call and plunged into non-cooperation with the British, Congress workers led by Sasmal toured the districts speaking out against the economic ruin of the country through colonial exploitation.[184] They also taught the villagers self-sufficiency through spinning, weaving, settlement of disputes through arbitration courts and nationalist education. All of this served to prepare the ground for confrontation between the inhabitants of Midnapur and the government from the earliest days of non-cooperation. The union boards became targets of peasant wrath. At a meeting of the BPCC held on 14 April there was a resolution, moved by C R Das, to refrain for the time being from boycotting municipalities and other district and local boards, including the unions. But for the villagers of Midnapur the union board and its taxation rules was a symbol of foreign exploitation that had a direct impact on their lives. Sasmal reported that the village self-government scheme was being opposed chiefly on economic grounds as it would increase taxes to seven times their present rate. Under the village *chaukidari* act the villagers already paid 12 rupees annually as *chaukidari* tax. But this enactment increased their tax burden to 84 rupees per year.[185]

Thus the implementation of the village Self-Government Act came at the right moment when the atmosphere was already tense with the non-cooperation propaganda. This fanned the resentment among the local people and caused spontaneous uprisings against union boards in eastern Midnapur. In Tamluk the president and the members requested that the district magistrate abolish the boards. In Contai the excited villagers resorted to violence. S N Ray, the joint magistrate, wrote in a report dated 1 November 1921 that at Contai Bazar he met some shopkeepers who vented their disapproval, saying that they had not had a good harvest for years and could hardly afford to pay for their food and clothing in the present state of the market.[186] Nationalist leaders also realized that government-controlled union boards would prove a deterrent to nationalist work.

Propaganda against union boards began. The leaders argued that these boards were really unnecessary because the principal cause of mortality in the villages was lack of proper food, not the problems with health and hygiene dealt with by the union boards. The people were unable to pay for improvements to health and hygiene which should have been entirely financed by the government. Moreover, union boards were under the control of the rich, who would force the people to bear the burden of extra taxation. Thus, continuous propaganda in the *Sabhas* and meetings created a strong feeling against union boards.[187] For about six months the villagers resisted and made no payments. After this, when the authorities appointed *Tahsildars* to sieze their property, the villagers openly invited them in without resorting to violence. Sasmal reported that 'poor women tax payers delivered their only utensils on the one hand and blew the conch shells on the other. There is actually gladness and contentment in every face'.[188] The cartmen and the labourers, in sympathy with the villagers, refused to carry the attached property. Even the *chaukidars* refused to assist the process in any way.

The first move towards boycott was made in the police stations of Contai Sadar and Ramnagar. The local Congress leaders organized villages with the help of volunteers. Five or seven *Palli Samities* made a *Palli Sangha* and a number of *Palli Sanghas* together formed branch Congress committee. From May the people of Contai stopped paying union board taxes. They also refused to pay *chaukidari* tax if the receipts were issued by the union boards. The inhabitants also resisted the tax collectors.[189] They refused to pay tax to the president of the union boards in Ram Nagar police station, Fatehpur village, because Sasmal had asked them not to. Even attachment of the belongings of the villagers could not cover the amount that was unpaid. Nobody attended the auction of the attached property.

From Contai the opposition to tax collection and non-payment spread to Tamluk, Ghatal, and eastern Sadar Mahakuma. In Ghatal Mahakuma the *chaukidars* resigned their posts as serving the government was considered shameful. Eventually the government was forced to remove union boards from Midnapur except at Gopalnagar in Tamluk Mahakuma.[190] The government tried to put the blame on the non-cooperation propaganda, but *The Musalman* reported Sasmal as saying that the 'government ought to be satisfied now that the non-cooperation movement had nothing to do with the agitation here, but that people themselves do not want the Act'.

The rural police naturally felt the brunt of rural unrest. In Rangpur the uniform of the *chaukidars* was burnt and complete boycott of police and government servants was enforced throughout the district.[191] In Tippera in Chaudagram police station the rural police had ceased to work since November. Taxes were not being paid and no agricultural rents could be collected, either by the government or by local landlords.[192] Villagers assaulted the officers who came to execute distress warrants or took recourse to criminal procedures, and when armed police went out to make arrests the villagers simply evacuated the area.[193]

The *adivasi* revolt against the Midnapore Zamindari Company in Jungle Mahals and neighbouring tracts of Bankura and Singbhum was another instance of Congress trying directly to involve the tribal groups in nationalist politics.[194] The Jungle Mahals in Midnapur district never saw any Congress attempt at organization until 1921. In the wake of the non-cooperation movement, *Deshbandhu* sent Satcowripati Roy to organize political movements in Midnapur. At Gidni he was joined by an old acquaintance Sailajananda Sen, a briefless lawyer, who joined the nationalist movement at Roy's persuasion. Sailajananda worked along with Murari Mohan Roy to involve the tribals in the non-cooperation movement. A branch Congress committee was opened at Gidni and members were enlisted.[195] The cult of non-cooperation was preached to the people of the district and the main target was the Midnapore Zamindari Company. A *zamindari* of this European concern was situated in Pargana Silda. The non-cooperators held meetings in the area to preach anti-British ideas and to exhort the people to unite against the European *zamindars*.[196] They persuaded these hapless tribals that if they stood together the *zamindars* would never be strong enough to possess the Jungle Mahals.

From May 1921, the Congress workers organized meetings among the *Santhals*. In one such gathering of 700 aboriginals, they resolved to give up drinking. The leaders also preached boycott of foreign cloth. In July 1921, 200 *Santhal* women led by Sailajananda Sen blocked the path of paddy carts belonging to the local *zamindar* to demonstrate their opposition to the export of paddy from their area when there was a shortage.[197]

Satcowripati Roy organized a strike of the tribal labourers of the company. They were paid the meagre sum of four paisa (a paisa being one hundredth of a rupee) for transferring wood over a distance of 14 miles. The company retaliated with force and an employee was killed in the encounter.[198] The strike developed into a widespread tribal agitation as they vigorously attempted to re-establish their conventional claims and ownership of their habitat, the Jungle Mahals. The *Santals* explicitly told the officials that 'they had full rights over the jungles and could not be stopped'.[199] They threatened to ravage the forests. The Midnapore Zamindari Company went to court seeking an injunction. The district magistrate, L Birley, intervened but Satcowripati Roy forced the company to accept the terms of the Congress, under which a Congress worker was to inspect working conditions in the area.

Congress gained such immense popularity in the area that the inhabitants, instead of going to the subregistrar's office, took deeds for the sale and transfer of lands to the Congress office. The deeds were registered at the Congress office and the Congress put its own seal on them. An attempt at equitable distribution of crops among the tribals was initiated. Congress leaders established *dhangolas* or granaries where the people accumulated their surplus paddy and those who had less borrowed paddy from this reserve to be returned later. The local Congress established its own post-office as the government post office had stopped functioning due to the agitation. Satcowripati claimed that the Congress had struck such fear in the hearts of its opponents that the manager of the Midnapore Zamindari Company removed his hat in deference while passing the Congress office.

Sailajananda Sen addressed several meetings in which he told the masses that if *Swaraj* was obtained, the jungle and the country would become theirs. They were asked to pay four annas to the *Swaraj* fund and nothing to the *zamindars*. They were also encouraged to oppose the traders in the Jungle Mahals.[200]

Once the tribal consciousness found expression through collective spontaneous action against the oppressive landlordism of their *Sahib zamindar*, the resultant movement acquired a dynamism of its own and broke away from political control by the Congress. The official dictum of non-violence could hardly be applied to the people of the area. After the Congress campaign against foreign cloth, several *hats* were raided and in the Dehijuri *hat* even indigenous merchants were not spared.

The affinity and cohesion that developed between the tribals of the Jungle Mahals and the Congress volunteers during the days of non-cooperation proved extremely important. At a trial of four Congress workers a crowd of 1,000 tribals surrounded the court. They remained absolutely non-violent. The subdivisional officer adjourned the case but an exorbitant 700 rupees was set as bail for each of the accused. There was no protest against the action but the only demand was to free the volunteers immediately.[201] Once the non-cooperation movement was called off in 1922 the confrontation between the tribals and their *zamindar* overlords still continued under the patronage of the local leaders, Sailajananda Sen and Murari Mohan Roy. In 1923 when Sailajananda Sen was arrested, the tribals destroyed the company's office at Kankrajhore and killed one man.[202]

While analysing the support base of the Congress we find that the method of mobilization adopted by the leaders, while successful in drawing many different occupational groups into the movement, failed to appeal the members of the caste groups, especially the *Namasudras*. They remained antagonistic to the Congress throughout.

III

The non-cooperation *Khilafat* agitation sparked off popular discontent that tended to breach the barriers of Gandhian non-violence. Even within the Congress there was controversy among the leadership regarding the extent and nature of mass involvement in the movement. In Midnapur for example, Sasmal decided to start the movement without the formal consent of the provincial Congress committee.[203] Earlier in February the working committee of the provincial Congress had resolved not to boycott union boards. So Birendra Nath sought the permission of Gandhi for inaugurating a boycott movement. Gandhi replied that since civil disobedience was complicated and still in its experimental stage, he wanted to carry it out himself. But if Sasmal still insisted, he could start a movement on his own responsibility. On the other hand in eastern Midnapur the resentment against union boards had reached such a height that it became impossible for the local Congress leaders to remain inert.

The Congress as an organization was averse to any political movement in the rural areas that might spark off anti-landlord agitation. But within Congress there were leaders who felt that, if the Congress was to establish itself in the rural areas, it must protect the peasants from the oppression of the landlords. Someswar Prasad wrote in his reminiscence *Nilkar Bidroha* that C R Das, although he knew that Congress would not cooperate with Someswar, did not object to his work in the rural areas. Personally Deshbandhu felt that if the indigenous landlords suffered some loss in the process of ending oppression by the European companies, it would help the cause of *Swaraj*. Among the rank and file of Congress workers too, differences of opinion existed regarding the Congress programme. Bijaylal Chattopadhyay believed Someswar's move in stirring up the peasants to be a revolt against the Congress, while Someswar believed that unless the villagers were freed from servitude, Congress would never be able to make progress with its programme for the attainment of *Swaraj*.

Even while stirring up labour strikes the Congress leaders often differed in their opinions. Chitta Ranjan Das was severely criticized by Shyam Sundar Chakrabarti, editor of the *Servant*, for encouraging the East Bengal strike. Das described the East Bengal strike as part of the non-cooperation movement and wired to Aswini Datta on 11 June not to allow labour grievances to be mixed up with it.[204] Shyam Sundar Chakrabarti, presiding over a public meeting held under the auspices of the Bengal Central Labour Federation on 16 June, severely criticized Das's statement to the press that the strike was a part of the general non-cooperation movement and hence should be actively encouraged by the Congress.[205] The difference between Das and Chakrabarti becomes apparent from an article in the *Servant*, which opined that the coolies should have been repatriated before 'manly course of corporate action was decided on'.[206] Gandhi himself was very critical of the strikes in eastern India and wrote in *Young India* 'whosoever instigated it did an ill-service to the labourers. In India we want no political strike. The only way we can help the strikers is to give them help and relief when they have struck for their own bona fide grievances. We must sedulously prevent all other strikes. We seek not to destroy capital or capitalists but to regulate the relationship between capital and labour. We want to harness capital to our side. It would be a folly to encourage sympathetic strike'.[207]

While conventional historiography tends to consider the mass movement of the 1920s as part and parcel of the nationalist movement and the subaltern emphasis upon its autonomous character running parallel to the nationalist movement, a close study of the non-cooperation movement reveals a constant interaction between radical militarism of the non-institutional movements and organized nationalist opposition to imperialism. This intermingling of the two forces of politics not exclusively on terms of congress ideology or conditions of peasant autonomy, helped the strengthening of the popular base of the Congress during the days of non-cooperation. In the process, new areas in politics were opened and new social and economic groups were drawn into politics. Organizational endeavours from the sphere of institutional politics matched with the spontaneous response of the people to create a volatile political situation.

The involvement of agriculturists and labourers in the anti-imperialist movement gave focus and purpose to a pre-existing revolutionary tendency among that class. Religious and social bonds influenced the response of the agrarian society to the political moves of the elite.

Religious leaders, *moulavis* and *wahabi* leaders exercised a great influence over the mass of the Muslim population. Many of them preached non-cooperation among the masses which left a deep impact. For example, itinerant *moulavis* preached the cause of *Khilafat* among the peasants of Bogra who for weeks heard nothing but tales of outrages against Islam. Besides, places of worship were made the venue of political meetings. Someswar Prasad wrote in *Nilkar Bidroha* that he deliberately planned to use the mosques as a meeting place and regularly visited the mosques during Friday prayers to hold discussions on the state of the country with the Muslim inhabitants. He made them vow by touching the Koran that they would obey his orders for the good of the country. Then, they would pray together and finally arrange the next meeting, which would be at another mosque.

Religious songs and symbols very often became weapons in the hands of the rebels. In Midnapur during the boycott of the union board the villagers began to sing *Hari Sankirtan*, a form of devotional song, wherever the tax collector entered the village as a warning to the others. This kept the villagers united and also kept officers at bay. In Bankura, the Congress leaders roamed around the villages accompanied by *kirtan* singers.[208] Govinda Prasad Singa of Gangajalghati organized *Sabhas* for the villagers to discuss religious discourses from the *Shastras* and also held prayer meetings at which he preached the ideologies of Ramkrishna and Vivekananda. On religious festivals like *Janmastami*, processions by local people were organized. In Kotulpur, Congress workers joined in the discussions on the *Shastras* held at the local *Hitasadhani Sabha's* premises.[209] Bankura had a considerable population of *Santhal, Khavia, Bhumij, Mahato, Bauri, Bagdi* and other such backward tribes. These men, who remained outside the fold of the Hindu society, were brought within its fold by the *Gauriya Vaishnav* preachers. Through *Sankirtan* and other ceremonies they gained social acceptance. The Congress workers who organized the movement at village level were able to establish a rapport with the populace through such social and cultural meetings. During times of flood and famine the local Congress camps arranged for *Hari Sankirtan*. The singers received flour. Jaidayal Goenka, a rich *Marwari* trader of Bankura donated the provisions. He was interested in spreading the preaching of the *Gita* and involved the Congress workers in this task.[210]

In the popular mind, religion and miracles – especially the miraculous removal of evil – were inseparably associated. This definitely influenced the political behaviour of the peasants, especially the tribals, and their response to the call of the leaders. The myth of the Gandhi *Raj* affected them immensely. The *Santhals* of Jalpaiguri believed that they were immune from bullets as they were wearing Gandhi Maharaj's cap.[211] The *Nagdis* of Bilmaria *Kuthi* informed Someswar Prasad that they had great respect for Gandhi.

Often, rumours of oppression stirred peasants into action. The villagers in the novel *Ganadevata* were overcome with tension as settlement operations began in their village, the basis of this trepidation being mainly the rumours of oppression and increased taxation that they had heard associated with these operations. The concept of Gandhi *Raj* was more dominant among the tribal peasants. The Muslims of North Bengal or the Mahisyas of Midnapur were not gripped by this frenzy. Their movement was characterized by strenuous efforts of organization, mobilization and planning on the part of the leaders and a conscious acceptance of their plans on the part of the peasants.

The actions of the non-cooperation movement were often almost experimental to begin with and when these experiments proved successful they became an accepted course of action. For example, Someswar Prasad and the *mandals* held prolonged discussion on whether to strike. *Hartal* was first declared in one *mauja* and once it proved successful, the other *maujas* decided to strike. Not all the headmen accepted Someswar's lead. Similarly, in Midnapur, boycott first began at Contai. The participants had no great aim of establishing the Gandhi *Raj* but were interested in redressing specific wrongs. Once that was achieved opposition was withdrawn.

The methods of protest did not always remain non-violent as prescribed by Gandhi. *Hat* looting, burning down the symbols of oppression like the *Nil Kuthi* and the uniform of the *chaukidars*, assaults on English officers and their Indian agents and social boycott were occasionally resorted to. These other methods that emerged out of popular initiative alarmed the officials the most.

The methods of mobilization adopted by the Congress leaders were many and varied, but what was most important was that they aroused in the people a hope of a better world once *Swaraj* was achieved. This mass campaign won a widespread support for Congress at grass root level. Despite this mobilization process, there sometimes remained a gap between elite ideology and popular aspirations. Use of religious associations for mobilization created future problems. As a result, once the nationalist fervour subsided, it became difficult for the Congress to hold together popular interest by its organizational superstructure. It had to find other means of keeping alive its link with the people. However, it can be argued that the non-cooperation movement proved to be somewhat successful as far as interaction of institutional politics and politics of the people is concerned.

Chapter 4

Congress in the Post Non-Cooperation Period, 1922–29

I

The Chauri Chaura incident followed by the Bardoli Resolution brought the non-cooperation movement to a sudden halt. Its participants were left without any clearly defined and intelligible objective and the result was confusion. But once the initial despair was overcome, the non-cooperators began to reconstruct a programme on lines that would appeal to the popular imagination.[1]

In Bengal, the Bardoli Resolution slowed down the pace of preparation for civil disobedience. In some places like Noakhali, Birbhum and parts of Rajshahi the activities of volunteers picketing excise shops did not stop stop immediately, but at Rangpur, in Gaibandha and Kurigram, the volunteers began to follow the Bardoli Resolution programme and engaged themselves in social reconstruction. In most of the districts, constructive social work, such as popularizing the use of *charka* among the poorer people, continued unhampered.[2] Organizational reconstruction, like enlistment of Congress members by district Congress committees, also continued as usual. Official records show that 'almost everywhere, the political atmosphere remained calm, marked by a general disappointment among the people'.[3]

Earlier in 1922, Chitta Ranjan Das and his lieutenants were arrested in connection with the boycott of the visit of the Prince of Wales in December 1921 and the BPCC was dominated by Shyam Sundar Chakrabarti and his followers. Later in the Chittagong conference of 1922 C R Das introduced the concept of obstruction and non-cooperation from within the council. Shyam Sundar Chakrabarti and the other Congress leaders in Bengal, who at the time were enjoying the support of the no-change group at the centre, refused to accept the

Swarajist programme.[4] Among the 40 representatives from Bengal, 25 supported the Gandhian followers and only 15 were with Das and the *Swarajists,* when at the national level the Gandhites led by C Rajagopalachari successfully passed an anti-council entry resolution in the subject's committee with a vote of 203 to 87.

From the end of 1922, the Congress was split into two sections: the *Swarajists* (pro-changers) and the Gandhians (no-changers). Das resigned as the Congress president in 1922–23. In 1922 soon after the report of the Congress civil disobedience committee was published, Das openly expressed his intention of changing the programme of the Congress. He was in favour of contesting the elections and of non-cooperation with the bureaucracy by obstructing every function of the council.[5]

The *Swarajya* Party was formed on 31 December 1922 with the aim of non-cooperation from within the council. The manifesto of the *Swarajya* Party signed in February 1923 declared that it was formed as 'a party within the Congress and as such an integral part of the Congress'.[6] The party also reiterated the creed of the Congress as its objective. The two criteria for eligibility to membership of the party were attainment of the age of 18 and devotion to the object, constitution and programme of the party. The annual subscription was eight annas, or four annas for those who enjoyed dual membership of the *Swarajya* Party and the Congress. The number and the geographical limits of the provinces were to be the same as prescribed by the constitution of the Indian National Congress.[7]

The party also gave an option for all those nationalists who did not agree with the principles of non-cooperation and *satyagraha* to sign the Congress creed and at the same time to join the council entry section of the party and contest elections.[8] The *Swarajya* Party was born out of a compromise resolution adopted by the Congress at the Delhi session. It was in essence the political wing of the Congress which was to function constitutionally as a party, as distinct from an organization. But it did not deviate from the path of non-violent non-cooperation as set down by the Congress.

Once established in his position at the national level as the leader of a new party, Chitta Ranjan Das established his control over the BPCC and got himself elected as the president of the Bengal Provincial Congress.[9] *Maulavi* Akram Khan and Lalit Mohan Das were elected as vice-presidents.[10] In the executive committee only six members won from the no-change faction. The *Swarajists* thus secured complete control of the provincial Congress committee.

In Calcutta the high caste, western-educated professionals were dominating politics. Among them Sarat Bose and Nirmal Chandra Chunder had lucrative practices at the Calcutta High Court. Dr Bidhan Chandra Roy was a medical practitioner. Nalini Ranjan Sarkar was a self-made businessman who had made a considerable fortune with the Hindusthan Cooperative Insurance Company and other enterprises. Tulsi Charan Goswami belonged to the *zamindar* family of Sreerampore. He was educated in Calcutta at St Xavier's School. After completing Senior Cambridge, he went to England and became a graduate of Oxford University, then in 1921 he became a barrister. He was practising in Calcutta, when he joined the non-cooperation movement.

Among these leaders Nalini Ranjan Sarkar began his political career as a volunteer in the *Swadeshi* Movement and Nirmal Chandra Chunder as the president of the provincial Congress committee and as a councillor in 1915. The others were comparatively new to politics. They had begun their political career in the 1920s with the non-cooperation movement and on the insistence of the Congress.

Besides this group, Subhas Chandra Bose, whose political role began with the non-cooperation movement, was emerging as an important figure in the provincial and ultimately the nationalist politics of Congress. He was appointed the chief executive officer in the newly organized Calcutta Corporation by Chitta Ranjan Das. Under his charismatic leadership, they had matured from professional into active politicians. All five of them held important posts in the provincial Congress committee and the *Swarajya* Party.[11] This group, later to become famous as the Big Five, was already exerting considerable influence in the politics in 1923. These men, who were all Western-educated established professionals belonging to high caste families and living in Calcutta, were endeavouring to control politics in opposition to the leaders from the districts. However, as long as Das lived, he was the centre around which the newly emerging galaxy of leaders revolved.

In the city of Calcutta, the politicians who were interested in constitutional politics provided the main source of support for the organization. They included mostly high caste, affluent professionals, aristocrats or business families. Many of these leaders had made their mark organizing popular movements in the districts during the non-cooperation movement. Convinced of their ability, Das had invited them to work at provincial level to build up an organization that was to rest on the extensive political support of the masses. Moreover, as the *Swarajya* Party was going into the elections, it became imperative to involve the district leaders in provincial politics so that through their candidature, the *Swarajya* Party could win the election.

The most prominent among these leaders were Jatindra Mohan Sengupta, who became the secretary of the *Swarajya* Party and Birendra Nath Sasmal who was elected as a member of the *Swarajya* Party executive committee. Kiran Shankar Roy from Dacca emerged as an important party functionary and Anil Baran Roy from Bankura became the secretary of the BPCC. Jnan Chandra Majumdar was another leader who had organized the Congress movement in Mymensingh and was later transferred to Calcutta politics.

The end of the non-cooperation movement found a section of the revolutionaries increasingly associating themselves with the Congress organization. Rabindramohan Sen from Dacca Anushilan Samiti in a letter to Gopal Chandra Das observed in February 1923, 'it will be our advantage if we work with the party of C R Das but there will be some difficulty in Barisal owing to the strength of the Congress Party there'.[12] Finally they joined the party of Das. In the AICC elected in November 1922, the representatives from Bengal included four important members of the *Jugantar*, Amarendra Chatterjee, Upen Banerjee, Bipin Ganguly and Satyen Mitter. These men, along with Bhupati Majumdar and Gopen Roy, were among the 60 members who were elected to the BPCC. Monoranjan Gupta was one of the assistant secretaries of the executive council of the Congress committee which also had Gopen Roy, Amarendra Chatterjee and Bipin Ganguly among its members.[13]

Most of the members of the *Jugantar* group nurtured an anti-council-entry feeling and were opposed to the idea of fighting the elections. When Das, after his release from jail in 1922, proposed to contest the elections, the *Jugantar* group refused to cooperate. But before the Gaya Congress in December 1922, Chitta Ranjan won them over to his side. Out of the 900 delegates who visited the Gaya Congress from Bengal, the majority were supporters of Das. The *Swarajya* Party had evolved an agreement with the revolutionaries ensuring cooperation 'so long as the latter abstained from overt acts'.[14] Chitta Ranjan Das himself had reached an understanding with Amarendra Nath Chatterjee and Upen Banerjee that they would support the cause of the *Swarajya* Party, provided the party did not interfere in the policies and work of the revolutionaries.

Many of the revolutionaries and ex-detenues who reverted to join the Congress, held official posts in the organization. Satyen Mitter who in 1921 had acted as private secretary to Das became one of his trusted lieutenants in 1923, a status shared equally with Subhas Bose. In February 1923, Upen Banerjee and Monmohan Bhattacharjee were appointed in the publicity board of the *Swarajya* Party. Satyen Mitter, Pulin Das, Basanta Majumdar and Nagendra Guha Roy were also included in the propaganda board of the party.[15]

Atmasakti, the pro-change revolutionary weekly controlled by the *Jugantar* group took up the cause of Das. As early as 1922 *Atmashakti* expressed pro council-entry views. The other news weekly which in spite of being an organ of the revolutionaries accepted the pro-changer viewpoint was *Bijali*. This newspaper was printed at Amarendra Chatterjee's press, *Atmashakti Library* in Bowbazar Street. This building, which was a secret meeting place of the revolutionaries, also became the headquarters of the *Swarajya* Party until Chitta Ranjan Das captured the BPCC.[16] In the Allahabad Conference at the end of February 1923 (which was held to discuss the split in the Congress caused by the formation of the *Swarajya* Party) Chitta Ranjan was accompanied by, among others, Satyen Mitter, Pulin Das, Jadugopal Mukherjee, Satish Singha and Sachin Sanyal.[17] Thus the revolutionaries constituted a major strength of the Congress during this period.

In most of the districts, the *Swarajists* dominated the district Congress committees. The BPCC and the *Swarajya* Party had become increasingly important for the politically ambitious, whether interested in constructive politics or electoral politics. In Dacca for example, a breach had occurred in the Dacca Congress Committee between the old Congress workers and the *Swarajists*. C R Das accompanied by Anil Baran Roy and Sris Chatterjee proceeded to Dacca to preside over the annual general meeting of the committee. Dacca District Congress Committee had two rival groups. Atul Gupta, Upendra Bhattacharjee, Abdul Karim and Sris Chatterjee formed one faction and the other included Monoranjan Banerjee, Pratul Ganguly, Purnananda Dasgupta, Nalini Dutta and others.[18] The breach however was healed up by the interference of Das. He was elected the president and Kiran Shankar Roy became one of the two secretaries of the committee.

But there were also some exceptions as in Dinajpur and Rangpur where the *Wahabis* held sway over the district Congress committees. *Moulavi* Abdullahel Baki of Dinajpur was a leading figure in the Congress.[19] He was educated in a *Madrassah* at Rangpur and then in *Jami-ul-ulum*, a *Madrassah* in Kanpur. He was one of the leading organizers of *Anjuman-i Ulema-i Bangla*. He took an active part in the *Khilafat* non-cooperation movement.[20] The president of the Dinajpur

District Congress Committee, *Moulavi* Maniruddin Anwari was also a *Wahabi*. *Moulavi* Abdullahel Baki, *Moulavi* Maniruddin Anwari, *Moulavi* Hussain Ali (pleader) and Muhammad Aftabuddin Chaudhuri of Nawabganj, all of them *Wahabis*, were elected as members of the BPCC. The Dinajpur Congress Committee under the leadership of the *Wahabis* was still active in the process of reorganization. Abdullahel Baki had started a branch *Khilafat* committee at Mahatabpur village in Dinajpur.[21]

In Rangpur, the *Wahabis* and the *Hanafis* had been elected as the office-bearers of the Congress and *Khilafat* committees. In the Gobindaganj police station, the *Wahabis* of Mohunganj, Kumedpur, Manoharpur, Pabnapur, Krishnapur and the adjacent villages were working in cooperation with the Congress. In Rajshahi District Congress Committee as well, the *Wahabis* played a prominent role. Meetings organized by the Congress committees were often attended by *Wahabi* leaders. Jogesh Chandra Sarkar, a Congress worker of Charghat Congress office in Rajshahi organized a meeting which was attended by *Wahabi* leaders like Haji Sadukullah, Muhammad Yakub Sarkar and Abdul Samad Khalifa of Gopalpur, Daman Shah and Gopal Sarkar of Jhikra and Jamiruddin Sardar of Khardah.[22] The *Wahabis* of Chabbisnagar in Rajshahi formed a local Congress committee after attending a meeting organized by the Congress. The president was *Maulavi* Jinnatullah of Kupakandi and the secretary was *Maulavi* Muhammad Sarkar of Chabbisnagar.[23]

In Hooghly, the Gandhites led by Prafulla Chandra Sen made Arambagh the centre of their work. In Sreerampur, Satish Chandra Sengupta, Ratanmani Chattopadhyay and other former revolutionaries were convinced of the efficacy of winning *Swaraj* through the Gandhian ideals of non-violence. They took charge of the Congress work in Sreerampur where a Congress office was formed.[24] *Hooghly Vidya Mandir* was the centre of political work in this district.

Between 1921 and 1929, Anil Baran Roy played a significant role as the secretary of the Bankura Congress Committee. During this period the Bankura District Congress Committee remained actively engaged in organizational work through constructive programmes. But after 1927 when Anil Baran Roy left politics and joined the Pondicherry *Ashram*, leadership of the Congress committee fell into the hands of Govinda Prasad Sinha. Following Gandhi's ideals, he engaged himself in constructive works. In 1924 after clearing the jungle of Machranga, he founded the *Amarkanan skisha o karmapratisthan* and transferred the Gangajalghati National School to this place.[25] But the political influence of Govinda Prasad Sinha remained confined to Gangajalghati. As a result, after Anil Baran Roy's departure, dissension within the Bankura District Congress Committee created divisions within the organization. It was split up into a number of units only large enough to include a few police stations, unions or villages.[26]

Upon his release from jail and after gaining control of the BPCC, Chitta Ranjan Das endeavoured to influence the important Muslim associations in the province to win Muslim support for his party. Among the Muslim members in the Congress, Mujibar Rahaman, Maulana Akram Khan, Haji Abdur Rashid Khan and Shamsuddin Ahmed supported Das. In 1924, during the Calcutta *Khilafat* Conference, Das ordered Purushottam Rai, the secretary of the Barabazar Congress Committee to induce the Hindus to participate in the reception.[27]

There was, however, considerable difference of opinion between the Hindu Congressmen and the members of the *Khilafat* Party. Muslim opinion was not easily won over to the proposition of council entry. The decision of the *Jamait-ul Ulema* that Council entry was *haram* or going against the faith still influenced the majority of Muslims. The flow of events in the direction of communal violence combined with the preaching of communal-minded religious leaders like Abu Bakr had stimulated the latent apprehension of the Muslim population that the much hoped for *Swaraj* would in reality be a Hindu *Raj*. A letter by Abu Bakr to the Ali Brothers urged the leaders to consider carefully before contributing to the movement for *Swaraj* by means of obstructing the councils from within.[28] They feared that it would lead to the formation of a parliament consisting mainly of Hindus.[29] Articles in the *Muslim Hitaishi* had stirred the imagination of the Muslim masses. The defeat of the motion on ministers' salaries in the legislative council had been considered by the *Khilafatists* as a direct assault on the Muslims by the Hindu *Swarajists*. The province witnessed a hectic preparation to revive the *Khilafat* organization and to prevent its incorporation with the *Swarajya* Party.

Leaders like Maulana Akram Khan, the President of the Bengal Provincial *Khilafat* Committee and Mujibar Rahaman, its secretary, favoured a more forward programme. Both the *Swarajist* leaders supported Das.[30] As a result, while the Bengal *Khilafat* Committee sided with Das, the Calcutta *Khilafat* Committee expressed its antagonism against him. But by 1924 in a secret meeting attended by Abul Kalam Azad, Chitta Ranjan Das, *Maulavi* Nazimuddin Ahmed and Mohsin Ali, it was decided that the Calcutta *Khilafat* Committee would support the *Swarajya* Party.[31] The *Swarajist* Muslims leaders also entered the Bengal Provincial Muslim League. Abul Kalam Azad, Nazimuddin Ahmed, Mujibar Rahaman, Suhrawardy and others from the *Khilafat* Party also joined the Muslim League. There was, however, a section of the Moderate Muslims led by A K Ghaznavi who were opposed to the *Swarajya* Party. In a meeting on 25 November 1924, they decided to form a pact with the Europeans, Anglo-Indians and the Moderate Hindu leaders to oppose the *Swarajists*.[32]

It is generally believed that in his endeavour to rally the Mohammedan elected members to support the *Swarajya* Party, Das formulated the Bengal Pact. However the initial proposal for an understanding between the Muslims and the Hindus came from the Muslim leaders themselves. Chitta Ranjan Das, reiterating his faith in the pact during council while moving amendments on the bill 'Muhammadans in Government Service' disclosed that 'the suggestion…came from the Mohammedan leaders'.[33] This had also been corroborated by Abdul Karim with whom Das held a meeting. According to him 'it was not Mr C R Das who first moved in the matter with a view as supposed, to court the support of the Musalman members of the Legislative Council of Bengal. On the contrary, the proposal in its inception came from the other party concerned and was developed in its final form after careful consideration on both sides'.[34]

By December 1923, Das was successful in coming to an agreement with the nationalist-minded Muslims on the Bengal Pact. The Muslims were promised a majority share in the administration and the government of Bengal, once *Swaraj* was attained. The banning of music before mosques, the permission of unrestricted cow sacrifice during the *Id* festival and the assurance of greater opportunities in the *Swarajist*-controlled Calcutta Corporation drew the *Khilafatists,* who had so long opposed council entry, to support Das and join the electoral battle.

It was not merely electoral politics, however, that prompted Das to agree to the proposal. Das's ultimate aim was for a *Swaraj* secured through Hindu–Muslim cooperation and to make sure that 'no misapprehension, no doubts may arise as to whether it is going to be a Hindu or a Mohammedan Raj'.[35] Das aimed to lay down in this pact the share of each community in the self-government that was to come. Das in an emphatic speech declared:

> I believe in the Pact and I believe in it as firmly as I believe in any article of my faith. So far as the Swaraj Party is concerned and the

members of the Swaraj Party who signed this Pact, it is a concluded Pact with them and they have taken upon themselves the charge of putting it before the whole country. But it is a suggestion for the country to adopt. I have got no doubt that the country will accept it. Those who are doubtful I challenge them to call a public meeting anywhere in Calcutta in any place except Burra Bazar and I undertake to get the resolution passed by an overwhelming majority.[36]

Political experience and vision had prompted Das to ensure 'for the educated Bengali Muslims, a share in the benefits of victory'.[37] The Hindu–Muslim Pact, however, aroused resentment among the members of the Congress, and Congress continued to voice protest against the pact. In the second half of January 1924, several meetings were held. The pact had also antagonized a large section of the Hindu middle class. The up-country Hindu element in Bengal had been alienated from the *Swarajya* Party on account of the Bengal Pact. The Burrabazar Congress Committee which was composed entirely of up-country Hindus had struck up a rapprochement with the no-change group in Bengal, led by Shyam Sundar Chakrabarti.[38] Condemnation of the Hindu–Muslim Pact continued among the general populace as well and a signed protest was circulated among the Hindus in Mymensingh.[39] On the other hand, in East Bengal especially in the districts of Mymensingh, Malda and Noakhali, leaflets were being circulated in the name of Maulana Abu Bakr of Furfura urging the Muslims to refrain from joining the *Swaraj* Party. The rejection of the pact at the Coconada Conference naturally met with the general approval of the Hindus but created resentment among the Muslims. The pact had aimed at a 'strange marriage of a religious-communal consciousness with institutional forms of representative politics'.[40] Kenneth Macpherson writes that it was primarily aimed to satisfy only a small group among the Muslims and Hindus such as the professionals, wealthier merchants, property owners and the enfranchized elements in the elected bodies. But in the end it even failed to achieve its primary aim.[41]

From the mid 1920s the Hindu Mahasabha was emerging as a major force defending Hindu interest. In Bengal, however, the Mahasabha never became a very important organization and the Congress generally remained aloof from its programmes. Still, there was always an attempt on the part of the Congressmen to capture the Hindu *Sabha*. Often individual Congress leaders took part in the deliberations and conferences of the *Sabha*. In the Mymensingh session of the Hindu Sabha held on 29 March 1925, there was a strong rumour that the *Swarajists* would attend in full strength to capture it. At Kishoreganj, local Congressmen had forced entry into the Hindu *Sabha* and its members feared that the organization would pass into the hands of the Congress.[42] Organizationally, the Congress and the Hindu *Mahasabha* remained aloof from each other at provincial level. But local interactions continued between the two organizations and they could not exist as totally separate entities.

Similar trends of interaction could be noticed between the Muslim organizations and the Congress. In 1923, the efforts of the Arya Samajists to reconvert the Malkana Rajputs and the *Suddhi and Sangathan* movement aroused the indignation of the Muslims. In July 1925 Dr Kitchlew started the *Tanzeem* movement. In Bengal Dr Surhawardy, a prominent Congress leader, took part in the movement, although initially he had chosen to remain aloof from it because of its revolutionary nature.[43] He became the secretary of the *Jamait-i-Ulema* and induced Abu Bakr to become its president. He also applied to the central *Khilafat* committee for affiliation.[44]

Under the dynamic leadership of Das, the *Swarajists* acquired a strong foothold in the Bengal Congress and at the same time fulfilled their aim of council entry. With the abatement of the non-cooperation movement and the fury of mass politics, institutional politics now oriented itself towards waging an electoral battle against imperialism. Outside the council too, the activities of the party continued unabated. They were mainly confined to strengthening the *mufassil* organizations of the party, canvassing for the *Swarajist* candidates for local bodies and spreading propaganda in support of the Hindu–Muslim Pact.

During this period, the *Swarajists* concentrated mainly on attempting to capture the local bodies. The Calcutta Corporation was an obvious first target and all five aldermen of this local body were elected from among the supporters of Das. In Dinajpur, the Balurghat and the Sadar local boards elected only *Swarajya* candidates to the district boards. In the Bogra municipality, the ten elected commissioners consisted of five *Swarajists*, three Independents and two with no definite political links.[45] In the Kalna municipality in Burdwan, six out of ten elected commissioners were *Swarajists*. In the municipal election of Mymensingh, the *Swarajists* won a substantial majority especially in the Tangail municipality where they gained a majority among the elected commissioners. They also carried on active campaigns in Nadia, where they won the elections in June, and in Dacca where they gained some seats in the Munshiganj and Manickganj subdivisions.

The *Swarajya* Party also adopted a programme of village organization. This was mainly the initiative of C R Das, who outlined the scheme in *Desher Dak* which was circulated during the *Swaraj* week in December 1924. In effect his village reorganization scheme was an attempt to drum up popular support for the *Swarajist* programme of participation in the elections. He made appeals for men and money, estimating that a sum of three lakhs was needed to finance this scheme. The first week of December 1924 was declared as a *Swaraj* week during which collections were made to finance the scheme. A number of meetings were held addressed by Abdul Hamid Deopuri, Hemaprova Majumdar, Sasadhar Chakravarti, Atul Sen and Protap Chandra Guha Roy. The sentiment of the people was aroused by eulogizing speeches on the romantic deeds of Khudiram, Kanai lal and Gopi Nath Saha. The youths were especially targeted by these speeches and they were asked to emulate their example. Abdul Hamid Deopuri also added that an awakening of the peasants and the rural folk would further strengthen the movement. As a result, at the Belgaun conference held immediately after the *Swaraj* week in December, resolutions were adopted to start a fund to assist the political sufferers. Collections for the scheme during the *Swaraj* week amounted to 50,000 rupees.

The scheme in its final form was adopted in August 1925, after the demise of its initiator. A village workers' training class was started at Dum-Dum under the patronage of the *Swarajya* Party. Jnananjan Neogy of the Bengal Social Service League and Suresh Das of the *Jugantar* Party were responsible for the training. Most of the appointees to the committee were revolutionaries.[46]

On the other hand, the Congress workers who opted for the alternative path of constructive non-cooperation took recourse to self organization and reconstruction. But there existed a strain of conflict between the two groups on issues like the release of the state prisoners. In the Faridpur Conference of 1925, which was attended by Gandhi, trouble began in the subject's committee when Das tried to get a resolution passed stating that the *Swarajya* Party would consider terms of cooperation with the government on condition of the release of Subhas Chandra Bose, Anil Baran Roy and Satyendra Chandra Mitra. The Gandhian group demanded that the condition should be release of all political prisoners without trial. Das left the meeting threatening resignation and ultimately Gandhi effected a compromise. It was agreed to demand the release of those arrested in October 1924, but not those arrested in 1923. The resolution condemning violence was passed in the open conference but of course was criticized by members of the revolutionary party.[47] Immediately after the Faridpur conference there was a lull in political activities in the province. Meanwhile the death of C R Das on 16 June obviously created a new situation.

With Chitta Ranjan's death, a void was created in the BPCC and the *Swarajya* Party leadership. On 28 June 1925, a meeting of the BPCC was held at the house of Chittaranjan Das to elect the president of the provincial Congress. The names of Sengupta, Basanti Devi and Lalit Mohan Das were proposed.[48] Revolutionaries like Sris Chatterjee and Basanta Majumdar were against the election of Sengupta as president. Sris Chatterjee went to the extent of suggesting the adjournment of the meeting. Hemendra Nath Dasgupta supported the candidature of Azad. Both Basanti Devi and Azad explained their unwillingness to accept the office.[49] That left Sengupta as the only suitable candidate for the post of president of the BPCC. In the absence of any other suitable leader (with Bose incarcerated at the time in Mandalaya jail), from among the names proposed at the meeting, Sengupta was unanimously elected president.

The tripartite struggle for supremacy among J M Sengupta, Subhas Bose and Biren Sasmal centred around the Calcutta Corporation, the *Swarajya* Party and the BPCC. Subhas Bose and Biren Sasmal both stood for the post of the chief executive officer of the corporation. Chitta Ranjan Das had promised the post to Sasmal. But the dominant *Kayastha* clique of Calcutta, headed by the Bose brothers, opposed the choice because Sasmal was a low caste *Mahisya* from the districts. The conflict between the metropolitan politicians not only revealed the hostility between high caste elite and the rising low caste gentry from the districts, but also the fear Calcutta-based politicians had of being dominated by the districts in the sphere of institutional politics. They feared the immense mass support enjoyed by district politicians like Sasmal, which could be used to advantage in the race for power centring around official posts.

By 1926, the Congress leadership was engaged in competing for domination in the provincial Congress committee. This power politics adversely affected the functioning of the Bengal Provincial Congress and finally resulted in the creation of two rival executive councils of the Congress committees in Bengal; one headed by Jitendra Lal Banerjee and Biren Sasmal and the other by Sengupta and his group. The AICC ultimately intervened to resolve the issue.

In November 1927, a new Congress committee was constituted. Subhas Chandra Bose, who had been released from prison, was elected president. Satyendra Chandra Mitra and Maulana Akram Khan became the vice-presidents and Kiran Shankar Roy was elected secretary. Dr Bidhan Chandra Roy was appointed treasurer and Nalini Ranjan Sarkar was the auditor. The new executive council was composed mainly of the anti-Sasmal group. Sasmal, who was elected from Midnapur, was not included in the executive council.[50] The domination of the Congress by the Big Five and their leader Subhas Bose was complete.

The contradictions within Congress between the pro-changers and the no-changers also pervaded Congress organizations at district level. In the districts such rivalry mainly centred around access to the organization's official posts and the contesting of seats in elective bodies. In Nadia, the *Praja Sammelan* played an important role in the elections of the office-bearers. It was an autonomous body and was not in any way connected with or affiliated to the Indian National Congress. The veteran pro-Gandhi Congress workers of the district voted for a motion of no-confidence against the office-bearers. Among them were Nripendrachandra Banerjee, Bijoylal Chatterjee, Satyendranath Roy, Indu Bhusan Bhaduri and Jogendranath Sarkar. They asked Jatindra Mohan Sengupta to settle the deadlock and organize a more representative Congress committee.

In the North Calcutta Congress Committee the secretary, Haran Chandra Ghosh, resigned and was replaced by Haridas Mitra who was a *Swarajist* and a member of the *Jugantar* party. The no-changer group alleged that they received no help from the BPCC. Their claims to be delegates of the AICC were ignored at the time of election and preference was given to the *Swarajist* claim.[51]

In Birbhum, the breach among the leaders centred around winning nominations for election to the Congress committee. The groups reflected the divergence that existed in the provincial Congress committee between Jitendra Lal Banerjee and Sengupta. The district Congress committee supported Jitendra Lal Banerjee and his group, while the election board of the Congress committee of Bengal gave its nomination to Abinash Chandra Roy who was the president of the committee. But the latter had not filed his nomination. The Raja Of Hetampur, who had been a loyalist and a non-member, was being supported by the Congress. Lal Mohan Ghosh, Madan Mohan Bhowmick and Surendra Chandra Chakrabarti were deputed by the BPCC to Suri in connection with the election of the Birbhum District Congress Committee. They too were canvassing in favour of the Raja. Bose and Sengupta, in a joint telegram, requested the Bar Libraries of the district not to support

Jitendra Lal Banerjee who was ultimately forced to seek the involvement of the AICC.

Thus in Bengal the leadership was divided, both at provincial and at district level, on issues of domination over the official posts, council entry and elections. While in 1927 the Congress committees in most of the districts of Bengal presented a dismal picture of dissension, a BPCC report affirmed that by 1929 'in Bengal all the districts have got properly elected district Congress Committees except Faridpur where there is a dispute'.[52]

II

In October 1923 Subhas Bose in a letter to Dr Saifuddin Kitchlew wrote that: 'We are in opinion that the first step in the direction of Civil Disobedience is a reorganization of the branch Congress Committees and a proper financing of national institutions'.[53] In the post non-cooperation period many of the institutions of mass contact that the Congress had built up had become defunct. So reorganization to broaden the social base of the Congress became the prime concern of the Congress workers at the local level.

In the districts, the major problem that preoccupied the Congress workers was recruitment of new members to reinforce the organization. A survey of membership of the Congress in the districts revealed a decline from 3,169 to 1,721 within a period of six months in 1925.[54] The people had lost all enthusiasm for politics and the leaders felt that only constructive work and election propaganda for council entry could provide some incentive for launching another effective campaign. So rebuilding the organization was given the first priority.

In Mymensingh a batch of *Tarakeswar Satyagrahis* started a new Congress camp at Dhallabazar in the shop of a local resident, Ganesh Nath. In Faridpur there were 20 Congress committees and three *Khilafat* committees in 1922. In Darjeeling, a Congress committee was formed at Kurseong Bazar with 380 members. Pershadi Ram, a shopkeeper of Kurseong, Padamlal Kharka, the collector's clerk and Biswanath Ram Teli, a *Swadeshi* shopkeeper were keeping the organization going. In Siliguri, a combined Congress and *Khilafat* committee existed and in Midnapur district 130 Congress committees and four *Khilafat* committees were still functioning.[55]

But what sustained the Congress organization in the post non-cooperation period, both at the district level and below, was its link with institutions which apparently acted independently but in reality worked in conjunction with the Congress. Among them, a network of *Ashrams* and *Sanghas* set up by the revolutionaries to consolidate their scattered organization, indirectly influenced and aided the Congress movement.

In Dacca a new organization of the *Jugantar* group was set up in 1922. This was a scheme initiated by Purna Das while he was in jail. This particular organization recruited workers from among the members of the various Congress committees in the district. Paramananda De was a volunteer of the Dacca Congress Committee. Jibanlal Chatterjee was an active member of the Munshiganj Congress Committee. He also started a branch of the Jugantar party at Munshiganj. The centre at Munshiganj was under Narayan Chandra Banerjee who was the ex-secretary of the Brajajogini Congress Committee and also taught at the Munshiganj National School. Other members of the centre were also Congress workers: Himangshu Roy was a leading member of the Dacca Congress Committee; Priya Kumar Goswami was the secretary of the Narayanganj Labour Association; Tarini Kanta Dey was a member of Rupganj Congress Committee; Dhirendra Mohan was a member of the Brajajogini Congress Committee; Sushil Kumar Das was a member of the Satura Congress Committee; Jiban Kumar Mitra Biswas was a member of the Kaliganj Congress Committee Brahmangaon; Nihar Chandra Dutta belonged to the Munshiganj Congress Committee Panchsayar; and Ratul Krishna Ghosh was a member of the Karimganj Congress Committee. The *Srigauranga Ashram* at Mymensingh had been in existence since the inception of the non-cooperation movement. It functioned in the house of Kulada Shankar Ray. According to official reports, the ostensible object was to help the poor and the needy and to give them medical attention. But actually the members were recruiting workers from the neighbouring districts.[56]

The Dacca Congress Committee was dominated by the members of the *Anushilan Samiti*. The secretary of the Dacca Congress Committee, Naren Sen, and other members of the *Samity* including Pratul Ganguly, Tarini Shome and Kulada Bose were opposed to the Dacca *Jugantar* party and its organ, the Saraswati Library. But once Pratul Ganguly and Naren Sen absconded their cooperation was re-established. Tarini Shome and Kulada Bose visited the Saraswati Library at Dacca.

In Bankura, the revolutionaries in the Congress committee developed secret organizations which were actually independent bodies comprised of few suitable and select Congress members. They received pecuniary help from the Congress committees and only the secretary or the president of the district Congress committee could establish contact with them.[57] In Bankura town, *Deshbandhu Tarun Sangha* was an organization comprised of Congress workers and acting as a feeder to the Congress organization of the town. The secretary and the president of the *Sangha*, Mani Bhusan Sinha was the secretary of the Bankura Congress Committee. It was through constructive social work that the *Sangha* kept the masses aware of their colonial bondage so that they could be mobilized and drawn into the struggle for *Swaraj*. The *Sangha* undertook to hold night schools and educate the masses.[58]

Secret Muslim revolutionary organizations also existed and in the initiation of Muslim revolutionary activities, the Muslim *Swarajists* and Congress members played an active role. Abul Kalam Azad, Akram Khan, Maniruzaman Islamabadi, Kutubuddin Ahmed Fazlur Huq Salisbury, Nazimuddin Ahmed (a *Swarajist* and the sub-editor of *The Mohammadi*) associated themselves with the revolutionary organizations.[59]

In the 1920s, the non-cooperation movement had mobilized students and youths into action. In the post non-cooperation days, student and youth associations were formed to provide the young people with a focus for organized expression and coordination. The All Bengal Youngmen's Association (ABYA) was the brain child of Dr Prafulla Chandra Ghosh. Initially the association's main objective had been to improve the economic condition of the country and it had no intention of concentrating on political programmes. Prominent non-cooperators, leading members of the *Anushilan Samiti* and *Jugantar* took an active interest in the association from its inception. On 6 August 1922, a meeting was held in the Rammohan Library Hall which was presided over by Dr P C Roy. Students thronged to the meeting in large numbers. Congress leaders Satcowripati Roy, Kumar Krishna Dutt, Sundarimohan Das, Basanta Kumar Majumdar, Haridas Haldar, Hemoprova Majumdar, Purushottam Rai and Bhupendra Kumar Dutta took a keen interest in the meeting. The presidential address of Dr P C Roy, which exhorted the students to dedicate themselves to constructive work like popularizing *khadi* and removing untouchability, reflected the initial aim of the association. Finally, a working committee was formed and Dr Prafulla Chandra Ghosh and Sasadhar Chakravarti along with representatives from the colleges, ex-students, teachers and professors were recruited as members. They were to draw up a scheme of work for the association. Not only students but also ordinary young men were encouraged to join the association.

The association held its first All Bengal Youngmen's Conference in September 1922. A reception committee for the conference was constituted. Sasadhar Chakravarti, the convenor of the conference and a member of the BPCC stated that the conference was taking place with a view to settling and arranging the duties of the young men of Bengal towards their country and devising practical measures of work. In the discussion that ensued Jibesh Dasgupta of the South Calcutta District Congress Committee and Jogesh Bhattacharjee, a non-cooperating student of Chattogram proposed important changes.[60]

Subhas Bose was the obvious choice for chairman of the reception committee as he was also the principal of the Calcutta *Vidyapith*. Professor Narendra Roy Choudhury of Bangabasi College was appointed secretary. The office of the committee was located in the residence of Dr Sundarimohan Das. The committee held several meetings and initially it was decided that Bipin Ganguly was to be president of the association, but subsequently the name of Meghnad Saha was proposed. Young men employed or engaged in other spheres of activity were called upon to attend the conference and with their cooperation, a practical programme of constructive work was to be launched with immediate effect. Such a call from Subhas Bose naturally caught the imagination of the younger generation of Bengal. The euphoria reached such heights that even government servants employed in the Bengal Secretariat and the Education Department enlisted as members on the payment of regular fees. Students of the *Kalikata Vidyapith, Jatiya Ayurvigan Vidyalaya* and some Bengali Boy Scouts enlisted as volunteers under Bose. Proposals to start a weekly paper, *The Student*, as the organ of the youths was accepted. Its main aim was to organize the student community into a corporate body and to utilize its strength in the interests of the country.

In the conference that was held from 16 to 18 September, the attendance varied from 200 to 250 delegates, including Muslims and district delegates. The agenda included mainly programmes of social welfare like the establishment of night schools and schools for the children of labourers. The conference passed resolutions on the propagation of the dignity of labour, the establishment of cottage industries, encouragement of the use of vernacular language, propagation of *Swadeshi* and unity among different sections of the society. Among other welfare activities, organization of cooperative societies, improvement of cotton cultivation, the introduction of handloom *charka* and settling of disputes by arbitration courts were given priority.

The conference was followed by the establishment of a permanent organization, the All Bengal Youngmen's Association. Dr Meghnad Saha was elected president and Dr Prafulla Ghosh, Subhas Chandra Bose and *Moulavi* Muazzam Hussain were joint vice-presidents. Professor Nirendra Nath Roy Chowdhury and Promotho Nath Sarkar were appointed secretaries. Naresh Sen and Rajkumar Banerjee were appointed assistant secretary and treasurer respectively. In accordance with the resolutions passed in the conference, the association began functioning by providing relief to the distressed and carrying out other forms of social service. It contributed to the North Bengal Flood Relief Committee more than 7,000 rupees collected locally.[61]

It was resolved that youths aged 16 and over could become members of this association by paying a monthly subscription of four annas. A yearly subscription of one rupee was fixed for the branch associations affiliated to the central body. Preliminary work on mass education, improvement of villages, removal of untouchability and *Khaddar* propaganda began almost immediately. The association not only initiated works of social welfare but, for the first time, attempts were made to awaken among the masses a consciousness of their heritage, a knowledge of language and culture of other countries. The association also made arrangements to hold regular classes on the economic, political and cultural history of India at City College, Calcutta. Besides Hindi and other Indian languages, foreign languages such as French and German were also taught.

Similar intensive propaganda was carried on in the districts to organize branch associations affiliated to the main body. In the first general meeting of the association, held on 31 August 1924, it was decided that all organizations of young men in Calcutta and its outskirts were to be merged into a central association. Every association had to earn affiliation to the core organization by paying a subscription fee of one rupee. They could then send representatives to the general committee of the association.

At about the same time, in Dacca, the *Anushilan Samiti* member Madan Mohan Bhowmick organized the *Dacca Sammilani*. They began to operate with the aim of propagating constructive social work, and organized protest rallies against such political actions as arbitrary arrest under Regulation III. Chitta Ranjan Das had asked Bhowmick to urge the Moderates as well as the neutral populace to join such protest rallies. In a general meeting of the *Sammilani* presided over by Swami Karunananda and H S Suhrawardy, a resolution was taken to spin 20 yards of yarn daily. The young members vowed to make special efforts to establish Hindu–Muslim unity.[62]

Soon afterwards, propaganda work began in Rajshahi, Pabna, Bogra and other districts in North Bengal. The *Bogra Sammilani* was organized by Naresh Sen. Sailesh Pakrasi of *Pabna Sthall Sammilani* got the association affiliated to the Youngmen's Association. At Thakurgaon, in Dinajpur, Khitish Chandra Roy started an association of young men. Almost all local college students and ex-students enlisted as members and willingly paid the subscription of four annas. Nalini Nath Roy, a political suspect and a member of the Thakurgaon Congress Committee was a member of the association and took keen interest in its activities.

In Faridpur Pratap Chandra Guha Roy, the *Swarajist* leader organized an association affiliated to the central organization. In Chittagong, a branch of the ABYA had been started. The president was a local doctor, Kiran Chandra Sen, and the vice-president was Amant Khan, a *Swarajist* member of the legislative council. Among its members were non-cooperators Ambica Charan Das, Jalal Ahmad, the secretary of the district *Khilafat* committee and Charu Bikash Dutta and Surja Sen, both revolutionaries. Another branch association was set up in Baranagar where the *zamindar* of Taki agreed to cooperate with the association. The Santipur *Kalyan Sangha* was operating as a branch of the ABYA and at Contai, the *Hara Naren Yubak Sangha*, Gopalpur, was a branch of the ABYA.

H S Suhrawardy had played an active role in giving the youth movement in Bengal organization and direction. He accepted official posts in the association and participated in its activities. Suhrawardy also arranged a conference of the Mohammedan young men of Bengal at the Muslim Institute. He wanted to form an association of Muslim young men and affiliate it with the ABYA.[63]

Initially the ABYA began as a social organization with little or no political agenda. But soon, at the initiative of leaders like Suhrawardy, Naresh Sen and Provat Ganguly, it was decided at a meeting held on 8 November 1924 that the association would henceforth help the BPCC. In a separate meeting held on 25 November 1924, Surhawardy openly declared his intention to develop this mass-based social organization as a force to pressurize the government in coordination with the activities of the Congress leaders in the council. He was a political man who did not want social organizations to remain aloof from politics. He asked the young men to infuse a spirit of nationalism in the masses through social service. The association published weekly bulletins called *Tarun*

Bangla. It also observed youth week as *Swaraj* week to collect funds. The membership roll of the association numbered between 1,000 and 1,500. The core association at Calcutta had 150 members with 42 affiliated associations in the countryside.

Nari Karma Mandir, a woman's organization was opened at the house of Deshbandhu's brother-in-law, Ananta Sen. Urmila Devi was in charge of this institution. The main purpose of the *Mandir* was to provide vocational training for women so that they could become self-sufficient in earning their living. But during the non-cooperation movement, the institution was utilized as a centre for political activity. Later it was transferred to Russa Road and was transformed into a recruiting ground for women volunteers. The expenses of the institution were partly borne by public subscription and partly by the BPCC.

In response to Gandhi's call for constructive non-cooperation, the entire period from 1920 onwards saw the establishment of institutions to develop self-realization through service to the motherland. *Abhoy Ashram* was such an institution, originally started at Dacca in 1921 but later moved to Comilla. Its main aim was attainment of *Swaraj* by developing self-reliance among the people. The members had to observe the vow of *Abhoy* or fearlessness.[64] The governing body of the *Ashram* was elected annually and was composed of seven members.

In Tippera, the *Ashram* had centres at Comilla, Barkanta, Panchpukuria and Chaudagram. In Noakhali, the centre was situated at Feni, in Chittagong at Munshirhat and at Muthachara in Bankura. Branches were also set up in Dacca, Faridpur, Jalpaiguri, Murshidabad, Nadia and Calcutta. The *Ashram* had a *Khadi* department. The production and sale of *khaddar* in 1925 amounted to 90,000 rupees and 74,620 rupees compared to 21,013-11-0 rupees and 21,822-13-3 rupees in 1924. The *Ashram* had four schools, *Ashram Vidyalaya*, *Methar Vidyalaya*, Ashram's Girl's school and four night schools. The *Ashram Vidyalaya* had 108 students, mostly Muslims and low caste Hindu boys. The *Methar Vidyalaya* had 45 students, six of whom were Muslims, five of whom were the children of prostitutes and 34 belonging to the same caste.[65]

The Girl's school had 30 students, a combination of *Namasudra* and Muslims. The students of the night school were mainly wage earners who worked during the day and attended the school at night. The *Ashram* had a library. The propaganda department of the *Ashram* arranged for tours to promote nationalist ideals among the masses and awaken nationalist consciousness. Magic lantern lectures were held in Comilla, Krishnanagar and Nawabganj centres. National medical schools were opened to train medical workers to work in the localities. The *Seva Samiti* had 70 members, mostly local students.

Within two years of the establishment of the *Ashram* at Dacca, three branches were opened in Maliakanda, Furshali and Nawabganj. In 1923 the *Ashram* was shifted from Gandaria to Dhulipara in the suburbs of Comilla town, which became its headquarters. Most of the founder members were orthodox non-cooperators imbued with Gandhian ideals. Suresh Chandra Banerjee of Faridpur, Nripendra Nath Bose of Burdwan, Ananda Prasad Chowdhury of Midnapore, Sushil Chandra Palit of Betur Bankura, Ramesh Chandra Majumdar of Chandpur Tippera and Chandroday Bhattacharjee of Burichang Tippera were some of the active members of the *Ashram*. It had branches in Noakhali, Chittagong, Faridpur, Jalpaiguri, Nadia, Murshidabad, Bankura, Midnapore, Calcutta, Barisal, Rangpur, Dinajpur and Agartalaand Tipperah.[66]

The *Ashram* at Comilla, although it initially subscribed to the non-violent creed of the Congress, in later years developed connections with the revolutionaries. Jogesh Chandra Chatterjee of the *Anushilan Samiti* Comilla, Govinda Kar of *Anushilan Samiti* Dacca (both associated with the Kakori Conspiracy case) and Upendra Dhar of *Jugantar* Sylhet (Deoghar Conspiracy case) were closely associated with it. The *Ashram* it seemed was not confined to those who believed in non-violence. It was utilized as an open platform for organizational and propaganda work by the nationalist leaders. Pratul Bhattacharjee, ex-state prisoner convicted in the Mechuabazar Conspiracy case, was connected with the Calcutta branch of the *Abhoy Ashram*. It was often used as a store house for arms and ammunitions by the revolutionaries. Many terrorists became members of the *Ashram*.[67]

The Feni branch of the *Ashram* had contacts with the revolutionaries of Chittagong like Ananta Singha, Surya Sen, Charu Bikash Dutta and others even before the Chittagong Armoury Raid. The connection was so close that this particular branch was practically under the control of the revolutionaries. In almost all the branches of the *Abhoy Ashram*, a considerable number of revolutionaries enrolled as members.

In Midnapore between 1921 and 1931 the *Abhoy Ashram* played an important role in the propagation of the Congress programmes through education. In Contai, a national school was established at a remote place. This school was run by Sasmal, Pramatha Banerjee and Basanta Das and conformed with the ideals of the Congress. Its students were engaged as Congress workers in each *thana*. Many of them were also appointed as teachers in the sub-national schools. They were sent to the *Abhoy Ashrams* of Dacca, Comilla, Sadghat and Patna for special training in the Congress creed and they in turn educated the people. At the same time, many of them enrolled as members of revolutionary groups, especially *Jugantar*.[68] The *Abhoy Ashram* at Feni, which was a branch of the Comilla *Abhoy Ashram*, was started in 1924. From 1929, the production of *khaddar* became a secondary objective of the *Ashram* while its primary object became the training of boys for revolutionary activities.

Besides the *Abhoy Ashram* there were other organizations which were engaged in social constructive work aimed at bringing the masses into the nationalist fold. Almost every village had a rehabilitation centre popularly known as *Deshbandhu Palli Sanskar Samity* and *Pallimangal Samity*. The *Khadi Pratisthan* enrolled 144 members who took to spinning. They were then enrolled in the Manicktolla Congress Committee. A school for training in *charka* was also opened by the *Khadi Pratisthan*. The North Calcutta Congress Committee formed the North Calcutta Spinning Association. The main object of this association was to increase the number of spinners among the Congress members. On the other hand the Bhowanipur Congress Committee urged people to enroll as members by spinning and depositing 2,000 yards of yarn every month.[69] In Bogra some members of the local Congress committee were associated with the Bogra *Jana Hiaishi Samiti* of Sonatala. Its main aim was to improve the villages of the district. The *Dakshinpar Pratisthan Sangha* was established in 1923 at Palong Faridpur. It was situated in the Palong Congress office and it engaged in constructive social work to encourage the use of *khaddar* and *swadeshi* goods. It had the unique aim of acting as a link between the federated *Pratisthans* or institutions in the area consisting of girls' schools and libraries to foster good feeling. The majority of the office bearers were Congressmen.[70]

The national schools, which were founded at the height of the non-cooperation movement, helped to sustain the Congress organization even after 1922. Although much reduced in numbers as well as in the extent of their activities, these institutions became centres for training in nationalist political activities. In some districts like Midnapore, nationalist schools became centres around which the Congress-led nationalist movement gathered strength. Not only Congress activities but also revolutionary activities received impetus from them. In Bankura, the *Amar Kanan Ashram* was part of the national school at Gangajalghati. It was under the supervision of the national school authority and the entire institutional network and was named Amarkanan and Gangajalghati National School. This school was patronized by C R Das, P C Roy, Anil Baran Roy of the Bankura District Congress Committee, Bijoy Krishna Chatterjee, lawyer and member of the *Swarajya* Party, Ramananda Chatterjee and Swami Basudevananda.

National Schools and *pathsalas* were introduced by the *Swaraj Sevak Sangha* at various places in East Bengal, especially in Barisal. The Kosliabar police station, Rupsia, Kotwali Mohanganj and Babuganj police station saw the introduction of institutions for spreading knowledge and nationalist consciousness among the masses.[71]

In Midnapore, at places like Contai and Ghatal, efforts were undertaken to use the national schools for nationalist mobilization and training. In Contai, a national school was established at a remote place. This school was run by Sasmal, Pramatha Banerjee and Basanta Das in conformity with the ideals of the Congress. The students of this school were engaged as Congress workers in each *thana*. About 13 subnational schools were opened in the subdivision by November 1993. In Ghatal, Mohini Mohan Das and Dr Jyotish Ghosh took the initiative to start the Ghatal National School.

The *Hooghly Vidya Mandir,* which originally began as national school at the height of the non-cooperation movement, became a centre for Congress activity including constructive work. The statements of several attendees of the *Hooghly Vidya Mandir* revealed the kind of activity that went on there. Prafulla Barman, the son of Biswanath Barman of Dighalia, Faridpur, stated that he was admitted to the *pathsala* in his village which he left after class VIII. In the wake of the non-cooperation movement he joined the *Santi Sena* and was sentenced for picketing. After his release he went to Calcutta, was enlisted as a volunteer of the Barabazar Congress Committee and was sentenced to jail. Here, he met one Sushil Chandra Bose from Barisal who told him that workers were needed for the Hooghly Congress Committee. After his release he went to *Hooghly Vidya Mandir* and worked as a Congress volunteer under the Bansberia Congress Committee.

Barada Kanta Bhowmick from the district of Tippera worked in the weaving department of the *Vidya Mandir* and was paid at the rate of ten rupees per *mensem* plus free board and lodging. He too left his studies and joined the non-cooperation movement. He learnt weaving from Narendra Nath Datta of Sakrail,[72] a skill he used later both for social work and as a means of earning a living. Dhurlav Chandra Das of Shyampur police station Pursura, Arambagh came to the *Vidya Mandir*, inspired by a meeting where a group of workers had lectured on the advantages of weaving and spinning.[73] Ambica Dutt Misir of Baghora,

Nizambad district Azampur, Uttar Pradesh, worked in the weaving department and earned 15 rupees plus free board and lodging. Salikram was a shop keeper at Bandel regularly bought *khaddar* from Maharajpur district, Saran, and sold them at the *Vidya Mandir*. Ammbica Dutt Misir became acquainted with him and on his advice came to work in the *Hooghly Vidya Mandir*.[74] The *Hooghly Vidya Mandir* received support from the local Congress committee, most of whose members believed in constructive non-cooperation. However, the institution also attracted revolutionary leaders like Jyotish Ghosh.[75]

Several sports clubs were opened for training and mobilizing young boys and they also instructed the students to work as volunteers. Such sporting clubs were always led by a nationalist-minded teacher who trained the member students in *lathi* and dagger play and also in other physical exercises. These students were encouraged to participate in boycott, meetings, processions, picketing of liquor shops and political agitation of all kinds.

In Jessore, Magura High English School, Sripur High English School and Binodepur School had sporting clubs attached to them. The students of Kalia High English School had a club well-known as Kalia Benda Youth Club. In 1929, a students conference presided over by Subhas Bose and Purna Das was organized at Kalia. *Smriti Mandir,* a sporting club organized by the students of Lohagara High School, also admitted Congress and youth volunteers.[76]

A surfeit of such sporting clubs emerged in Nadia districts under the leadership of one Jagadananda Goswami. Among these clubs were the Kashyappara, Ramnagarpara, Duttapara, Kanasaripara and Fatakpara. As the names signified, these clubs were situated in a *para* or small local area and they served to organize the youths of the neighbourhood. Club members were mainly local school boys who often worked as volunteers picketing excise shops.[77] In Howrah, most of the *Akhras* or sporting clubs which were connected with the youth movement got merged with the Congress organization.

According to official reports in the Rajshahi division, especially in the towns of Pabna and Bogra, the *Akhras* were mostly quasi-political associations run by political parties or by the Congress. Among them *Samaj Sevak Sangha* near Rajshahi Collegiate School in Rajshahi town had strong pro-Congress sympathies. The *Bogra Bayam Samity* was organized by the local Congress committee and most Congress volunteers in the town were members. Suresh Chandra Dasgupta was its president and the *Samiti* became the centre of all political activities in the town. In Pabna, at Serajganj, *Moulavi* Ismail Hussain Siraji, *Moulavi* Asad ud Daulah and *Moulavi* Seraj ul Huq, all of them ex-convicts, organized the *Tarun Sangha*. The *Chandiskon Akhra* at Chaudagram, Tippera, was a part of the local district Congress committee. The secretary, M Aftabul Islam, organized the students of Chaudagram High English School for picketing and boycott. The Brahmanbaria *Akhra* (which was to all intents and purposes the Brahmanbaria Congress office) was the centre of all political activities in the area. It organized lectures on *swadeshi* and picketing against sale of opium, liquor, *ganja* and foreign cloth.[78]

Within Congress a new organization, the Congress *Karmi Sangha*, evolved and ultimately came to dominate Congress politics in Bengal. Initially it was formed 'to reunite the Congress workers in a solid and disciplined group, to consolidate their energy and influence and to bring about a common understanding for a cooperation among them'.[79] Although the organization was launched to protest against the methods of the BPCC, they adopted the Congress creed of winning *Swaraj* by peaceful means and abided by the decisions of the Kanpur Congress. The organization intended to function as a socio-political force which would improve conditions in the villages, form labour unions and peasant unions, reconstruct the rural economy and build up cooperative credit societies. But over time the *Karmi Sangha* became so important that it began to exert an influence on the decision-making process of the Congress. The political prisoners who were released joined the *Sangha*. Amarendra Chatterjee was chosen as president and Suresh Das as secretary. In 1928, with the help of the *Karmi Sangha*, Subhas Bose was able to become president of the BPCC and at the same time to cut away Sengupta's political support in Bengal.

Bideshi Bastra Barjan Sangha was formed as part of the Congress organization but was a group which protested against the inactivity of the provincial Congress leaders in furthering the programme of boycott. It was formed along non-party lines, mainly to push the Congress programme of boycotting foreign cloth. They had the approval of Subhas Bose, president of the BPCC, and also of Jatindra Mohan Sengupta. This institution was composed mostly of Congress members like Urmila Devi, Jyotirmoyee Ganguly, Mohini Devi, Bimalprativa Devi, Mithi Ben (a Gujarati lady Congress worker from Barabazar), Sarala Bala Devi, Basantalal Murarka and Jagadish Nath Tewari (vice-president of the Barabazar Congress Committee). The other members were Satin Sen of Barisal District Congress Committee and Hemanta Kumar Bose.[80]

The volunteer movement, which had gathered a strong momentum during the non-cooperation movement, suffered a setback in the years following. The BPCC in Calcutta had no standing volunteer corps attached to it. However, efforts to organize and train volunteers did not altogether stop. The Bengal Volunteer Corps was initiated at the efforts of Subhas Bose and it enjoyed the patronage of the BPCC.

Sachin Mitra and his associates pushed to organize a provincial branch of the *Hindusthani Seva Dal* in Bengal for the recruitment of volunteers. In June 1924, the BPCC held a council meeting attended by Anil Baran Roy, Satyendra Chandra Mitra and Surendra Mohan Ghosh, at which formation and organization of the *Hindusthani Seva Dal* was the main topic of discussion. The *Hindusthani Seva Dal* was intended to train Indians for national service and also to coordinate the function and discipline of the existing volunteer organization and to start new organizations. Suren Ghosh, Aswini Ganguly and Anil Baran Roy formed a subcommittee.[81]

In February 1925, a volunteer corps branch of the *Hindusthani Seva Dal* was formed at Tippera under the 'captaincy' of Govinda Dutta. In the meantime, Bengal Congress leaders were debating the question of whether they should organize a branch of the *Seva Dal* in Bengal connected to the BPCC. Pursuing the decisions of the AICC, Tulsi Goswami held discussions with N S Hardikar. Both the *Jugantar* and the *Anushilan* members were keen to open branches of the *Hindusthani Seva Dal* in Bengal. In 1930, Pratul Ganguly wrote to Hardikar: 'We want one solid organization which still have branches throughout India. We want an all-India mentality. The *Dal* will serve this purpose.' It is quite clear that the *Anushilan Samiti* was ready to cooperate with the *Seva Dal* branch in Bengal.[82]

While Congress leaders were still debating the issue of organizing the *Seva Dal* in Bengal, some districts witnessed independent efforts at forming volunteer corps. By 1928 Subhas Bose was thinking in terms of amalgamating the Bengal Volunteer Corps with the *Hindusthani Seva Dal*. It was decided that the *Hindusthani Seva Dal* would be known as the All India Volunteer Corps, with Hardikar as its general secretary and Bose as president. A board of 21 members was formed from members of the 'All India Volunteer Corps' in the different provinces. Subhas Bose, Harikumar Chakrabarti and Pratul Ganguly represented Bengal. Two cadets from each province would receive military training in the physical cultural centre of Hardikar. In Bengal, a provincial branch of the All India Volunteer Corps was opened. Ramesh Chandra Acharya, an ex-detenu, was made secretary. The executive board had Nripendranath Banerjee, ex-detenu Rabindra Sengupta, Harikumar Chakrabarti, Nalini Ghosh, Pratul Ganguly and Monoranjan Gupta (both revolutionaries and members of the BPCC) as members. The Bengal Volunteer Corps was a subdivision of the All India Volunteer Corps.

Several districts also accepted the programme for an all-India volunteer corps. In Nadia and Faridpur, the arrangements to amalgamate the existing volunteer organizations with the *Hindusthani Seva Dal* started immediately. In Pabna, the Pabna National Militia was absorbed into the *Hindusthani Seva Dal*. It was directly affiliated to the *Dal* and its main object was the physical training of the district's young men, and to teach them how to spread anti-British propaganda to the villages in an organized way.

Individual efforts at setting up volunteer organizations also became a popular trend among local leaders. Aftab ul Islam, an ordinary *Khilafat* worker at Chaudagram and the secretary of the Tippera *Khilafat* Committee, started a volunteer corps, the *Tippera Seva Bahini* and he became the *Senadhakya*. He attended the Serajganj Conference in 1924 with his volunteers and was appointed vice-president of the *Krishak Samiti* in Comilla. He was also associated with the Congress and *Khilafat* workers of the district and organized a volunteer corps in Comilla, the Comilla *Santi Sena*.[83]

The *Anushilan Samiti* leaders were also making plans for an all-Bengal volunteer corps. In May 1926, a conference was held near Calcutta where Dharani Goswami, Nirode Chakrabarty and Peari Das agreed to bring the volunteers of the Krishnanagar Conference under the control of the Bengal Volunteer Corps. Nalini Ghosh secured the sanction of Hardikar to organize an all-Bengal volunteer corps. He had joined the *Anushilan Samiti* and maintained links between the organization in Bengal with that of the whole of India. In 1924, after his release from prison, he began to work through the Congress organization and utilized his connections at the all-India level for this purpose.[84]

Sporting clubs organized by school students also generated volunteer corps. The headmaster of the Bandabilla Middle English School launched a local no-tax campaign and raised a volunteer corps from among his the students. Sometimes these *Akhras* provided volunteers for the local Congress committee. The *Bogra Bayam Samiti*, for example, supplied volunteers to the Congress committees in the districts.

In the decade prior to the civil disobedience movement, it was quite apparent that organizational activities of the Congress failed to keep up the pace of the earlier years. The BPCC and district Congress organizations failed to coordinate and harmonize political activities at all levels or to conciliate the refractory elements. It also failed to sustain the well-knit organizational structure of the non-cooperation days. But the province was not lacking in political energy; it simply needed a catalyst. The people's enthusiasm may have abated, and the leaders may have been concentrating their energies on electoral politics and competing for official posts, but Congress as an organization was not yet a redundant element in the nationalist politics of Bengal. It was the most important institutional expression of anti-imperialist feeling. Even the revolutionaries needed its support to revive their inert organization.

Much has been said about the moribund condition of the BPCC and the Congress committees in the districts. It is true that membership was decreasing, that very few new Congress committees were created during this period and that squabbles among the leaders had left a section of the populace disillusioned. But factionalism was a common feature of all modern politics and had been part of Congress politics since its inception in the nineteenth century. Institutional politics had managed to survive despite the onslaught of factionalism. Therefore, it would be unimaginative to cite factional politics as an indication of the decay of institutional Congress politics.

An important feature of Congress politics in Bengal was that it channelled its activities through various formal and informal institutions which fed into the central organization and vice versa. Sometimes they were directly affiliated to the official Congress committee. Others were revolutionary organizations or institutions for the Gandhian constructive programme. Independent efforts at mobilization through organizations like *Akhras* or sporting clubs provided links that were essential to the structural network of an organization like Congress. Of course Bengal did not present the picture of a strongly knit organization centrally controlled by an official Congress committee. Diffusion and decentralization were marked features of the nationalist institution which evolved in the interim period between the two Gandhian mass movements. But nationalist workers, representing institutional Congress politics, sustained their efforts to keep in touch with the people and their politics, thereby keeping the spirit of nationalism alive.

The Congress organization did of course have certain serious weaknesses which left wide gaps in the anti-colonial movement it was trying to organize. The organizational structure of Congress and the nationalist institutions which fed into it did not accommodate the rural and industrial working class who had been so active in the earlier period. The Congress was criticized for not organizing labour and peasantry. So the Labour and *Swaraj* Party of the Indian National Congress was formed to promote the interest of the Indian National Congress. Any member of the Indian National Congress subscribing to the object, constitution and programme of the party could become a member with the approval of the central executive. The party stated its objective to be the attainment of *Swarajya* or complete independence based on economic, social and political emancipation of men and women by means of non-violent mass action.[85]

The Peasants' and Workers' Party of Bengal (transformed from the original organization, the Labour and *Swaraj* Party of the Indian National Congress), dominated by the Communists, was actually against the use of the Congress by the landlords and capitalists for their own ends. The Communists of Bengal did not initially contemplate an organizational break away from the Congress. The report of the executive committee of the party in Bengal issued on 31 March 1928, stated that 'the original motive of the formation of the party as a group within the National Congress was dissatisfaction at the stagnation of the Congress and the apparent inability of its leaders to originate any fruitful policy'. Members of the party were delegates to the Delhi and the Kanpur session of the All India Trade Union Congress in 1927. Also, three members of the party were elected to the BPCC and AICC. At the Madras session of the Congress, Communists from Madras, Bombay, Ajmer, Merwara and the Punjab formed a faction to express their views in the subjects' committee.

The party came into existence in November 1925 as the Labour *Swaraj* Party. Later an all-Bengal tenants' conference was held on 6 February 1926 at Krishnanagar, presided over by Dr Naresh Chandra Sen Gupta. A delegation of representatives of the peasants and tenants was present. It was decided to form the Peasants' and Workers' Party of Bengal, incorporating the Labour *Swaraj* Party. The party intended to work in coalition with other national bodies to develop a mass movement for national freedom which would involve the workers and peasants. The Congress, which was not following a definite programme to uphold the economic and general interest of the peasants and workers, was criticized as being 'indifferent to the welfare of the great majority of the nation'. However, at the same time the party openly declared that 'our policy and tactics in connection with the national movement and the Congress require careful determination... We must be careful not to oppose the National Congress without sufficient definition of our opinions or we shall enable our opponents to claim that we are anti-Congress or even anti-national or that we stand merely for the sectional claims of labour... The basis for our opposition to the Swaraj Party is not that it is bourgeois, but that it is not whole-heartedly for national independence.'[86]

III

It has often been argued that of the major weaknesses of Congress politics in Bengal, it was factional dispute among the leaders that ultimately proved disastrous for the organization. But in spite of this breach among the leaders, which mainly centred round rivalry for official posts, events like the appointment of the Simon Commission could still inflame nationalist fervour. This commission was deputed by the British Parliament to assess the effectiveness of the Montague-Chelmsford reforms of 1919, in response to a demand by the Swarajya Party for dominion status. It was also responsible for evaluating the real need for further reforms and deciding whether the administrative capabilities of the Indians were equal to the management of affairs, should India get dominion status. The Simon Commission was an all-white body, with no Indian representation, and was headed by Sir John Simon and seven other members of the British Parliament. A day of *hartal* was declared on 3 February 1928, to protest against the arrival of the Commission in Calcutta. Subhas Chandra Bose issued a manifesto calling all sections of the community to cease work on that day. Processions and meetings were regularly held to raise awareness of the boycott programme. He issued letters to the principals of the schools in Calcutta asking them to close on 3 February in support of the agitation against the Commission. The boycott of British cloth was revived with vigour. The boycott left a deep impact on the student community. The fortnightly reports which rated the boycott as a failure had to accept that 'there is considerable unrest in the educational world and there is no doubt that the student and school-boy community is being adversely affected by the agitation leading to the *hartal* on the 3rd and the proposed boycott on 20 February'.[87] The students of the Presidency College had been agitating for over a month. The students of the Bethune College had also been observing strike. The students of a district high school at Uttarpara picketed the school. The headmaster tried to stop the agitating students but they were supported by the local people who united to start an agitation against the headmaster.[88]

The Bar associations also resolved to observe 3 February as a day of strike. The Sealdah Police Court Bar Association, Division of Incorporated Law Society, the Alipore Mukhtear Association, the Bagerhat Bar Association, the Tamluk Bar Library, the Suri Bar Library and the Noakhali Bar Association observed a day of protest.

With a definite target of attack against imperialist excesses in the form of the Simon Commission, the political energy of the nation was activated. On 1 March, Meetings and processions were organized at different parts of the city to reinforce the boycott programme. The North Calcutta Congress Committee organized meetings at the various wards and at almost all the major cross-sections of roads and parks. The Barrabazar, Central Calcutta and South Calcutta District Congress Committees also arranged mass meetings. Across the city, 30 boycott meetings were held simultaneously and processions from the BPCC were to attend as many of these meetings as possible. Lantern lectures describing the ruin of the cloth industry of India and the need for *swadeshi* were shown under the patronage of the various district Congress committees. The *Khadi Pratisthan* too organized lantern lectures at the *Bhukailash Rajbati*. This popular visual media attracted a large audience and in this case women, and working class women in particular, attended in large numbers.[89]

Boycott meetings were held also in the districts. The people of Barisa, including many women, assembled and took the vow of *swadeshi*. In Hooghly the District Congress Committee organized meetings at the important centres. One such meeting was held in Bandel Bazar to declare a boycott of British goods and to enlist Congress members. Lantern lectures were delivered by Prafulla Chandra Sen. The meeting was attended by the villagers of the neighbourhood who took the vow of *swadeshi*. It was at this meeting that the Kodalia Devanandapur Union Congress Committee was formed. The president of the newly formed committee presided over a congregation of workers from the *Palli Sevak Samity* at Devanandapur. Dwijendra Nath Dutta, the president, exhorted them to push for the sale of *swadeshi* articles and *khaddar,* which in turn would solve the unemployment problem in the villages. Accordingly, three workers of the *Samity* were sent out every day to hawk *swadeshi* cloth and *khaddar* to the Bandel market and in the surrounding villages. The district *Khadi* board supplied *khaddar* and the workers sold all the cloth. Induction of the villagers to the concept of *swadeshi* was also attempted through weekly *kirtan* processions, which patrolled the villages and the market areas. The Tippera Congress Committee made elaborate arrangements to ensure the success of the boycott movement. Basanta Kumar Majumdar and Hemaprova Majumdar visited the villages and carried on regular propaganda. In Chandpur, under the leadership of Hardayal Nag, meetings were organized urging boycott of foreign goods.

Subhas Bose's whirlwind tour of the districts of Bengal proved immensely successful in rousing anti-imperialist fervour. In Kishoreganj, the occasion of his visit was the Mymensingh district conference. Bose's direct appeal to the young men was received with fervent enthusiasm by the youth of East Bengal. After the conference Bose addressed a huge public meeting of 8,000 people (with Muslims forming the majority) presided over by Abdul Hamid Khan, the *zamindar* of Jawair.[90] At Kustea, in an informal conference of Congress workers, Bose insisted on the need for the boycott of British goods, particularly cloth, and a reduction in the area of jute cultivation. It transpired that Kustea was an important distributing centre of foreign cloth and that the supply of *swadeshi* cloth at Kustea was not at all adequate.[91]

The Namasudra Independent Association also adopted resolutions that British cloth, cigarettes and other luxury items should be given up. They also adopted a resolution in favour of the use of *swadeshi* cloth and other *swadeshi* goods. The *Bangiya Gupta Mahisya Samaj Sanskarani Samity* under the presidency of M N Sarkar took resolutions in favour of boycott of the Simon Commission and a general boycott of British goods.

The Peasants' and Workers' Party declared its intention to cooperate with the Congress to boycott the commission. In its manifesto it declared that 'the appointment and arrival of the Simon Commission confront the national movement with a serious responsibility... It gives the nationalist movement a chance to rally once more to the call of Independence and the solution of its problems of poverty and misery. This opportunity must be seized... It is necessary in the interest of the immense majority that the campaign for boycott and independence be carried forward with the greatest possible energy in spite of any sabotage or position... The *hartal* must be complete and strikes of workers be held on as large scale as possible. Demonstrations must be held demanding independence and the solution of our pressing economic and political problems.'[92] The Workers' and Peasants' Party wanted the occasion to be used to launch a demand of complete independence and not just boycott. On 3 February they organized *hartals*, strikes and demonstrations with the slogans: 'Down with imperialism and Simon Commission. Complete independence. National Constituent Assembly. Votes for all. A living wage. The eight hour day. Land to the peasants.'[93]

The other area which attracted the attention of the agitators was the need for the reduction in the area of cultivation of jute. The overproduction of jute had resulted in the fall of the raw price of the crop. The Congress organizations in the jute-growing districts of Bengal began an extensive propaganda campaign among the cultivators to reduce the area of jute cultivation. Accordingly, the local Congress committee at Mymensingh carried out vigorous propaganda on the subject through mass meetings and pamphlets. The Dacca District Congress Committee sent workers to the subdivisional centres for propaganda and meetings were regularly held. The cultivators responded to the propaganda. *Moulavi* Ashraf ud din conducted meetings in Nadia especially in Kustea. The Rajshahi District Congress Committee also undertook a widespread programme to make the cultivators aware of the need to reduce jute production.

The Basirhat session of the Congress committee endorsed the plan and Amarendra Nath Ghosh, the secretary of the jute propaganda committee took an active interest in it. He held a meeting with the workers of the *mofussil*.[94] Large numbers of handbills and pamphlets were sent to the districts for distribution among the peasants.

Under the direct guidance of the Central Jute Propaganda Committee of the BPCC, centres were opened in 24 districts of Bengal. Local workers were placed in charge of the district centres. They in turn employed volunteers who penetrated the remote areas carrying out vigorous propaganda. They distributed leaflets and other literature on the subject prepared by the BPCC jute Committee. The volunteers met the cultivators and explained to them the evils of growing jute in excess of demand. They also explained the elementary principles of trade and how the monopoly of the foreign merchants was ruining the cultivators, urging them to unite against the traders. Faridpur became a hotbed of agitation against the cultivation of jute. Twenty-five workers travelled around the districts visiting the villages. They held meetings with the cultivators in the *hats* and bazaars of the locality and in the houses of the village heads. From the response of the cultivators it was expected that Faridpur would reduce the land utilized for jute production by more than half.[95] The volunteers also preached the boycott of British goods and Hindu–Muslim unity.

From the general political condition, it was evident that Bengal was affected by intense social tensions. Interestingly, the report of the magistrate of Khulna said that 'the present tension seems considerably to be due in part to the development of class consciousness which was fostered by the Non-Cooperation Movement. It may also be traced to the emphasis which communal representation is bound to give to communal differences and to anxiety each community is beginning to feel as to its ultimate position in the Constitution now that the meaning and trend of the Reforms is becoming clear.'[96]

In East Bengal, tension between the *bargadars* and the tenants was reported in official records. Among the peasantry, an open antagonism towards the *zamindari* system often found expression through violence based on communal and class identities. In certain areas peasant unrest was linked with the Communist elements, as in the case of the agitation in Atia Forest. Faizuddin Hussain of Mymensingh, a member of the Peasants' and Workers' Party attempted to organize the disaffected element of Atia Pargana. He wanted to protect the peasants from the transfer of lands to the forest department and sought the help of the party. A branch of the party was opened in Atia. The inhabitants who conventionally used the forest resources refused to comply when these lands were transferred by the landlords to the forest department and were brought under the government's regulations on forests. The peasants were supported by a local *zamindar*, Wajed Ali Khan Panee or Chand Mian who was also a prominent Congress worker.[97] This period also saw prolonged labour strikes in the jute mills and strikes in the oil depots of Budge Budge in 1929, led by Subhas Bose.

Thus it is shown that the BPCC in the post non-cooperation period might not have made many direct efforts to restructure the existing Congress organization in Bengal or to undertake an active programme for effective mobilization of the masses, but at local level the Congress committees mobilized the masses for the nationalist cause through various institutions of mass contact. In Bengal, the institutions for the constructive programme and revolutionary organizations maintained their links with the Congress committees. They appeared to function as independent institutions but in fact maintained links with Congress organizations and built up a structural base which was to be the launching pad of future nationalist mass agitation. Besides, as has been demonstrated, local Congress committees also undertook independently to develop a relationship with the people in the areas where they worked. This was to help the Congress to draw a positive response from the people during the civil disobedience movement.

Chapter 5

The Civil Disobedience Movement In Bengal, 1930–34

The resolution of *Purna Swaraj* adopted by the All-India Congress in Lahore resuscitated nationalist spirit, despite the hardships caused by the international economic crisis of 1930. According to official reports the resolution of independence and the decision to celebrate Independence Day on 26 January initially aroused little enthusiasm in Bengal.[1] The major reason, as cited by the magistrate of Rangpur was 'rivalry of leadership and split in the Congress itself'.[2]

Yet as Gandhi launched his *Dandi* March and placed before the public a positive programme, the salt *satyagraha*, enthusiasm for civil disobedience developed rapidly in Bengal. An All-Bengal Council of Civil Disobedience was formed and it was decided to violate the salt law in the coastal districts of Chattogram, Noakhali, Barisal, Khulna, 24 Parganas and Midnapur. Every district was to form a civil disobedience committee comprised of the important personalities of the district *suder* and *mahakuma* and also make provisions for raising funds.[3] The civil disobedience movement, with its clear anti-imperialist agenda, once again helped to crystallize efforts towards linking elite politics and the relatively spontaneous politics of the people into an organized movement.

The civil disobedience movement in Bengal was organized by special Congress district civil disobedience committees which were affiliated to the local Congress committees. *Satyagraha* camps were organized to train volunteers who would spread the message of civil disobedience to the far corners of the province and carry on the movement. The civil disobedience councils even organized mail services to East Bengal, North Bengal and Central Bengal to act as a link between Calcutta and the *mofussils*.[4]

Unlike the non-cooperation movement when the official Congress committees at various levels undertook to organize the movement, the civil disobedience movement rarely saw direct involvement of the

Congress committees at provincial, district, and village level. As most of the Congress committees were torn by schism in leadership, any united effort to build up the movement became impossible. Consequently in almost every district, the civil disobedience movement was conducted by local civil disobedience committees.

The centre of Congress activity during the civil disobedience movement was Midnapur. The district Congress committee formed a civil disobedience committee to supervise the movement organized by the subdivisional Congress committees. The branch Congress committees were revived. A subdivisional Congress committee was formed in Ghatal and Jyotish Ghosh was elected president.[5] Besides the district civil disobedience committee, a civil disobedience committee was also formed at Tamluk, and responsibility for organizing the movement was devolved to them.[6] The Tamluk Civil Disobedience Committee sent its representatives to meetings of the civil disobedience committee of the BPCC. Initially it was decided that Tamluk would be an affiliated branch of the Bengal Civil Disobedience Committee (BCDC). As this was constitutionally impossible to achieve, it was unanimously resolved by the president of the BCDC, Satish Chandra Dasgupta, and the members of the Tamluk Civil Disobedience Committee that Tamluk would organize the movement independently but would not be an autonomous institution. The BCDC was to provide men and money and Tamluk was to co-opt into their committee three representatives of the BCDC.

In Tamluk the local people allowed their houses to be used as offices by the Congress volunteers. In *Mouja* Basudebpur in Sutahata, Kumar Chandra Jana allowed his house to be made into a Congress office of the Tamluk War Council.[7] The Contai Civil Disobedience Committee was also permitted to launch civil disobedience on its own and could raise volunteers, collect funds, and control local policy. In North Bengal, civil disobedience committees were opened at Rajsahi, Bogra, Rangpur and Malda and Natore. In Bogra the Adamgiri Congress established four branch Congress committees. Their funds came mainly from subscriptions collected from the members and also from the sale of contraband salt.[8] The committee enlisted 250 members. The Bogra District Congress Committee set up local Congress subcommittees. In the Adamdighi police station Congress subcommittees were opened at Raikali, Kanchanpur, Sherpur and Sonamukhi.[9] In Bogra enthusiasm for civil disobedience provided the incentive for the revival of the organization. In Rangpur a subcommittee for civil disobedience was formed at the instance of BPCC. The Malda District Congress Committee held a meeting under the presidency of Gossain Baladevananda Giri. A subcommittee for civil disobedience was formed consisting of Priya Nath Chaudhuri, Krishna Gopal Sen and Atul Chandra Kumar. They toured the district to enlist volunteers. Atul Chandra Kumar was elected to organize meetings at suitable centres in the *mofussils*.[10]

In Comilla, the district Congress committee was the guiding force in all district politics. The civil disobedience movement had caught the special attention of the district Congress committee. The district had about 150 branch Congress committees which, under the leadership of the district Congress committee, organized processions, boycott propaganda and a no-tax campaign.[11] A new Congress office was opened at Chhaudagram, at the house of a local resident, Kobbat Ahmed. The shopkeepers and store owners of Chhaudagram bazaar paid subscriptions for its maintenance. A branch Congress committee was started in Gangohar, Comilla town, in the house of Taijuddin, a fuel dealer. He and Rebati De of Gangohar became joint presidents. Ajharal Haq and Tota Mia were secretaries of the committee.[12] The Brahmanbaria subdivisional Congress committee formed a subdivisional civil disobedience committee on 28 March. Lalit Mohan Barman was elected secretary. The Noakhali District Congress Civil Disobedience Committee passed a resolution agreeing to follow the orders of the provincial civil disobedience committee.

The Dacca District Congress Committee undertook to organize the civil disobedience movement in Dacca. The district Congress committee was dominated by the *Swarajists*, most of whom were ex-revolutionaries. In Dacca, new branch Congress committees were formed in the wake of the civil disobedience movement. Significantly, some branches of the Congress committees at Brahmandi and Sibpur had Muslims as their members. Among the secretaries were Hakim Shahab-ud din Ahmed, *Moulavi* Hajrat Ali Murdha and Abdul Gani Bhiya, all of them residents of Brahmandi. Civil disobedience committees were also formed at Narayanganj, Barisal and Mymensingh. In Jessore, the district Congress committee selected Haripada Bhattacharjee the 'Dictator'[13] of the civil disobedience movement and authorized him to form a committee for disobeying the Salt Laws. Haripada Bhattacharjee was helped by Upendra Nath Ghosh, the secretary of the committee and Aswini Kumar Kar, the 'Captain' of the volunteer corps.[14]

In Sylhet the leadership of the movement came from B N Chaudhuri, a former member of the legislative council.[15] In Noakhali, the leader of the Bengal Provincial Civil Disobedience Camp appointed Basanta Kumar

Majumdar as the 'General' of the civil disobedience campaign at Noakhali. An advisory board was also formed for coordinating the movement. The members of the board were noted Congressmen like Manmohan Kanjilal, Girindra Nath Sen and Mahim Chandra Das, the presidents of the Noakhali, Sylhet and Chittagong Congress committees. It also included nationalists like *Moulavi* Ashraf ud din Chaudhuri, *Moulavi* Mukuleswar Rahaman, Hemaprova Majumdar and Atul Chandra Sen of Dacca.[16] This board proved extremely beneficial for the movement since it brought together the organizers of the neighbouring districts. In 24 Parganas, local Congress committees in Dhakoria, Haltoo and Kasba were particularly prominent in organizing the movement. Financial support for the movement came mainly from the sale of contraband salt.

Mofussil towns like Kanchrapara and Naihati that had remained untouched by nationalist outbursts were also astir during the civil disobedience movement. New Congress committees were formed in Kanchrapara and Naihati. Rudal Singh, a labour leader, was elected president of the Kanchrapara Congress Committee and Tarak Nath Choudhury became president of the Naihati Congress Committee. Occasionally, as in Palliarah and Howrah, the initiative to start a Congress committee came from local residents.[17] A new centre for the civil disobedience campaign was opened at Kalna with Ananda Prasad Mondal as president and the centre enrolled many volunteers. Centres for the civil disobedience movement were opened at the initiative of local people in remote areas. At Sreebera, Shamganj the local people opened a centre for salt making. Solna, a small village on the banks of Vidyadhari started a new centre for the campaign under the auspices of the BPCC's civil disobedience committee.[18]

In Birbhum preparation for the civil disobedience movement began from May 1930. Branch Congress committees were set up in several localities. Atul Krishna Ray Gupta of Kharia was made the president of the Muhammadbazar Congress Committee. In Bolpur Dhurjati Das Chakravarti, a local pleader, was elected president. In Ilambazar another Congress committee was opened. Guru Charan Sinha, Brojokishore Kar, Jadupati Bhattacharjee and Bhutnath Chatterjee were elected president, vice-president, secretary and assistant secretary. In Muraroi police station at Jajigram a Congress committee was formed. Jasodanandan Majumdar, a local man, became the secretary and 14 young men were enlisted as its first members. The Dubrajpur Congress Committee was revived with local pleader Jatindranath Chatterjee as president and Lachmi Narayan Bhakt, a local merchant, as secretary.[19]

In Birbhum the Congress organization was dominated by caste Hindus, independent professionals and merchants.

Associations, some functioning independently and others in conjunction with the Congress committees, also played an important role in expanding the social base of the movement. Among them, workers' and peasants' organizations were the most important. In March 1931, members of the executive committee of the Tippera District Congress Committee initiated a separate organization, the Tippera *Krishak Samiti*, under the auspices of the Congress, to look after the welfare of the labourers and cultivators.[20] In a general meeting held in Mahesh Pargana, the organization Comilla was reconstituted. The office bearers were mostly Muslims. *Moulavi* Mukuleswar Rahaman was the secretary. *Moulavi* Ir udatullah was the assistant secretary and *Moulavi* Abdul Malek, *Moulavi* Abdul Wayhed and *Moulavi* Habibur Rahman were members of the executive committee. The *Krishak Samiti* was established in April 1919 with its headquarters at Comilla and Syed Emdadul Huq, popularly known as Lal Mian of Bhoukshar, was elected its president. The object of the *Samiti* was to protect the interests of the *rayats* against the *talukdars, zamindars* and their representatives. Eminent Congress leaders of the district like Kamini Kumar Datta, Hemaprova Majumdar, Nibaran Ghosh, Dhirendra Datta and Habibur Rahman associated themselves with the *Samitis* activities.[21] According to official records, these were directed towards spreading the ideas of Communism among the cultivators and labourers. Very often the cause of the Krishak *Samiti* was espoused in the guise of the Congress.

The Gandhian *Ashrams* were also crucial in popularizing the civil disobedience movement. *Abhoy Ashram, Vidyashram* Sylhet, *Swaraj Ashram* in Khalishpore Khulna and *Khadi Mandal* in Arambag became important centres of the civil disobedience movement. The *Khadi Pratisthan* at Sodepur was transformed into a *satyagraha* camp. It also made arrangements for training the volunteers. This camp was later transferred to Belur and Mahisbathan.[22] Krishnadasji was in charge of the volunteers. In this area an important trend within the movement was the initiative taken by the local people. Local merchants and shopkeepers undertook to provide the volunteers with goods for their daily needs. A local Congressman, Kali Charan Sukul of Titagarh, in cooperation with a cloth merchant called Sital Singh, had managed to enlist the sympathy of the local shopkeepers. They supplied the volunteers of the Sodepur camp with 60 *maunds* of rice, 12 *maunds* of flour and 8 *maunds* of potatoes.[23] Centring around the *Pratisthan*, brisk canvassing and fundraising went on across the whole area in the name of Congress. The Gandhian *Ashrams* provided the centre and the atmosphere necessary for training and propaganda. For the salt *satyagraha,* such *ashrams* gave the initial structural support. Prominent Gandhians like Satish Dasgupta and Dr Suresh Banerjee organized the first violation of the Salt Law in Bengal.

In Arambag the Congress committee had been organizing constructive social work since the days of non-cooperation. The *Khadi Mandal* was set up for production of *khadi.* A major centre was established at Duadanda. The weavers collected cotton from these centres and wove them into yarn in return for a daily wage. The centre provided *charka* to the weavers. Most of the poor local people earned an extra living in this way. Congress workers also helped them at times of distress. It was through their work, writes Hitesh Ranjan Sanyal, that they became a part of the Congress although none of them were formal members of the Congress committee.[24] Often local residents themselves formed *ashrams* to facilitate propaganda work. At Chalmari police station in Palta a group of 20 volunteers set up the *Govinda Ashram,* which provided an organizational base for the civil disobedience movement in the Barrackpore mill area.

National schools also developed as centres for inspiring young minds with patriotism. Schools opened during the non-cooperation days were still particularly important in this respect; even as late as 1933 new schools were opened in Contai and Tamluk subdivisions. The Rama Krishna Misson in Tamluk was known to shelter nationalist volunteers. This branch had opened two national schools which had been sheltering the *satyagrahis.*

As in the non-cooperation movement, in the 1930s too, the volunteer movement proved to be crucial in organizing the civil disobedience movement in Bengal. The Congress committees had official volunteer corps and volunteers were trained to mobilize the people. The *Hindusthani Seva Dal* primarily oversaw the volunteer movement in Bengal. A number of associations like the Bengal Volunteer Corps, Burrabazar *Banar Sena, Nawajawan Sabha* were formed in Bengal on the eve of the civil disobedience movement.[25]

In Midnapur, Debendra Lal Khan and Sailajananda Sen enlisted and trained 5,000 volunteers.[26] Midnapur saw the volunteer movement reach its zenith of perfection. Volunteers were organized into batches of 11 and 12 and they toured each union asking the *chaukidars* to resign. Most of them were not local residents but strangers from distant places.

They explained the Congress mandate to the villagers, urging them to oppose imperial rule in every possible way so that rural administration would be brought to a stand still. In Contai, Congress volunteers from *Abhay Ashram* in Comilla worked alongside local volunteers. In Central Calcutta, a permanent volunteer corps was organized to give military training to the young men of the locality.[27]

In Hooghly the centre of Congress volunteer activity was at Borodongal. Nagendranath Mitra who was the president of the war council and a resident of Hooghly sent volunteers from Calcutta. Local people also took the initiative to enroll as volunteers. In the Borodongal area, 60 to 70 per cent of the low castes enlisted as volunteers.

The Tippera District Congress Committee set up an All Tippera Volunteer Corps. The male volunteer corps was led by revolutionaries like Jogesh Chakravarti and Amulya Mukherjee. The ladies' volunteer corps was led by Hemaprova Majumdar, wife of Basanta Kumar Majumdar. She was a member of the Comilla *Jugantar* Party and had joined the Congress in 1921, actively participating in the non-cooperation movement. The Boy Scouts in Tippera also rallied around the Congress. Throughout 1930 drills, *lathi* and dagger play were practised in Mahesh Prangan, the headquarters of the Congress.[28] The Scout movement attracted mainly schoolboys. In Comilla too, the Boy Scout movement was popular even among the Muslims.

The Bogra District Congress Committee issued instructions to the branch Congress committees and also other *Samitis* in the district to organize volunteer corps. Accordingly, the Adamgiri Congress Committee enlisted 21 volunteers, including eight girls. They practiced *lathi*, dagger play and wrestling in their gymnasium. They were trained to carry the message of no taxation to the Adamgiri Union Board.[29]

The Bengal volunteers of the provincial Congress' civil disobedience committee selected by lottery a group of volunteers who formed the fourth platoon of the civil disobedience corps. This was to be the first batch of volunteers that would start the civil disobedience campaign as volunteers of the provincial Congress committee.[30] All the volunteers were caste Hindus. In Contai the *Deshbandhu Satyagraha* Regiment was sent by the BPCC to offer *satyagraha*. Basanta Kumar Majumdar led the Comilla Brigade to offer *satyagraha* at Noakhali. The Dacca Congress Committee mobilized hundreds of volunteers to picket excise shops.

In Bhola, the revolutionary associates of Satin Sen worked as Congress volunteers in the civil disobedience movement of Mymensingh district. The *satyagrahi* volunteers of Birbhum toured the Sadar and the Bolpur circles. They held regular meetings urging the people to boycott foreign cloth, union boards and police.

Unlike the non-cooperation days, no front-ranking leader took initiative in organizing volunteer corps in the civil disobedience movement. Volunteers in the 1930s were recruited by the local civil disobedience committees or by youth associations. Local clubs and gymnasiums also provided volunteers who worked for the Congress. In Noakhali the Muslim youths of Dar Ul Aman *Ashram* had enlisted themselves as volunteers. In central Calcutta a permanent volunteer corps was organized to impart military training to the young men of the locality.

The volunteer movement, although less organized than it had been in the days of non-cooperation, was more instrumental than any other method of arousing popular sentiment. The volunteers worked in accordance with the guidelines of the civil disobedience council. The *satyagrahis* were to educate the villagers about the Salt Act, impart the true meaning of *Swaraj* and exhort them to disobey the civil laws. For their livelihood, the volunteers had to depend on the hospitality of villagers.[31] A *satyagrahi* had to sign a *Pratigya Patra* or trust deed issued by the civil disobedience committee, making certain promises:

> I promise to obey the following rules and become a satyagrahi.
> 1. I became the Congress member from 1930.
> 2. I shall wear khaddar at all times.
> 3. I am ready to face imprisonment, all sorts of torture and misery.
> 4. I accept Satyagraha as a vow to win purna swaraj.
> 5. I shall remain non-violent.
> 6. I shall obey the orders of the Civil Disobedience Committee.
> 7. If I am convicted on grounds of political offence, I shall not support myself.
>
> Signature.

Once the volunteers had been enrolled, a group of ten volunteers were to walk to the nearest salt-making centre to defy the salt law. All volunteers had to be at least 16 years of age to become a *satyagrahi*.

Public rallies, especially in the districts, also proved to be effective in mobilizing popular support for the civil disobedience movement. The Muslim population usually remained aloof from these meetings. Jessore was perhaps an exception where a civil disobedience meeting was held in early March and it was addressed by *Moulavi* Mujibar Rahaman.[32] At Neela, the first Congress meeting was able to inspire 38 men to join as volunteers. The group included a Muslim, and the rest belonged to the *Mahisya* and low agricultural castes.[33] The Adamgiri Congress Committee held 11 meetings in Bogra district and six meetings in Rajsahi district. The Hatshahar *Ganamangal* convened a meeting where 13 members enlisted for salt *satyagraha*.[34] They were mostly Muslims. In Bogra Town at Namajghat a rally was held which was addressed by the local leaders like pleader Naresh Chandra Bose and Mohini Mohan Neogy, *Mukhetar* of the Bogra Town. Cash and ornaments worth 300 rupees were collected during this meeting.

Meetings were often organized to appeal to a particular occupational group or section of society. At Katnarpara Bogra, a rally was held to popularize the civil disobedience movement amongst the local working class. It was attended by carters, *ghariwala* and *tomtom* drivers. The initiative for this was taken by the Bogra Congress Committee. The meeting was addressed by Suresh Chandra Dasgupta, president of the Bogra Congress Committee, who spoke on the problems of the working class and advised the audience to form associations under the Congress so that their grievances could be redressed. They were invited to enroll themselves in the Congress by paying a subscription of four annas. About 30 volunteers were enlisted.[35] The general secretary of the railway labour union at Kharagpur, Giri, advised the workers to wear *khaddar*, stop drinking and to picket liquor shops and cloth shops selling foreign goods.[36] In response to this incentive, a local leader of the Kollapa Union in Kharagpur declared that if peaceful picketing of liquor and cloth shops were stopped by the police, a general strike for higher wages would be declared in protest. It would therefore be wrong to contend that the labouring class in Bengal remained unaffected by the Gandhian movement.

Special meetings were also convened for students and women. For instance, a ladies' meeting was held at Noongola in April 1930 on private land belonging to Raja Peary Mukherjee of Uttarpara. Attended by about a hundred women from different professions, this meeting dwelt on the issues that affected women like the *purdah* system and female education, alongside Gandhian ideals such as boycott of foreign cloth, use of *khaddar* and the manufacture of salt at home.[37] Some cash and jewellery was also collected at the conference.

Often village level Congress committees organized meetings to discuss the economic plight of the country under colonialism. Such meetings were held in Tamluk, for example, and those who attended were entrusted with explaining the meaning of *swaraj* to other villagers.[38] Such meetings were attended by leading men of the villages and leaders from Calcutta. Villagers were also urged to demonstrate their unity and their solidarity. They were often made to take vows in local temples to demonstrate their loyalty to the Congress. The *Mahanta* of the Sidheswar *Mandir* in Tamluk was interested in the movement and contributed a sum of 10,000 rupees to the Congress fund. Villagers were forbidden to disclose the secret orders of the Congress to any government servant or to anyone with government connections. They were induced to suffer repression calmly and encouraged to take public vows of service to the Congress in local religious places like the Rameswar *Mandir* and Shidha *Mandir*. About 200 people from neighbouring villages assembled at Rameswar *Mandir* to take the vow.[39] Although the vows were taken at a Hindu *Mandir*, Muslims also participated in the ceremony and two presidents were selected for the meeting, Bhuban Jana of Katmani police station, Panchkura and Sayyid Abdul Latif of Uttar Mechogram.

Another instance of village mobilization around the civil disobedience movement can be seen in Shidha village in Tamluk.[40] Reorganization of the villages was given priority to ensure disciplined participation by the villagers in the movement. Each village had a president and two members. Every month four meetings were held and the president would receive instructions from Tamluk and Calcutta.[41] One particular meeting was attended by the *Santhals* and therefore resolutions to break the forest law were also taken. The Congress declared to support those who refused to pay *chaukidari* tax for the year. All civil and criminal cases were to be tried by the arbitration courts set up by the Congress.[42]

The press was another such vehicle for disseminating nationalist ideas. Besides the well-known and widely circulated nationalist newspapers published from the metropolis, local cyclostyled newspapers gained circulation and stirred the political imagination of rural Bengal. In the districts they spread detailed news of the nationalist movement and facilitated the exchange of ideas in the shortest possible time.

In the district towns like Contai, Tamluk, Danton, Sabong and Midnapur Sadar cyclostyle machines were set up.[43] Almost all districts published regular news bulletins. District reports showed an increase in the circulation of every bulletin whose number increased to 56. Placards were pasted everywhere in the important towns and by 1932 the publicity centres published about 60 bulletins, dailies and weeklies. The BCDC published daily bulletins, *Satyagraha Sanbad* in Bengali, *Challenge* in English and *Navjiban* in Hindi. The council re-cyclostyled *Young India*.[44] The Bogra District Congress Committee published

Abhisapta Desh. In Bogra town *Congress News Bulletin* was issued and distributed by the Congress. In Birbhum the *Congress News Bulletin* was released by Dr Sarat Chandra Mukherji, the secretary of the district Congress committee, while he was in Seori jail. Manuscripts were sent out with the convicts who had been recently released and they then distributed the copies among the Congress workers.[45] From the beginning of the movement a cyclostyled bi-weekly bulletin was issued from Arambag and it had about 2,000 copies in circulation.

In Midnapur, as well as the Congress bulletins one Radha Nath Das published *Satyagraha Bulletin*. From Tamluk came the *Tamluk Satyagraha Sanbad*. Most of the printed materials highlighted racial oppression, police atrocities on helpless villagers and the social and economic distress of the people. They highlighted the contrast between pre-colonial and colonial days with the obvious aim of stirring the sentiment of the people. An issue of the *Satyagraha Bulletin* published an article entitled 'What if the black man dies. Plenty of black bastards'.[46] The central theme of this article was racial discrimination and oppression meted out to the black subjects by the white masters. Police atrocities and brutal murder committed at Chorepalia village in the Contai subdivision of Midnapur were vividly described and as a background to this it outlined the programme of the Congress to enlist participation of the readers in the movement for *Swaraj*. Day to day reports of the movement, picketing of liquor shops, boycott of foreign goods and *chaukidari* tax movements were printed.

Pamphlets like *Desher Dak* were distributed or read out to the villagers and usually pictorial illustrations and bold captions were used to whip up imagination. One hundred and eighty men had been arrested for distributing unauthorized leaflets. The Bogra District Congress Committee distributed printed pamphlets *Abhisapta Desh* through the volunteers. *Swadeshi* songs and verses were printed in the form of pamphlets to extol the courage and self-sacrifice of the martyrs. Dissatisfaction caused by economic distress was articulated through themes of economic exploitation of the colonies and of these themes the favourite was the drain of wealth. Boycott of foreign goods, picketing of shops that sold foreign goods and the impact it had on the British export and import trade were regularly reported.

Two different kinds of leaflets were intercepted by the police in Jalpaiguri. They were in Bengali and headings read *Hatat ato darad keno* (why so much concern?) and *Congresser hukum na mene ai bipad* (this distress caused by not listening to the orders of the Congress).

Both were issued by the BPCC.[47] The aim, it seemed, was to convince the cultivators that their economic distress was not due to Congress activities but to the tactics of the foreign merchants.[48] *Ha mor durbhaga desh* (my unfortunate country) with a picture of Gandhi in prison was issued after Gandhi's arrest. The *Deshbandhu Palli Sanskar Samiti* also issued a leaflet insisting on boycott, *Chi Akhono Bilati Dhik*. In a Congress bulletin of 21 October 1930 excerpts from the *Statesman* were printed to prove that the boycott of foreign goods had an adverse impact on the import trade of Britain. Below a heading of 'Boycott Tells' it was reported that 'the import trade of Calcutta with foreign countries in September 1930 compared very unfavourably with previous months' accounts...'.[49] *Swatantra* in its editorial of 27 November 1930 wrote: 'Britain in the past used all her efforts to destroy the cloth industry of India. There can certainly be no political or legal objection if we try now to reorganize this industry. Today we have no other weapon than boycott. It is on account of this boycott that British trade in India is being ruined absolutely. To boycott British trade in India is to boycott poverty'.[50] As before, the nationalist press in Bengal was vociferous about achieving economic freedom, which they felt was indissolubly connected with political freedom. Boycott was justified on grounds that 'it was the only weapon that every one of us is able to use in this struggle for freedom'.[51] *Gandhi Gospel*, a book of selections from Gandhi's writings and speeches, was proscribed in February.

Nationalist newspapers published from Calcutta and the districts took a keen interest in the movement and through their editorials were able to influence intelligent minds. *Advance*, a *Swarajist* newspaper begun by Das noted that 'the Congress movement had spread far and wide and was not confined to particular areas and particular sections of the population. The inspiring message of the Congress has permeated masses and classes alike'.[52] *Advance* was also irked by 'the senseless groupism of Congress politics' which was rendering this organization into a moribund state.[53] Talks of a possible rapprochement between the BCDC and 'the Bowbazar rump led and patronized by men like Nalini Ranjan Sarkar and Sarat Chandra Bose' evoked a violent reaction from the editor. *Panchajanya*, published from Chittagong, also showed concern at the indifference of the Bengal leaders.[54] *Modern Review* felt that 'the experiment of running a movement without any prominent leaders would have to be tried again and again'.[55] *Modern Review* identified the three main points in the Congress programme as: the boycott of foreign especially British made cloth; the setting up of parallel popular institutions to function side by side with, if not to displace government institutions; an extension of no-tax agitation. *Modern Review* argued that if carried out successfully the last of these would hit the government the hardest. It urged the people to be non-violent and to suffer without protest.[56] It showed a positive attitude towards the arbitration boards that were constituted for settling civil disputes. The newspapers thus directly influenced the educated section considerably, but very often the ideas gained from the newspapers were spread among the non-literate sections of society by the paper-reading public.

II

The civil disobedience movement in Bengal began with the violation of the salt law in the coastal districts where the respective district Congress committees opened camps to organize the manufacture of salt. The BPCC had 30 centres under its direct supervision. The local Congress committees supervised 12 more centres sanctioned by the BPCC. For example, Mirjakalu was the place where the Salt Law was violated in Barisal. Local volunteers were reinforced by volunteers sent by the BPCC and other district Congress committees. In 24 Parganas, Mahisbathan, Kalikapur and Neela were selected as centres. Among these three centres, Mahisbathan and Kalikapur became important as volunteer headquarters from the very beginning of the movement. They also became centres for picketing activities and intensive propaganda against the union board administration of their immediate areas and also of the surrounding region. Mahisbathan was a part of the Rajarhat police station. The area was inhabited by Hindus, mainly *Rajbansi, Goala, Pod, Kaora* and *Dom*. Some of the local people worked in the various factories at Dumdum, Dakshindari and Maniktala Bengal Chemical. It was through the latter institution that the workers, many of whom were natives of Mahisbathan, imbibed the spirit of *Swadeshi*.[57] At Mahisbathan, a local *zamindar*, Lakshmikanta Paramanik, who was also the president of the local Congress committee, opened his house and the surrounding compound for the use of the *satyagrahis*.[58]

In Noakhali, the Bengal Provincial Congress Civil Disobedience Committee sent Mukuleswar Rahaman to inspect the centres for making salt. He was accompanied by Hardayal Nag, the president of the Tipperah District Congress Committee. After consulting with the prominent workers of Noakhali, they selected a place of attack, north-east of

Noakhali Station.[59] Young men from *Darul Aman Asram* who had enlisted as volunteers for civil disobedience were to participate in the salt *satyagraha* at Noakhali. They included both Hindus and Muslims. Dhirendra Nath Dasgupta, the president of *Vidyashram* and *Swaraj Sangha* opened a new camp at Noakhali.

A conspicuous trait of the salt *satyagraha* in Noakhali was the absence of local volunteers. Throughout April, volunteers were imported from the neighbouring districts to keep the movement going. They came mainly from Sylhet and Comilla. The secretary of the provincial civil disobedience committee directed the district civil disobedience committees to engage volunteers from Comilla in the campaign at Noakhali. Basanta Majumdar and Hemaprova Majumdar arrived from Comilla with 16 volunteers and prepared salt near Noakhali *bandh* (dam). From Sylhet, Dhirendra Nath Dasgupta of Bidyasram led his group of volunteers to Noakhali. From Chandpur, Hardayal Nag, accompanied by 17 volunteers, went to Datterhat where he appealed to the shoppers gathered in the *hat* to defy the law by making salt. The volunteers made Lakhipur, Sonagazi, their base camp from where they visited in small batches the surrounding *hats* and bazaars. Thus in Noakhali, salt was manufactured not only on the seashore or in the remote places but in the thickly populated towns, *hats* and market places to draw large crowds.[60] A list of the centres of civil disobedience in Comilla and the attendance at these camps show the depth to which Congress had been able to reach organizationally.[61]

Centre	Attendance	Centre	Attendance
Comilla HQ	6,000	Subil	300
Fakirhat	700	Chemta	1,000
Rajapur	900	Kunda	800
Jagannathpur	150	Ahmedabad	400
Golmanthan	200	Durgabari	300
Jaltal	80	Nasirnagar	2,000
Bhat	250	Kalikachha	2,500
Nutanbazar	300	Mogra	40
Mainamati	4,000	Bitghar	500
Ramchandrapur	1,000	Raitala	500
Dargabari	300	Hajiganj	1,000
Sripur	500	Chandpur	7,000
Dharmanagar	600	Puranbajar	–
Jalan	100	Chaltatali	–
Gopinathpur	700	Shakdi	–
Laksham	200	Paikpara	–
Bardia		Bhotal	–
Brahmanbaria	2,000		

In Midnapur, Contai and Tamluk were selected as centres of *satyagraha*. Both these areas had a history of continued mass participation in Congress programmes. Contai had attained fame by opposing the establishment of the union board and by being the first place to offer mass civil disobedience. For the last nine years, Congress workers had been active in Contai establishing national schools, *khadi* centres and arbitration boards. The Congress had also captured almost all the seats in the local bodies and in the provincial legislature. The BPCC civil disobedience committee opened a centre in the subdivision of Contai to disobey salt law on 6 April. The centre was directly supervised by the BPCC civil disobedience committee.[62] In Midnapur, the movement started in April 1930 with organized violation of the salt law. In March 1930, a district workers' conference was held which resolved to collect money and workers for the civil disobedience movement.[63] Delegates from Tamluk and other subdivisions of Midnapur attended this conference. On their way back they held public meetings at various localities to spread the message of the movement. The Tamluk District Congress Committee reported that the people of Tamluk received the Mahatma's message enthusiastically and encouraged volunteers to launch the campaign of salt *satyagraha*.

In Tamluk a planned organization by the Congress leaders ultimately resulted in the successful launching of the salt *satyagraha*. Once the Tamluk Civil Disobedience Committee was formed, members of the Bengal Civil Disobedience Committee, Sushil Chandra Banerjee and Ajit kumar Mallick, visited Tamluk to choose a site for salt *satyagraha*.[64] Throughout the summer, the inhabitants of Tamluk saw representatives of the BCDC working in cooperation with their own leaders to launch the salt movement in their locality. They attended a public meeting on 5 April 1930 and heard Pratap Chandra Guha Roy of BCDC delivering the message of Gandhi. He also led the movement until he was arrested.

The movement in Tamluk received considerable impetus from the provincial civil disobedience committee. Capable organizers like Jyotirmoyee Ganguly, Krishnadas Chakravarty, Bhagabati Shome, Lalmohan Maitra, Kshemankari Dasgupta and Provat Kumar Ganguli were deputed to Tamluk by the BCDC.[65] Thanks to the help rendered by the BCDC the movement in Midnapur, especially Tamluk, never faced a setback even when large-scale arrests created a dearth of leadership. To keep the movement going, Lalit Mohan Sinha and Benode Behari Dasgupta were deputed by BCDC to Tamluk. They led the people until they were relieved by a prominent local leader, Kumar Chandra

Jana, a member of the Tamluk Civil Disobedience Committee, after his release from jail.[66]

Another area in Midnapur active in the civil disobedience movement was Contai. About 30 subcentres were opened at Contai subdivision on 26 April 1930 under the direction of Prafulla Chandra Sen.[67] The centre at Contai was directly under the control of the district civil disobedience committee. By the end of the season about 60 centres were opened in the subdivision where thousands of people gathered to manufacture and export salt. The civil disobedience committee of the provincial Congress committee promised to help such centres opened by the district Congress committees. The movement in Contai was strengthened by volunteers from other provinces. For example *satyagrahis* from landlocked regions like Ram Nagore in Bihar's Jallesore *thana* participated in the salt *satyagraha* at Contai.[68] A remarkable feature of the salt *satyagraha* of Contai was that here the people participated of their own volition, even when there was no effort by the leaders to involve them. A committee comprising of J N Bose, P Mukherjee, Member of the Legislative Council, P R Sen, professor of Calcutta University, Khitish Neogy and B N Sasmal, visited Contai in the midst of the campaign. As the committee arrived, crowds of villagers gathered to make salt. The committee also received registered letters from Behuna, Subarnadighi and Pichaboni carrying the message of the people that they wished to break the salt law.[69]

Narendia Khal in Ramnagore had been a centre of illicit salt making for a long time. On 21 May some volunteers arrived at Ramnagore and gave a call to make salt openly. On 6 June 1930, between 800 and 1,000 men gathered on both sides of the Narendia Khal to make salt. The sub-inspector who crossed the canal where salt was being made, broke the salt *chulas* and *handis* and asked the crowd to disperse. When the crowd refused to obey, he arrested a local volunteer who was leading the protesters. The crowd immediately flew into action trying to rescue him. They attacked the police with brickbats, stones, clods of earth and *lathis* which they had kept hidden in the canal.[70] In Pratapdighi, Contai subdivision, on 31 May some volunteers arrived at the Pratapdighi *hat* to manufacture salt. The volunteers erected a tin shed with the help of the villagers. The *daroga* who appeared on the scene explained to the villagers the illegality of this action and asked them to leave. Some relented but most refused. As the sub-inspector was leading the volunteers away one villager, Lakshmi Narayan Das of Mazna, shouted 'I have all along hid my opinions. I now come out in the open to do something for the cause.'[71] He then tore his *belati ganji* and burned it. He also collected some more and burned them. With the sound of conch shells the crowd began to increase. They embraced the volunteers, brought flowers for them and honoured them with *chandan phota* and by touching their feet, the usual custom of sending patriots on their way. The crowd continued to follow the volunteers demanding not their release but the arrest of the entire village. They even threatened to set fire to the house of a local doctor where the police had sheltered. The frightened *daroga* fled from the place.

The next day however the *daroga* arrived with armed reinforcements and searched several houses in Baghmari, Kalika Patna and Moghulpur villages. The villagers in the meantime had armed themselves with *lathis* and *kataries* and as they confronted the assistants of the *daroga* they gave vent to their anger and attacked them. The *daroga* ordered his constables to fire, but the mob remind fearless. They continued to pursue the police shouting 'it is blank fire catch them; beat them'.[72] One of the pursuers had actually been hit by a bullet and died instantly but such was the intensity of the crowd's frenzy that his death went unnoticed. The crowd pelted the police out of the Kalika Patna village. Another round of fire was ordered by the Assistant Superintendant of Police when he failed to pacify the crowd which began to spread and surround his small force.[73]

Such incidents certainly crossed the Gandhian boundaries of political action. These were instances of self-organization by the villagers. There were other instances of self-mobilization of the peasants, for example in Basudebpur Sutahata where a police assault on the *satyagrahis* caused people from distant villages to come and break the salt law. The angry villagers even pelted the police and tore down police camps.[74] Yet such popular actions were not divorced from organized politics.

In Midnapur, it was evident that the Congress organization gained in strength due to popular support. The omnipotence of the Congress was becoming clear from some of its resolutions declaring, for example, that all orders of the Congress should be obeyed and that if a person was required to serve in distant places he should on no account refuse the call.[75] Such was the harmony between villagers and volunteers that the former never disclosed anything about volunteers to any stranger. Such was the wave of sympathy for the *satyagrahis* that the villagers on their own accord often resorted to social boycott of the police. They refused to sell anything (especially betelnut and cigarettes) to them or allow them to draw water from their wells.[76]

In the 24 Parganas the salt movement took a peculiar turn. The *satyagrahis*, instead of manufacturing salt at the centres improvised for disobedience of the salt law, toured the local villages. They involved the villagers, especially the rural womenfolk, in the process so that they could manufacture salt even in their own homes.[77] Aswini Kumar Ganguly, the assistant secretary of BPCC, accompanied by Dhirendra Nath Chakrabarty, Mohini Devi, Nistarini Ganguly, Shivani Chakravarty, Santilata Ghosh and Sailabala Roy visited Kalikapur. The ladies of the neighbouring villages came to watch them make contraband salt. They then assembled in a meeting where Santilata Ghosh explained to them the political condition of the country and the duties of women in this situation. She exhorted the women to make salt in every home in order to spread the anti-British agitation. The women promised to do so and also help the Congress in the campaign of civil disobedience.[78]

A close relationship developed between villagers and volunteers at Kalikapur in 24 Parganas. The villagers supplied earthenware pots to volunteers free of charge. They helped the volunteers to erect shelters of palm leaves and bamboo. They also devised their own methods of non-cooperation with the government, ostracizing the police by not allowing them to draw water from their tanks and refusing to sell betelnut, cigarettes and other items of daily consumption.[79]

By the end of the summer of 1930, as the monsoon arrived the enthusiasm for salt *satyagraha* began to wither away. But during this phase of the movement, when popular initiative was gaining in strength, institutional politics still had a significant role to play. Villagers, even when they were taking initiatives for organization, maintained close contact with the Congress volunteers. There were also organized efforts to reach the people in order to keep up the momentum of the movement. The masses showed a conscious response to these efforts. An intermingling can be seen of organized mobilization from above with more spontaneous self-mobilization of the people themselves. The role of the Congress volunteers in forming this connection was particularly important. It was through them that a direct link was established between the Congress and the masses. They toured the villages delivering lectures, holding magic lantern shows and involved the people into salt making and the anti *chaukidari*-tax movement.

The Dacca Congress Committee had 100 volunteers picketing the excise shops. In Bogra the Adamgiri Congress Committee enlisted 21 volunteers including eight girls. Practicing *lathi*, dagger play and wrestling in their gymnasium, they were being trained to carry the missive of no taxation in the Adamgiri Union Board. The revolutionaries from Bhola, the associates of Satin Sen had been working as Congress volunteers in the Civil disobedience movement of Mymensingh district. The *satyagrahi* volunteers of Birbhum toured the *Sadar* and the Bolpur circles. They held regular meetings urging the people to boycott foreign cloth, union boards and police. In Tamluk, soon after the salt *satyagraha* was begun by the regular volunteers, the masses, including the women, showed unprecedented enthusiasm in working for the Congress and the reins of the agitation were transferred to their hands. The no-tax campaign then began in Tamluk with the initiative from the people.

In Contai, Congress volunteers from *Abhay Ashram* Comilla worked jointly with the local volunteers. Brutal repression of the volunteer movement failed to stop the inflow of workers. Regular volunteers were joined by the villagers who offered *satyagraha* at various centres. At Pichaboni, Kholakhali, Protapdighi and Balisai the *satyagrahis* were mercilessly assaulted. On 8 May 1930, the government captured all the camps and arrested about 200 volunteers. Volunteers from other parts of the province were forced to leave or were convicted but local volunteers were released. As a result, their method of action had to change and *satyagrahis* offered *satyagraha* in groups, with a new batch ready to come in and replace those who had been arrested. With the approach of the rainy season the Contai Civil Disobedience Council held celebrations on 11 June to mark the triumph of the salt campaign. In different salt centres large processions paraded through the streets. Contraband salt was sold in every market.

In the Ghatal subdivision the volunteers had influenced the villagers to such an extent that they could organize resistance to official repression and even dared to resort to violence as in Chechuahat under Daspur *thana*. A well organized and strong footing of volunteers at Nandanpore headed this violent action. Nandanpore was a prosperous village with a large population of rich Calcutta excise vendors. A large group of volunteers had been recruited who, under the guidance of the Bunder Dal and the branch organization at Sonakhali, held sway over the locality.[80] These volunteers from Bunder, Sonakhali and Nandanpore had been visiting the *hats* and spreading anti-imperialist ideas. At the same time they collected funds for their parent organization at Bunder from the villages. Unhampered by the authorities, the volunteers organized the villagers into some sort of pseudo-military discipline and gradually prepared them for open defiance of law and authority. The police had to admit that the 'whole area of about ten miles around Chechua *hat* is absolutely out of control, and is under the full sway of the volunteers of Bunder, Sonakhali and Nandanpore'.[81]

Police reports testify to the constant contact maintained by these volunteers with the revolutionary organizations in Calcutta. They received material and moral support from the villages around. They also trained the Bagdis and other low classes in *lathi* play and drill and taught them discipline in a military fashion.[82] Nandanpore and Sonakhali were their base of support in the Ghatal subdivision. The volunteers visited the *hats* and the villages regularly, picketing foreign goods. Their special target were the womenfolk whom they urged to break the *belati churi*. The 'Captain' was Provakar Ray who, along with Hari Sadhan Maity, a student of Scottish Church College, Brajakishore Chakrabarty, Sudhakar Ghosh and Pulin Dwari, carried on propaganda in this region for quite some time. A fraternal relationship developed between these young volunteers and the villagers. To the villagers, these young men with their simple lifestyle and their earnest belief in *Swaraj* were the very image of patriotic sacrifice. Moreover such specific actions as making salt by boiling water, picketing of *belati bastra* or breaking *belati churi*, and the consequent police repression helped the villagers to conceptualize the change that would come with *Swaraj*.

In Kakdwip the volunteers, many of whom were from outside the locality, passed on the message of civil disobedience as they travelled through the villages begging for subsistence on their way to the centres of salt *satyagraha* in Sagar and Mathurpur.[83] The inhabitants of Namkhana responded to such moves by preaching boycott of foreign goods. The villagers prepared salt at home and collected subscriptions to help the volunteers at Midnapur and other centres. Dr Hiralal Seromani led a group of boys of the *Anchal Balak Samiti* to picket the subregistrar's office in Bogra. In Jalpaiguri and Darjeeling volunteers from other districts were spreading the movement. Schoolboys were recruited as volunteers and they visited the *hats* at Garirkata and Dhupgiri distributing leaflets to spread the movement of civil disobedience. A group of young Gurkha volunteers from Darjeeling joined the civil disobedience movement, which gave an impetus to the movement in the district.[84]

Along with the violation of the salt act the civil disobedience movement in Bengal was also associated with a move to boycott British cloth. Picketing of shops that sold foreign cloth began from early April 1930.

The BPCC had been carrying on vigorous picketing of cloth shops in Calcutta and the districts until the *Durga Puja* when the sale of cloth reached its peak. The *Marwari* Chamber of Commerce which was against boycott reported that due to stringent activity of the Congress workers in picketing and propaganda the merchants made barely five per cent of their usual sales in 1930. In Midnapur, intensive propaganda against foreign cloth by Congress volunteers was instrumental in stopping its sale. Debendra Lall Khan and Sailajananda Sen were active in organizing the volunteer movement and held regular meetings in the house of Debendra Lall Khan to decide on the boycott programme.[85] A remarkable feature of the boycott movement in Midnapur was that the shopkeepers and small businessmen of the local markets took the initiative in resolving not to sell foreign goods.

In Pabna too the *gomasthas* and *mahajans* of a local market refrained from selling any foreign goods. A Congress committee was formed at Natore where the Congress movement was slowly winning popular support. Volunteers were recruited and vigorous picketing of liquor and cloth shops was carried out. Local dealers of foreign cloth assembled and agreed to refrain from selling foreign cloth but only till the *Pujas*. They had not indented any foreign cloth and also agreed to impose fines on those who would buy and sell British cloth.[86] At the insistence of the Congress committee in Uluberia, the local shopkeepers hoisted the national flag outside their shops and expressed their determination not to sell foreign goods. The next day obeying the mandate of the AICC, the area observed a complete *hartal*. All shops were closed and the local high school had to be closed due to non-attendance of the students. The members of the Balurghat *Mahila Samiti* led by Belarani Chatterjee picketed excise shops at Balurghat *hat*. In the interior villages of Khulna, the young men of Jessore Khulna Youngmen's Association picketed foreign goods. In May the *Marwari* Chamber of Commerce, the Indian Importer's Association and the Cloth Merchants' Committee unanimously decided not to place any orders for foreign cloth until 31 December.[87]

Picketing under the auspices of the BPCC continued even during the *Pujas*. In October the shops around Clive Street, Mullick Bazar, were picketed by the volunteers of the BPCC. The volunteers of the Bengal Provincial Students Association (BPSA) and the Central Calcutta District Congress Committee picketed the foreign cloth shops in the Entally Market. With the onset of winter the sale of woollen garments had begun and the BPCC directed its efforts towards checking the sale of foreign warm clothing in Calcutta. *the Liberty* published a comparative study of imports of piece-goods into India in 1929 and 1930 to prove the success of *swadeshi*.[88]

Swadeshi Succeeds
Crores Saved In Cloth.
Value Of Piece Goods Imported Into India.

	In 1929	In 1930
Grey	165	33
White	118	30
Coloured	153	54

The Swadeshi Board of the BPCC had circulated a list of mills in India working with *swadeshi* yarn. The *Bangiya Pradesik Rashtriya Samiti* also issued a leaflet entitled *Pujar Bajare Swadeshi Drabya,* asking the people to buy *swadeshi* cloth and they published a list of mills that used *swadeshi* threads to weave cloth. It included: Dakeshwari Cotton Mill, Dacca; Bangalakshmi Cotton Mill, Srirampore; Mohini Mills, Kustea; Kesoram Cotton Mills, Calcutta; Bharat Abhudaya Cotton, Howrah; Bharat Cooperative Weaving Mill, Bagerhat; Jagatdhatri Cotton Mill, Tangra; and Sri Radha Krishna Cotton Mill, Salkia. They also published a list of mills that prepared *swadeshi* silk. Among such mills were the Bengal Silk Mill; the Bihar Silk Syndicate; Benaras Cotton and Silk Mill; Bengal Home Industries Association and the Indian Silk House.[89] People were urged to buy the products of such *swadeshi* enterprises.

In September 1931 the Mymensingh District Congress Committee formed a *swadeshi* board to stop the sale of foreign cloth and to propagate the use of *swadeshi* among the people. The board was also to revive the cottage industries, introduce *charka* and spinning and spread the sale of *khadi* in the *hats* of the villages. Almost all the Congress committees had taken up the picketing of foreign cloth. The district Congress committees issued instructions to all the branch committees to picket cloth shops so earnestly that no foreign cloth business would be able to continue in any area that was under Congress influence.[90]

Throughout 1931 picketing went on in different parts of the province to stop the sale of imported cloth. In Calcutta, shops in the Manohar Das Katra, Sadasuk Katra, Parekh Kuthi, Ganesh Bhakat, New Monohar

Das Katra and Puggeapatty were picketed by volunteers including ladies.[91] In September, at a meeting of the executive committee, the Ballygung Lake Congress Committee formed a picketing board with Bimalprativa Devi as the president and Ananta Lal Ganguly as the secretary. This committee was to organize picketing of the foreign cloth shops in Bhowanipur, Ballygunj and Lake area. The Congress *Bideshi Barjan Sangha* also organized their volunteers to take part in a peaceful picketing of several *Katras* of Burrabazar. From 1 September 1931 the volunteers of the Howrah District Congress Committee had started picketing shops in Howrah *hat* that sold imported cloth. The lady volunteers of the Howrah Congress *Mahila Samity* led by Sushama Mukherjee and Sarama Mukherjee joined the volunteers.[92]

The BPCC also organized picketing of other foreign items like stationery, matches, toilet articles, sugar, cycles, accessories and electric goods.[93] Sugar and kerosine of British make were not allowed to be sold by the volunteers in Midnapur and Khulna. In Midnapur Sadar subdivision post offices were made targets of attack, especially at Contai, Sabang and Danton. Posters appealing for boycott were pasted on the walls of the post office buildings. In Bankura in the local fairs the sale of foreign-made sugar, glass bangles and other luxury articles was forbidden. While addressing a mass meeting at Jharia, Subhas Chandra Bose urged the Indian colliery owners and merchants to make an united effort to improve their own trade. He asked the Indian mill and factory owners to use coal extracted from Indian-owned mines and to boycott foreign coal and also foreign-owned coal mines.[94]

In a letter to the Bengal Chamber of Commerce, Imperial Chemical Industries (India) Ltd complained at the boycotting of one of their main products, soda ash, by the Congress volunteers. Their depot in Basirhat continued to be boycotted by the Congress and stocks of soda ash had to be carried from the depot under cover of darkness. The Bandar depot in Arambag subdivision and Khanapur police station, was situated six miles from Ghatal. Congress activists continuously picketed the light ash stocks in the area depots. One of the dealers who had 50 bags of light ash in stock was forced to return these bags to the Ghatal distributors. In Khakorda, Sadar subdivision, Naraingarh police station, Midnapur district, just five miles east of Contai, light ash boycott had been taken up by the Congress six weeks earlier. A mild protest against the sale of soda ash was made in Balighai of Contai subdivision in Midnapore District. Here the Congress encouraged the sale of *saji*. The dealers of the locality showed reluctance to hold large stocks of ash. In Radhamohanpur,

35 miles east of Kharagpur in Contai subdivision, boycott of light ash resulted in business worth 8 to 12 bags per month being lost. The worst affected depots were those situated in Baliachak in the subdivision of Sadar and police station Debra. To quote an official report:

> This small place about 30 miles East of Kharagpur is served by our Kharagpur distributors. It is reported to us about 2 months ago that 16 bags of our soda ash lying with the various dealers at this place had been sealed up by the local Congress Party who had forbidden the sale of our soda ash. These bags were subsequently returned to our distributors at kharagpur. We wrote to the District Magistrate at Midnapur asking him either to take action or advise us what action could be taken. No reply however has been received. The boycott propaganda appears to be the most intense in Midnapur with the Contai Sub-Division worse than the others. There appears to be a network of volunteers and passive assistance to the movement was given by the villagers and merchants.[95]

Thus, throughout the province all important towns as well as remote villages became scenes of daily excitement with picketing, boycott propaganda, meetings and processions. Through the collective actions of the leaders and the led, the symbols of foreign exploitation were attacked.

British administrative organizations and establishments were often dominated by nationalist-minded employees who utilized their power to direct attacks against them. In Charghat Bhaduria the president of the Charghat Union Board, Prafullanath Banerjee, rallied the villagers to boycott British goods in Basirhat subdivision. As the president he also urged the *daffadars* and the *chaukidars* of his union to resign and told the villagers to stop paying *chaukidari* tax.[96] In some districts the Bar libraries became centres of anti-imperial conspiracy. The Barisal Bar Library had contributed 25 rupees to the Bandabilla fund and also to the defence in the Mechuabazar bomb case. The Bhola Bar Library, in spite of the protest of their Muslim members, allocated funds similarly.

The civil disobedience movement in Bengal was also accompanied by a no-tax campaign. The villages were already angered by the raising of local taxes under the village self-government act. The civil disobedience movement now provided them with a channel for the expression of this dissatisfaction. For instance, in Mahisbathan persistent opposition by the inhabitants, under the leadership of Lakshmikanta Paramanik, had been successful in resisting government attempts to impose union boards. In the wake of the civil disobedience movement Mahisbathan became a stronghold of the no-tax rebellion. It was decorated with tricoloured flags and patrolled by youths dressed in khaddar with Gandhi caps and national badge. The spirit of agitation was so high in Mahisbathan that it blatantly proclaimed that the British government in that area was regarded as a non-entity.[97] So the groundwork for a no-tax campaign had already been laid in Mahisbathan.

The no-tax campaign often went hand in hand with no-rent campaign. At Bhanu Bil in Sylhet district the tenants of Prithimpasha refused to pay the enhanced rent.[98] The Congress had been preaching non-violent non-cooperation with the imperial authorities from the commencement of the civil disobedience movement. The tenants, mostly *Manipuris* and Muslims had enthusiastically taken up civil disobedience under the leadership of Baikuntha Sharma. In Panitola Dinajpur the police met with stubborn refusal when they made an effort to realize taxes. The attachment of household articles, cultivation tools and livestock in lieu of taxes failed to deter the villagers. No-tax agitation was also going on in Tipperah, at Luxum and eastern parts of Chandina and Chowdgram *thanas*. The *Krishak Samity* in Comilla organized processions with national flags and anti-government slogans. The instigators behind this were Mukuleswar Rahaman and Krishna Sundar Bhowmick of Tippera *Krishak* and *Sramik Samity*.[99]

The village of Uttar Raybar in Danton *thana* was a scene of a bloody encounter on 12 July 1932, between police and villagers refusing to pay *chaukidari* tax.[100] The police resorted to firing at the protestors in an effort to force them to capitulate. This village had already revolted against the salt law in 1930. Now once again the villagers were organizing under the leadership of a villager named Devendra Nath Pandit. They were required to pay off the arrears in *chaukidari* tax which amounted to 6 rupees. The head of the village, the *Barua*, failed to persuade the villagers to pay their dues. The *chaukidar* of the *mahalla* was also threatened. Every action of the villagers showed that they were resolute in their decision not to pay the taxes and in this they had the support of the *Barua* and other influential people of the village.

On the day of the incident the *chaukidars*, assisted by police officials, arrived to collect tax. The villagers immediately began to remove their cattle which were usually seized in lieu of payment. When the *chaukidars* took the cattle, the villagers reacted by surrounding the area. According to a police report:

Some 100 or 150 persons made their sudden appearance from the jungle or thickets surrounding a tank...and they carried with them bows and arrows, lathis, stones from the railway line and it is said spears and *tangis*. They were joined by other villagers including women and the crowd swelled upto 200 to 250 men. They attacked with lathis, stones and arrows. There is no doubt that these men were determined from the beginning not to pay any chowkidari tax and all attempts by requests, persuasions, takids and urgent takids failed and they were in no mood to listen to anything about the payment of the chowkidari tax.[101]

Village solidarity and collectivity was a central aspect of rural consciousness. It enabled them to organize in opposition to those who were illegitimately draining them of their hard-earned money. Even the *Barua* who had paid the tax himself dared not oppose them. By joining together the villagers had strength in numbers and the anonymity of a crowd, which protected their individual weakness and vulnerability. Collectivity was therefore a fundamental aspect of non-institutional politics of the rural folk, central to popular consciousness and action. It imbued them with a power and determination with which they could momentarily overpower their rival in a spontaneous upsurge. When necessary, institutional politics made use of this collective force to build a condition of inchoate insurrection.[102]

Another such example of collective peasant action was the boycott of the settlement operations in the Arambag subdivision of Hooghly. The movement was led by Prafulla Chandra Sen who had made Arambag the centre of his activity since the non-cooperation movement. This Gandhite had already created a strong base for Gandhian movements in Arambag through constructive work. The Hooghly District Congress Committee also resolved to oppose settlement operations by organizing a complete *hartal* on 27 November 1931, followed by a workers' conference in December. Opposition to the operations was so strong that even inhuman police repression failed to deter the agitators.[103]

While the non-cooperation movement had a distinct urban orientation, the civil disobedience movement had a predominantly rural face. Jawaharlal Nehru himself pointed out that 'the Civil Disobedience Movement of 1930 happened to fit in unbeknown to its own leaders at first, with the great world slump in industry and agriculture. The rural masses were powerfully affected by this slump and they turned to the

Congress and Civil Disobedience. For them it was not a matter of a fine constitution drawn up in London or elsewhere, but of a basic change in the land system, especially in the *Zamindari* areas.'[104]

Under the circumstances it was not unnatural that around the civil disobedience movement in Bengal there developed a no-rent agitation. The Congress, especially Gandhi, was opposed to no-rent agitation, but once it began the local Congress became involved. In the tiny village of Brikusta, Sadar subdivision of Rajsahi, peasants organized themselves into a *satyagraha* against the *zamindar*.[105] This area was suffering famine conditions as a result of failed crops. The excesses of the *zamindar* antagonized the peasants who sought the help of the local Congress committee. Pravash Chandra Lahiri, secretary of the Rajsahi District *Rayat Samiti* took up the matter and urged the *zamindar*, Panchanan Banerjee, to redress the allegations of the tenants against his officers. Satish Chandra Dasgupta tried to bring about a compromise which failed and the tenants launched a non-violent movement against the *zamindar*, refusing to pay rent.[106] In the later phase, the district Congress committee assumed leadership of the movement. This was a movement where the tenants were urged to be self-reliant, denying even the help of the BPCC. The movement received response mainly from the poor tenants. The secretary, Manas Govinda Sen and later Pravat Mohan Bandyopadhyay played a crucial role.[107] This was an instance where despite the official decision of not encouraging anti-*zamindar* agitation, the Rajsahi District Congress Committee adopted a resolution supporting a peasant upsurge against a local landlord.

In Nadia friction occurred in Kustia subdivision over the collection of fishery rent by the *zamindars* of Sadarpore. In Bahalbaria the peasants opposed payment of *abwabs*.[108] Non-payment of tax had hit the *zamindars* to such an extent that several estates were put up for sale, 22 *taluks* in Jessore, 227 estates of Bogra, 71 permanently settled and 433 *khasmahal* estates of Noakhali were auctioned. Several *taluks* in Chittagong, Jessore, Murshidabad, Pabna, Dinajpur and Tippera were sold for non-payment of tax.[109]

In the second phase of the civil disobedience movement, the agitation was spreading mainly through the volunteers whose activity was confined to printing and distributing bulletins and leaflets.[110] Unauthorized Congress manuscripts and leaflets preaching non-payment of *chaukidari* tax and boycott of foreign goods were in circulation. The 'dictator' of the Bogra Zilla Congress Committee, Dr Abdul Kader Chaudhuri issued a leaflet which urged the public to commemorate the day of the *Dandi*

March and to attend the Calcutta session of the Congress on 31 March. In Jessore, Nadia and 24 Parganas, leaflets urging non-payment of rent were distributed. In the Tehatta police station of Nadia, the Congress bulletin *Agni Sikha* was circulated.[111] In Dacca's Nawabganj, *Mahila Prachar Patra* a cyclostyled Congress bulletin, was circulated. Congress volunteers distributed leaflets even among the pilgrims of Jalpeswar fair at Moynaguri Jalpeshwar.[112]

In this phase of the movement, the local level leaders were entrusted to carry on the agitation. In Hooghly, for example, a workers' conference was called on 4 January 1932 when the Arambagh subdivision was divided into 12 circles, with one circle officer for each circle. They were entrusted to carry on civil disobedience in their circles. The circles included: Arambag Sadar, comprised of Chunote, Borodongal, Arambag and Mayapur; Khanakul, comprised of Krishnanagar, Nandanpur and Dhanyaghori; Goghat, comprised of Amarpur, Nakunda, Raikhan, Kamarpukur including some villages in Kotulpur *thana*, and Pursura.

In Tamluk, the power of the Congress executive committee was placed in the hands of the 'first dictator' Shrinath Das and his successors. The 'second dictator' was Lakshmi Rani Devi, the 'third dictator' was Induprava Devi, with Nitya Bala Gole and Subodh Bala Kuity the fifth and sixth dictators in line.[113] The Congress institutions in the area were declared unlawful. Throughout 1932 and 1933 Congress organization in Midnapur remained active although the earlier ebullience was lacking. In Keshpur police station a new Congress camp was started by the volunteers of *Abhoy Ashram*. According to the government reports, the spirit of civil disobedience still ran high in areas like Tamluk, Contai and Sadar of Midnapur district. Numerous processions took place on 26 January, '*Swadeshi*' day (symbolizing the demands for independence). Moreover, in the recent local board elections in the Contai subdivision, only a few people took part. In the two *thanas*, only 147 out of 3,508 voters turned out in one and in the other 175 out of 5,191 of those enfranchised recorded their votes. In the two *thanas* of the Sadar subdivision, the elections failed altogether for similar reasons. The district magistrate felt that 'this was an interesting proof of the hold which the Congress had over the minds of the people'.[114]

III

The second spate of nationalist mass upsurge in the 1930s once again involved different social and occupational groups. But the response of each of these groups to the movement and the extent of their participation definitely differed from the first Gandhian experiment of mass mobilization of the 1920s.

As for the students, the Congress was able to gain their support but not as vigorously as during the non-cooperation movement. In urban areas they organized the picketing of liquor shops and outlets for foreign cloth. As early as April 1930 a meeting of the Bengal Provincial Student's Association (BPSA) was held to discuss the attitude of the students in the ensuing civil disobedience campaign. It was decided that students who were willing to join the agitation should enlist as Congress members. Those unwilling to join the Congress could also participate in the movement as individuals.

Only when the movement had gathered strength and assumed a concrete shape as an all-round force for freedom would the BPSA start to mobilize the student community. For the time being the student political institutions ensured student participation only as a part-time engagement during vacations. As the Congress had not issued instructions to the students to leave their educational institutions, the president of the BPSA chalked out a course of action for them. It consisted of cooperating with the Congress in its boycott programme (a committee was formed for this purpose), picketing shops that sold foreign goods especially in the villages and inducting fellow students, relatives and neighbours with ideas of *swadeshi*. They were free to organize social boycott against those unwilling to follow the movement. They were to organize themselves in small groups and hold street corner meetings for civil disobedience. In the rural interiors, these meetings were held in the *hats* and bazaars. The BPSA asked all affiliated students associations to follow this programme.[115] The secretary of the All Bengal Students Association (ABSA) toured the districts to propagate civil disobedience. Throughout the summer months the workers of the ABSA visited the rural areas. Bholanath Mukherjee was sent to Midnapur, Khulna and Malda, Jitendranath Pal to Faridpur and Jessore, Babesh Chandra Chakrabarty to Murshidabad, Tipperah, Dacca, Chittagong and Dinajpur.[116]

The ABSA and the BPSA organized picketing of educational institutions such as Presidency College and Scottish Church.[117] The lady volunteers of *Chatri Sangha* picketed Bethune College. In Bankura, Charushila Devi was arrested for picketing educational institutions. There was, however, no mass exodus from schools and colleges to join the nationalist movement. The report of the ABSA showed that 'the present BPCC was evoking no response from the students and the youths of the province to the call of the Congress during the Civil disobedience movement'.[118] The ABSA was not on cordial terms with Bose and his associates. On the eve of the election of the executive council of the ABSA, Surendra Mohan Ghosh approached them to elect his nominees to the central and executive council of the ABSA. Bose's associates also tried to wreck the district students' conference because he was not given preference over Dr Alam of Lahore when the conference president was selected. Surendra Mohan Ghosh and his followers captured the reception committee which elected Bose as the president. A deputation of the members was plainly told by Nalini Ranjan Sarkar to accept Bose without opposition. The members of the ABSA however refused to ignore the verdict of the districts. This offended Bose and he set up a rival organization.[119]

Independent student and youth associations also joined the civil disobedience movement. Upon his release Subhas Bose formed a network of associations and clubs for young men. In Comilla the student and youth associations had joined the movement under the Congress. Local sporting groups like the Nabinnagar Athletic Club mobilized the village youths to form volunteer corps for enforcing *hartal* and picketing. *Kamal Sagar Chhatra Sangha, Tippera Chhatra Samiti*, Tippera Students Association and Bogra Students Association were also active in the movement.[120]

In rural areas the students provided a much needed workforce to carry the message of civil disobedience. It was only in June 1930 that the Indian National Congress decided to involve the students and the educational institutions in the movement. It called upon the students to place themselves at the disposal of the Congress. The students had to be prepared to completely suspend their studies in the cause of the national movement. Following this resolution, in July 1930, a convention of the students' organization was held in Albert Hall presided over by Basanti Devi. The convention was attended by Acharya P C Roy, Dr B C Roy, Sarat Chandra Bose, Nelli Sengupta, Mrs J M Dasgupta, Mrs Latika Bose, Makhanlal Sen, Satya Ranjan Bakshi, Mohit Kumar Moitra and Gopal Lal Sanyal. It adopted resolutions that all school and college students, in those districts where the student associations had permitted them to participate, would suspend their studies and join the national service as dictated by the Congress. Dr B C Roy, however, wanted medical students to be exempted from the main resolution.

The participation of women in the civil disobedience movement was more active and unconstrained than during the non-cooperation movement. Womens' associations helped particularly to mobilize the womenfolk. At *Kalyankutir* in Gandaria, the *Gandaria Mahila Samiti* organized a ladies' committee which preached the cult of *charka, khaddar* and other constructive work to help the Gandhian Movement. The Women's *Satyagraha* Committee enlisted women volunteers who were asked to enroll themselves to Santi Das and Bimalprativa Devi.[121] The *Tangail Nari Samity* held meetings to mobilize volunteers for the civil disobedience movement. Ashalata Sen had begun the initiative to start an organization for the training of women volunteers in 1927. The *Kalyan Kutir Ashram* was the result of this effort. In 1929 she and Sarama Gupta visited the Juran village which was a Namasudra majority area and established the Juran *Shiksha Mandir*.[122] With the help of magic lantern shows they tried to inspire the villagers to nationalism.[123] In 1930 they organized a *Satyagrahi Sebika Dal* from among the villagers and broke the salt law. The *Vikrampur Rashtriya Mahila Sangha* was established in 1931 with branches in different parts of Bikrampur that trained women volunteers for salt *satyagraha*. In Comilla's Nabinnagar a *Mahila Samiti* was formed and some lady volunteers were enrolled and a sum of 250 rupees was collected in a meeting. The Balurghat Mahila Samity trained women volunteers in dagger and *lathi* play and actively participated in the civil disobedience movement. It also arranged for home spinning with *charkas*.[124]

In early 1930, with the commencement of the agitation, the involvement of the women lay mainly in picketing activities. Women from established families were particularly active in Calcutta and organized boycott of foreign cloth. Bimal Prativa Devi, Shanti Das, the secretary of the Lady *Satyagraha* Committee and wife of Sardar Lachman Singh along with 50 volunteers of the BPCC began to picket foreign cloth shops and liquor shops from the junction of College Street. About 25 women volunteers of the womens' civil disobedience committee visited the Burrabazar area and picketed shops selling foreign cloth in Cotton Street, Dacca Patty and other places including Monohar Das Katra. In South Calcutta, the lady volunteers of the South Calcutta District Congress Committee, led by Labanya Prava Datta, picketed cloth shops in the vicinity of Russa Road. Many of these young picketers were volunteers of the *Jatindra Smriti Mandir*, who were helping the Congress committee volunteers.[125] About 45 lady picketers and 20 boys of the BPCC went to R G Kar Road and picketed the foreign cloth shops there. In the face of such vigorous picketing the shopkeepers ultimately had to draw down their shutters and stop all business in the area.[126]

In Comilla picketing was done entirely by women, including the wives of government officials, on the occasion of Mrs Naidu's arrest. About 400 women joined in the picket and absolutely paralysed *kutchery* work. In Noakhali a ladies meeting in the town prepared salt. After this the women started making salt in almost every house in Noakhali. Women inspired by Gandhian ideology dared to do challenging deeds. Pratibhamayee Sen and Kamala Devi of the Baherek Satyasram in Munshiganj were sentenced to prison for holding meetings of the Congress at Kamarkhara to celebrate Jalliwanwala Bag Day.[127]

Participation of women in the salt *satyagraha* was particularly strong in Dacca. Sarama Gupta, Ashalata Sen and Ushabala Guha led a group of volunteers to Noakhali and collected salt water from the sea. They brought this to Dacca and prepared salt at the Coronation Park. Many who watched them and bought the contraband salt were arrested. In Munshiganj, Surabala Basu, a housewife from a middle class family, wrote to the Munshiganj Congress Committee asking for one *chatak* (a small measure) of contraband salt so that she could break the salt law at home. She also declared that if the government did not take action against her, she would openly join the civil disobedience campaign. She broke the salt law by purchasing contraband salt and also made a gift of her gold *Sankha* to the Congress.[128]

In Dacca, Ashalata Sen organized the women in different areas and with them courted arrest. In Bikrampur, Kiranbala Kushari and Prabhaslakshmi Devi along with Ashalata Sen established the *Nashankar Mahila Sibir* and preached *satyagraha* in the villages of Dacca. It was only at the high tide of the nationalist upsurge that women were politically motivated to act. In the urban and rural centres women were collectively activated into acts of resistance. At Arambag, tax collection was impeded by women activists. In Bankura at Indas, 250 women prevented attached property from being taken.[129]

At a later stage, when large scale arrests had removed the men from leadership, women were allowed to lead the agitation as 'Captains' of the war councils, but few women enlisted as Congress members or took an active leading role in the decision-making process of institutional politics. When women did emerge from their domestic confines, the

Gandhian ideology of non-violence protected their feminine image and role. In rural areas the rich peasants like Jhareswar Majhi of Contai or Lakshmikanta Pramanik, a *zamindar* of Mahisbathan, showed the way by permitting their womenfolk to join the agitation. This set the trend for the 'lesser peasant nationalists'.[130] Equally important were the sacrifices of those women who helped the *satyagrahis* in day-to-day matters, nursed them when sick and hurt or fed them when hungry. Satyabati was a prostitute of the Terpakhya village, Nandigram, Tamluk. She took care of the wounded *satyagrahis*. Later she herself joined the *satyagraha* movement. In Borodongal, Baradamayee, better known as 'Habur Ma' took care of the *satyagrahis* daily need for food.[131]

According to official report:'the civil disobedience movement whatever else it may be was essentially Hindu in its conception and in its aim, while its agents are predominantly Hindu... The whole philosophy of the Civil Disobedience campaign is Hindu.'[132] Although unequivocal support was not forthcoming from the Muslims they did not remain totally insulated from the Gandhian call of civil disobedience. Most western educated Muslim politicians spoke in favour of civil disobedience. The Bengal Muslim Political Conference was held in Chittagong in April 1930, presided over by Ashrufuddin Ahmad Chaudhury and attended by an audience of 500 including *ulema* and Muslim educationists. The resolutions were drafted by Abdur Rahim, discussed for five hours at the subjects committee and passed unanimously in the conference. *The Musalman* reports that 'though there was a fairly long debate on the main resolutions, there was not a single voice raised in dissent, protest or amendment'. The Bengal Muslim Political Conference 'identified itself entirely and wholeheartedly with the national goal of independence for India and a common motherland of all sister communities'.[133]

The conference resolutions also instructed the Muslims to cooperate in every possible manner for the attainment of *Swaraj* and democratic freedom. Participation was justified once again on the religio-political grounds that *Quronaic* injuctions and Islamic tradition stipulated that Muslims should never be a subservient race. In a truly national government they should function as equal partners with their co-religionists. The resolution was proposed by Maulana Islamabadi, seconded by Yacub Ali Chaudhury and supported by Abdur Rahim, Moulavi Nazir Ali and Mukuleswar Rahaman.

The Muslims were also called upon by their leaders to enroll in the Indian National Congress in the largest possible numbers and to establish 'their inalienable claim to complete political, social emancipation and development'.[134] They were asked to participate and take a full share in all nationalist activities. This resolution was proposed by Shah Baidul Alam, seconded by Abdur Rahim and supported by *Moulavi* Abdul Aziz, *Moulavi* Muhammadullah and Moulana Ali Ahmad Wali Islamabadi. Muslim participation in the civil disobedience movement and in breaking the salt monopoly of the government was never forbidden. In fact, the conference accepted a resolution proposed by Abdur Rahim to motivate and legalize Muslim participation in the civil disobedience movement at all stages. Muslim students and youths were particularly requested to join the nationalist movement. So the conference was unanimous in its decision that 'it is practical and desirable to continue some separate Muslim organization for the sake of social reform, educational economic and incidental political work affecting only Muslims while working for main political emancipation and self development of the nation through the National Congress Organization.'[135]

As early as in March 1930, a public meeting was held in the local town hall of Noakhali, which was attended by the Muslims.[136] Attendees included: Faziullah, a member of the legislative council; Hasmatullah a *mukhetar*; Rezakul Haider Chaudhuri, a pleader; Sayid Abdul Majid, pleader; Fazaler Rahaman, a doctor and *Moulavi* Ali Ahmed, marriage registrar of Hatiya. Besides these local figures, Muslims of other districts also came for the meeting. *Moulavi* Asaduddowllah Siraji of Serajganj, Abdul Malek of Comilla and Fakiruddin, secretary of Tippera *Jubak Samiti* was invited to attend by the local district Congress committee. The Muslim middle class intelligentsia in Noakhali was not in its entirety opposed to the movement. Assaduddowllah Siraji appealed to Muslims to join the movement because a true *Musalmaan* had to be independent. In spite of differences of opinion this movement had to be given a free scope to survive. He also asked Muslims not to pay serious heed to those who were calling the anti-imperial movement seditious. This meeting was held at a time when official reports, describing the political condition of Noakhali, said 'there seems to be little or no real enthusiasm among the local people for the campaign'.[137]

In Bogra the Muslims did not turn away from the movement. On the contrary they participated so actively that the weekly report stated 'enthusiasm of the people in connection with the civil disobedience movement is on the increase. All the leaders here are supporting Gandhi's movement.'[138] Muslims were well represented among the senior Congress committee members in Bogra, so the movement there was directed by the Muslim leaders. Meetings organized at various places were addressed by the Muslim leaders. At Hili the branch Congress committee summoned a meeting and the committee secretary, Aftab uddin Chaudhuri, addressed the audience. Rajibuddin Tarafdar, president of the Bogra Congress Committee and All Bengal Praja Samiti spoke at various meetings urging the Muslims to join the Congress.

The *Moulavis* also were in favour of the Muslims joining the agitation. At Mirgaon in Joypurhat *Moulavi* Nader Ali of Hatshahar GanaMangal spoke on civil disobedience and boycott. After Gandhi's arrest the district observed a *hartal*. Muslim leaders held a separate meeting and decided to join the movement. *Moulavi* Muhammad Eshaque, Rajibuddin Tarafdar and Jamaluddin Talukdar of Bogra and Muzahar Hossain of Nagore preached the ideology of the new movement.[139] A procession of the Muslim populace of the town went through the metropolis to celebrate the occasion of the Muslims entering the movement.

In Bogra, Hatshahar *hat* was a popular recruitment and propaganda centre. A national flag was hoisted and a meeting was held there, and 13 volunteers were enlisted for the salt *satyagraha*, most of whom were Muslims. The speaker, Abul Jabbar of *Hat shahar Gana Mangal* read out the independence resolution of the AICC and when he enquired if they wanted independence, a number of hands were raised in affirmation. At Sonatala, a meeting was attended by 300 Muslims who declared the use of foreign goods as *haram* to a Musalman. In Bogra even local leaders like Mokleshuddin Khan of Loknathpara and Arafur Rahaman Sudharamani of Dubchanchia talked of Hindu–Muslim unity and boycott of foreign goods. Bogra, although a small district, had the highest proportional Muslim population of all the districts of Bengal. Muslims were mostly *Shaikhs* though there were *jolas*, *Kulus* and *Saiyid* and *Pathans*. A massive proportion – 87.5 per cent – of the population was dependent on agriculture and the rest on industries, commerce and professions. The fertile soil of Bogra was ideal for rice and jute and the jute trade had enriched the inhabitants of Dhunot, Shariakhandi and Shibganj *thana*. The *thanas* of Khetlal and Adamdighi were a hotbed of Congress activity. On the west side of Karatoya river there were extensive plains noted for the production of finer brands of rice.[140]

Dacca, along with the rest of the country, enthusiastically joined the movement. Several Muslim volunteers enrolled and together with their Hindu co-workers proceeded to Contai to make salt. Together they picketed liquor shops and observed *hartal* on 15 April 1930, the day of Nehru's arrest. All shops, including those owned by Muslims, were closed. Even the hackney coach drivers, most of whom were Muslims, joined the strike. The movement in Dacca gained in strength due to Hindu–Muslim unity.[141]

In Comilla the *Krishak Samity* conducted the movement under the leadership of Mukuleswar Rahaman who was convicted for participating in the civil disobedience movement. A district Muslim conference was held in Comilla, attended by 25,000 Muslim delegates and presided over by *Maulavi* Ashraf ud din Chaudhuri, which resolved that Muslims should be urged to join the agitation.[142]

In the Burdwan division there was a distinct tendency among the Muslims to join the Congress. But in East Bengal, while Muslim leaders showed pro-Congress attitudes, the masses kept aloof from the movement, because of the economic distress they were experiencing due to the falling price of jute. As peasant participation in the movement increased in East Bengal the Muslims joined the agitation. 'There was a great deal of unorganized discontent among the Muslim peasantry' of which the Congress could take advantage, observed *Sufi* Abdul Qadia, a pro-government religious preacher of the *Ahmadiyya* sect.[143] Muslim villagers began gradually to be involved with agitation after they became associated with the detenues. Students of the Deoband Seminary who had returned to their homes proved to be the most effective instrument in inciting Muslim opinion. Hussain Ahmad, an ex-student of Deoband school went to Calcutta to preach boycott and the use of *khadi*. It was suggested 'that the *mullahs* of the *mofussils*, who are products of Deoband are being influenced by him…in making anti-British propaganda in the villages.'[144]

Some Muslim newspapers also preached civil disobedience. *The Musalman* in its editorial of 12 April:'a question seemed to have arisen as to whether the Musalmans should join the movement and participate in the campaign for Civil Disobedience. The salt tax is a most inequitable tax. To fight against it is an assertion of the people's right not to pay any unjust tax. It affects the poor masses and Musalmans are mostly poor. It will accordingly be unwise on part of any section of the leading Musalman to dissuade the community from taking advantage of it.' *Mohammadi* too spoke in favour of the Muslims joining the movement. A number of radical nationalist newspapers with Muslim proprietorship and readership and a circulation figure above 1,000 had been described as 'extremist' by the government. Among them were *Al Kalam, Hind-e Jadid, Hamdard, Watan,* all dailies in Urdu and published from Calcutta. *Azad* was published from Noakhali, *Masik Mohammadi, Mohammadi* and *Moslem* were published in Bengali. The *Mohammadi* published a protest letter by a Muslim reader, Golam Gilani, under the heading 'The Present Movement And The Musalmans'. The article pointed out the sacrifice of the Muslim women and youth, specially the *Bangiya* Muslim *Tarun Sangha* of Serajganj and *Dar ul Aman Ashram* of Tippera. In almost every Bengali jail Muslim leaders and workers were imprisoned. The civil disobedience movement under the aegis of the Congress was thus joined by both Hindus and Musalmans and was not confined to any particular community.

Throughout 1928 and 1929 there were widespread organized labour strikes, especially in sectors like jute production. The other important labour strike was organized by the workers of the oil depots at Budge Budge. Work stopped completely at the factories of Burma Shell, the Standard and Indo Burma Petroleum companies. The oil company workers went on strike at the same time as the Budge Budge group of jute mills. They created the Budge Budge Oil And Petrol Workers' Union with Subhas Bose as president.[145] But after the Meerut arrests, the labour movement suffered a setback. Moreover, in the 1930s due to worldwide economic depression, there was a fall in the wages of skilled and unskilled labour and the scope of employment became limited. The coalfields of Asansol and Raniganj, which had been hotbeds of labour politics in the 1920s, employed only a few up-country and Ooriya coolies.

In 1930 attempts were made to stop retrenchment in the jute mills by organizing a general strike. In the beginning of March 1930 Miss Prabhabati Dasgupta and Bakr Ali Mirza from the labour research department of the Indian National Congress led a strike in the Titagarh Jute Mills.[146] At the end of March V S Deshpande, the general secretary of the All India Trade Union Congress (AITUC) came to Calcutta and after a meeting with the labour leaders drafted a leaflet '*Banglar chatkal sramikder prati Nikhil Bharat Trade Union Congreeser Istihar* (the manifesto of the All India Trade Union Congress for the jute-mill workers of Bengal)'. But the actual organization of the strike was left to labour leaders like Bankim Mukherjee and others. There were also a series of minor strikes at Kharagpur Bengal Nagpur Railway demanding better overtime rates. The most important labour agitation that occurred during this period was the carters' strike. Following regulation restricting the movement of the bullock carts to certain hours of the day the carters approached a Congress councillor who took them to the Workers' and Peasants' Party (WPP) office. The carters' strike was thereafter organized by Abdul Momin, Swami Viswananda, Madanmohan Barman, Bankim Mukherjee and D P Godbole. With the help of some carters like Raja

Singh and Kishore Singh, they 'built up a city-wide strike apparatus'.[147] The strike was extremely successful and the government was forced to negotiate with the union leaders. Throughout the civil disobedience movement carters often participated in the *hartals* and demonstrations.[148] Between 1932 and 1934 there were minor strikes by the working class.

Although these years between 1930 and 1934 saw labour strikes, unlike the days of the non-cooperation movement there was little connection between the labour unrest and the civil disobedience movement.

The civil disobedience movement in Bengal saw an interaction between mobilization from above and self-mobilization of the people from below. Congress activists at district and local levels provided the link between these two levels of politicization. Yet the civil disobedience movement did not have the intensity of the non-cooperation movement whose 'heady vision of *Swaraj* within a year had inspired sweeping millenarian hopes'.[149] Nevertheless the civil disobedience movement was crucial for strengthening the political organization of the Congress. As the Congress entered the arena of electoral politics in the late 1930s, the Indian National Congress could evoke memories of the civil disobedience movement to project itself as the sole representative of mainstream nationalism.

Chapter 6

Congress in Electoral Politics and After 1935–39

The end of the civil disobedience movement once again witnessed a division in the Congress leadership in Bengal. One section within the party preferred to return to constructive social work to keep up mass contact. Others opted to contest elections for local boards and legislatures. The latter felt that 'the members may not in principle recognize council entry as one of the means to fight the bureaucracy but it may reserve clear enunciation of its attitude towards the coming Reforms for future consideration.'[1] At the AICC meeting in May 1934 a new parliamentary board was formed to control electoral affairs. In Bengal, while Dr Bidhan Chandra Roy was in favour of the parliamentary programme, most Congressmen were opposed to council entry.

The Government Of India Act 1935 introduced provincial autonomy, which was to come into full force from 1 April 1937. Qualifications for inclusion in the electoral roll for the 1937 election was made dependent on taxation, property and education.[2] However, the Act granted separate electorate to the Muslims. This meant that they would vote as a distinct political community and they were allotted 119 out of the 250 seats.

The act was expected to enfranchise 16,600,000 voters. While Congress expected to win seats in the general constituencies, it did not anticipate an uncontested victory. There were strong indications of a decline in the popularity of Congress because of general disillusionment at the failure of civil disobedience movement.[3] Even the best efforts of such stalwarts as Sarat Chandra Bose and Dr Prafulla Kumar Ghosh failed to stir up adequate enthusiasm for prospective Congress candidates. In most places Congress election meetings aroused no response from the people. The only exception was the Burdwan Division where the Congress candidate was welcomed.[4]

On the other hand the *Krishak Samiti* attracted considerable attention in rural Bengal. The *Krishak Praja* Party (KPP) was formally started in July 1929 by those Muslim workers in the Congress who left under the leadership of Maulana Akram Khan and established *Nikhil Banga Praja Samiti* in July 1929.[5] They were subsequently joined by other Muslim members of the legislative council led by Abdur Rahim and A K Fazl ul Huq. The *Praja* movement was in the opinion of some scholars 'launched with an inclination towards the path of Muslim separatism'.[6] Affluent Bengali Muslim tenants allied with urban professionals to mobilize the *raiyats, bargadars* and poor Muslim peasants. On the basis of communal issues they mobilized the Muslim agricultural labourers, using class interests to create a political schism in agrarian Bengal, especially eastern Bengal. This primarily agrarian movement was given an institutionalized form by the *Praja* movement.[7]

At the Rangpur Conference in April 1931, the KPP declared its intention to participate at union level in all governmental and quasi-governmental institutions, legislatures, municipalities and other institutions. In a conference at Serajganj the party reiterated its decision to join all public bodies. A K Fazl ul Huq actively participated in the union board elections of 1935–36. While the Congress had always vacillated over the issue of participation in council politics, the KPP firmly resolved to stand in the legislative council elections and oriented its organization accordingly. At the Dacca Conference in April 1936, the KPP drew up and published the *Krishak Prajar Chaudda Dapha* (Fourteen Point Demands of the *Krishak Praja*). Its demands were:

1. Abolition of the *zamindari* system without any compensation.
2. Reduction of rates of rent.
3. Abolition of the *zamindar*'s rights of *nazar* and *salami* rights of pre-emption (the right to purchase property in preference to others).
4. Adequate measures for agricultural credit to meet the cultivators' current needs.
5. Remission of old debts and interests.
6. Enactment of a moneylending act for adequate protection to the tenants and cultivators.
7. Formation of a debt conciliation board.
8. Resuscitation of the dead and dying rivers of Bengal.
9. Establishment of adequate hospitals in each and every police station.
10. Free and compulsory primary education for all.

11. Fully fledged provincial autonomy for Bengal.
12. Reduction of administrative expenditure.
13. Fixation of ministry's salary at one thousand rupees.
14. Release of political prisoners.

This election manifesto was primarily pro-peasant and anti-*zamindar*, but it contained very little concrete promise to settle the status of the various categories of peasants.

The first two months of 1937 were eventful, as polling began in most constituencies by 18 January. Although the number of those entitled to vote for the lower house totalled about 6,700,000, in most constituencies only 40.5 per cent of registered voters actually turned out. Of the registered voters, nearly 1,000,000 were women. Of this newly enfranchised electorate only 5 per cent voted. According to official records in the scheduled caste constituencies only 27 per cent of the registered votes were cast.[8]

In Bengal the principal contestants in the election were the Congress, the Muslim League and the KPP. The Congress won all the territorial and general seats. Of the reserved scheduled caste seats Congress claimed only three or four wins. Niharendu Datta Majumdar, standing as a Congress Labour candidate won in the Barrackpore Factory Constituency and secured 51,526 votes. But in most of the reserved seats non-Congress candidates succeeded. The Congress however won both of the seats reserved for women.[9] The communal composition of the new house was 96 Hindus and 123 Muslims. None of the Muslims contested on the Congress platform. Official observation was that 'a few of the *Tippera Krishak Samiti* members and the Hooghly Sreerampore Factory Labour members had close connections with the Congress.[10] However, the Congress was still numerically the largest party, having secured 54 seats in the assembly.

Poll results showed that in urban areas the Muslim League was dominating the Muslim vote, while the KPP held sway in the countryside, especially the rural sector of Eastern Bengal. The Muslim League had secured 40 seats and the KPP had 38 seats. In the Labour constituencies five out of eight seats were won by the Congress, which the government interpreted as an indication 'of a remarkable swing towards the Left in Bengal politics'.[11] The following list shows party wise position of the Congress in the 1937 elections.[12]

1.	Santosh Kumar Basu	Calcutta East
2.	Prabhu Dayal Himatsinka	Calcutta West
3.	Dr J M Dasgupta	Calcutta Central
4.	Jogesh Chandra Gupta	Calcutta South Central
5.	Sarat Chandra Bose	Calcutta South
6.	Barada Prasanna Pain	Hooghly cum Howrah Municipal
7.	Tulsi Charan Goswami	Burdwan Div. N. Municipal
8.	Rai Harendra Nath Chaudhuri	24 Parganas Municipal
9.	Dr Nalinaksha Sanyal	Presidency Division
10.	Surendra Mohan Maitra	North Bengal Municipal
11.	Birendra Nath Majumdar	East Bengal Municipal
12.	Promotha Nath Banerjee	Burdwan NW
13.	Dr Sarat Chandra Mukherjee	Birbhum
14.	Asutosh Mallick	Bankura West
15.	Manindra Bhusan Singha	Bankura West
16.	Kamal Krishna Roy	Bankura East
17.	Govinda Chandra Bhowmick	Midnapur East
18.	Iswar Chandra Mal	Midnapur SW
19.	Nikunja Behari Maity	Midnapur SW
20.	Radha Nath Das	Hooghly NE
21.	Gour Hari Shome	Hooghly NE
22.	Sukumar Datta	Hooghly SW
23.	Manmatha Nath Roy	Howrah
24.	P Banerjee	24 Parganas NW
25.	Anukul Chandra Das	24 Parganas NW
26.	Haripada Chattopadhyay	Nadia
27.	Kishori Pati Roy	Jhargramcum Ghatal
28.	Sasanka Sanyal	Murshidabad
29.	Nagendra Nath Sen	Khulna
30.	Patiram Roy	Khulna
31.	Atul Krisna Ghosh	Jessore
32.	Rasik Lal Biswas	Jessore
33.	Satya Priya Banerjee	Rajsahi
34.	Atul Chandra Coomar	Malda
35.	Nishitha Nath Kundu (Independent)	Dinajpur
36.	Khagendra Nath Dasgupta	Jalpaiguri cum Siliguri
37.	Jatindra Nath Chakrabarty	Rangpur
38.	Mono Ranjan Banerjee	Dacca East
39.	Kiran Shankar RoyChaudhuri	Dacca
40.	Charu Chandra Roy	Mymensingh West
41.	Surendra Nath Biswas	Faridpur
42.	Narendra Nath Dasgupta	Bakarganj SW
43.	Dhirendra Nath Datta	Tippera
44.	Harendra Kumar Sur	Noakhali
45.	Mahim Chandra Das	Chittagong
46.	Miss Mira Dattagupta	Calcutta Gen, women
47.	Hemoprova Majumdar	Dacca Gen, women
48.	Dr Suresh Chandra Banerjee	Calcutta Suburbs
49.	Niharendu Datta Majumdar	Barrackpore Labour
50.	Sibnath Banerjee	Howrah, registered factories
51.	B Mukherjee	Colliery, coal mines

52.	Debendra Lal Khan	Midnapur Central
53.	Harendra Nath Doloi	Jhargram
54.	Narendra Narayan Chakrabarty	Bogra cum Pabna

Unfortunately for the Congress, Bengal was one of the provinces where it did not have an absolute majority. The Muslim League had secured 40 seats and the KPP only 41 seats. Since the Congress refused a coalition with the KPP, under the circumstances a KPP–Muslim League coalition government became inevitable.

In the seven provinces where the Congress accepted ministerial responsibilities, it had a wide scope to prove itself as a party of the people and thereby build its hegemony. In comparison, Bengal restricted the constitutional activities of the Congress. In September 1937, the Huq ministry placed before the house the Bengal Tenancy Amendment Bill. The bill was definitely anti-*zamindar*. The Congress bloc remained neutral. As leader of the opposition, Sarat Bose had a difficult decision to make. Bose, it has been argued, had 'dressed up his objections to the Bill in ultra leftist terms that it did not protect the rights of the under-raiyats'.[13] He called for an amendment that proposed suspension of rents paid by the under-tenants. Some historians interpret this defence of the under-*raiyat* as evidence that the Bengal Congress in the 1930s was a radical body.[14] Others feel that Bose's reaction to the Tenancy Amendment Bill was 'a compromise designed to placate his own restless left-wing and the members of the Legislative Assembly from the Krishak Praja Party who supported him, while at the same time trying to retain the support of the conservatives in the Party'.[15] They argue that in this case Congress was following its long-standing policy and commitment to *zamindari* interests.

Within the KPP, members like Tazimuddin Khan and Shamsuddin Ahmed were dissatisfied with Huq for not defending the interests of the cultivators firmly enough. They formed an Independent *Proja* Party in the assembly and joined with the opposition.[16] The Congress also opposed the KPP–Muslim League ministry's initiative to promote a number of legislative and executive measures in the interest of educated Muslim community.[17] Throughout 1938 the Congress Party in the legislature continued to form the core of the opposition, providing a focal point for the various groups that were hostile to or dissatisfied with the ministry. That year also saw several attempts to topple the government by a coalition dependent on Congress support.[18]

Significantly, Congress activity outside the legislature showed a marked improvement on earlier years. As an organization, Congress was contemplating ways and means to develop closer contact with the masses. The Lucknow Congress appointed a committee consisting of Rajendra Prasad, Jairam Daulatram and Jaya Prakash Narayan to devise amendments to the Congress constitution.[19] The Faizpur Congress of 1937 recommended the introduction of the village *panchayat* system. Membership was not confined to primary members who paid their four-anna subscriptions. Village or *mohalla* residents who had reached 18 years of age could become associate members.[20] The membership fee was brought down to two annas and could be realized both in cash and kind.[21] Twice a year the associate and the primary members would meet to consider local problems and carry out the Congress programme. The lower committees could also advise their superiors and influence their policy decisions.

Revitalization of the Congress organization was considered, aimed at extending the roots of organized politics down to the bottom of the hierarchy. The village was identified as the lowest unit from which to build up the organization. Moreover, the leaders were forced to acknowledge that due to the extension of the franchise the peasantry had become an extremely important factor in the body politic. In Bengal the Socialists gained in importance within the Congress during this period and they were mainly responsible for the organization of mass meetings and rallies of workers and peasants. More than 1,100 meetings were held to propagate Socialist ideas and according to official records the Congress was associated with every meeting. The changed attitude of the Congress towards political and economic issues, especially those concerning the agricultural population and labour, was most marked in Bengal. According to an official report: 'In 1937 the Communists and the Congress worked in comparative harmony, each being too useful to the other for any advantage to be gained from stressing their difference.'[22]

An analysis of Congress strategy showed that its resolution to build mass support was effected through the formation of *Krishak Samitis* in different parts of Bengal. As early as 1936 the district magistrate of Midnapur reported that in Bankura, as settlement operations commenced in the latter half of 1936, the tenants organized themselves under the leadership of Dr Bistupada Mondal (secretary of the Bankura *Tarun Sangha*) and Anath Bandhu Samanta. Earlier, some of the tenants in Jujeswar had succeeded in securing occupancy rights in Panchshila area despite *zamindari* opposition.[23] These peasant groups, created through protest meetings and rallies, often succeeded in forcing occupancy rights from their *zamindars*. In accordance with Congress resolutions the Congress workers actively mobilized these anti-*zamindar* peasant groups to form *Krishak Samitis*.

In early 1937 in the village of Panchshilla in Bankura, a *Krishak Samiti* was started after a meeting of peasants.[24] The secretary of the Bankura Congress Committee was appointed secretary of the newly established *Krishak Samiti*, which had its office at the house of Bistupada Mondal. The *Krishak Samiti* had many members of peasant stock, including Kangali Das, Sudhanya Dhara, Krishna Samanta, Purna Hazra and Gostal Samanta. The *Krishak Samiti* was basically anti-*zamindar* in character and its main object was to stop all illegal exactions by the *zamindars*. Provisions were also made for collecting funds to keep the *Samiti* going. But a distinction was made in the subscriptions to be paid by the peasants and the affluent; *Samiti* worker Nitai Mondal was to collect one rupee from the poor peasants and the four rupees from rich men of the locality. As the trend towards the formation of *Krishak Samitis* gathered momentum, peasant meetings were held to form such organizations throughout Howrah district. In Amta police station the peasants were drawn together into so many *Krishak Samitis* that the entire police station was honeycombed with them. Of course, ceaseless propaganda by local leaders had a definite role to play.

This institutionalization of peasant politics under Congress brought a distinct change in the peasant movement. The *Krishak Samitis* provided the support which encouraged the peasants to refuse rent to the *zamindars*. Deputations were sent to the more opulent *zamindars* demanding that the *Khut Khamar* system – a crop-sharing system between the landlord and the tenant (who was also the tiller) whereby the plough and other appliances belonged to the tiller – be substituted by money rent. When the *zamindars* refused to concede to their demands, the peasants didn't attend the yearly appraisement of crops. Soon the movement gained so much in intensity that it began to drift towards militancy. By the second week of April the tenants of Bahirmat harvested the crops without paying even the legitimate share to the *zamindars*. In Shibgachia and Kushberia too, the peasants refused to pay the *zamindar's* share.

By the middle of 1937, when the jute mill strikes were coming to an end, labour leaders transferred their attention to organizing the peasants. In the course of this work Shib Nath Banerjee, the Congress Labour MLA from Howrah, came into contact with mill workers who also worked on the land. They drew his attention to the predicament of the peasants of the Panchla police station where the *zamindars*, the Mannas of Jujeswar, were extremely unpopular with their tenants. Durgapada Banerjee, a college student and an ex civil-disobedience convict, and Hatem Ali Purak, a member of the BPCC and also a civil disobedience activist, were selected by Shibnath Banerjee as his aides. Together they began to unify the local peasants, primarily through meetings and demonstrations.

In February 1938 union board elections were held. This provided a unique opportunity for propagating the ideals of the Congress. In all the public meetings held for the farmers, posters and slogans indicated an openly hostile attitude to the *zamindari* system: 'Down with the zamindari system. Tillers of the soil are the owners of the land!' or 'We till with the sweat of our brow. What do we care about the *zamindars?*' In the unions of Jujeswar and Deulpur, the worst affected areas, Shib Nath Banerjee worked in coordination with the Howrah District Congress Committee and Howrah District Krishak Organizing Committee.[25]

Among other programmes, the coordinators also focused on anti-*chaukidari* tax payment. Since the *chaukidars* and *dafadars* were a part of the police force, it was felt that any extra financial burden for the maintenance of the *chaukidars* must be borne by the government and the money saved should be used by the union boards for rural reconstruction. Peasants were urged to put their problems to the rural arbitration courts set up by Congress leaders, instead of getting involved in litigation. Congress leaders also attended to local issues like the payment of tolls for the empty boats plying on Rajpur Irrigation Canal or the *zamindar's* refusal to grant separate *dakhila* (deeds for rental) for renting date palm trees released for extracting juice. Their involvement in such matters brought them closer to the masses.

The initiative for unifying the peasants came mainly from the Socialist leaders who had been organizing the working class movement and were in touch with the mill labourers from rural backgrounds. In Jagatballavpur police station the peasant movement was growing stronger under the lead of Shibnath Banerjee who practically controlled the situation. In the latter part of 1937 the lock-and-key workers of the Bargachia and adjoining villages in Jagatballavpur police station also organized themselves under the guidance of Shibnath Banerjee.

By the end of 1938 official reports were talking of the growth of 'a no-rent mentality' which had enveloped the countryside and was being actively encouraged by 'the Congress and other elements'.[26] The Sub-divisional Officer (SDO) reported that 'Krishak Sabhas continue to be formed under the leadership of the Congress...and a no-rent mentality is on the increase'.[27] In Tippera, there was a tendency to withhold rent in the Chakla Roshanband Estate belonging to the Maharaja of Tippera. Instead of realizing the *tahuri* and *uttarayan* (types of land tax) which had been abolished, the peasants were expected to pay interest on rent arrears with a maximum of one anna in a rupee. This interest which had not previously been collected had accumulated, totalling an amount equal to the old *abwabs*. The peasants demanded that the estate must accept arrears without any interest or *abwabs*.

In Chittagong, the *Krishak Samitis* of Patiya and Boalkhali *thanas* organized meetings and called for the reduction of rents. They also demanded complete abolition of the *chaukidari* tax. In Rajsahi, Someswar Prasad Chaudhuri led a meeting at which he attacked the *zamindars* and the Midnapur Zamindari Company. In Bogra, agitation reached such a height that the agitators were threatening social boycott of those who paid rent. The *bargadars* were insistent that rent should be fixed at the rate decided in the last settlement. The tenants also demanded that *khas* lands (holdings under the direct possession of the proprietor) should be settled with the original owners.[28] A public meeting was arranged at the *Kalibari* of Gopalganj town in Pabna where leading Communist activists like Muzaffar Ahmed, Dharani Goswami and Abani Lahiri spoke on the *Krishak* movement.

Peasant resistance movements were also spreading in different parts of Birbhum. The circle officer reported that 'the workers of *Amar Kutir* in Bolpur thana, some of whom were ex-detenus have been holding meetings in Bolpur to organize centres for the furtherance of the *Kisan* movement'.[29] They advised the peasants to refrain from paying illegal *abwabs* and cess. The circle officer of Bolpur confirmed that at a meeting of the *raiyats* held at Kirnahar on 11 December 1938, Jitendra Lal Banerjee suggested withholding rent until the grievances of the tenants were redressed. In another meeting at Radhanagar in Bankura, Dr Haripada Mukherjee urged the cultivators not to pay 'the very high water rate' imposed by the government.[30]

In Hooghly district, peasant meetings were held mainly in the Polba police station of the Sadar subdivision. Here, Congress and its supporters championed the no-rent mentality, motivated mainly by the forthcoming union board elections. They hoped to attract the support of the people by promising lower rents and the abolition of *chaukidari* tax if they were elected. Several leaflets in Bengali, like *Hal jar jami tar* (he who ploughs owns the lands), were distributed. In Birbhum, according to government reports, Congress leaders were holding meetings with the ostensible object of enlisting members, but were in fact organizing *krishak* activities. A meeting was held at Darpasila presided over by Pannalal Dasgupta and Surendra Nath Banerjee where the people were asked not to pay rent to the *zamindars*.

In the Presidency Division, the ex-detenus took an active part in forming *Krishak Samitis*. In parts of the division, *Krishak Samitis* were actively cooperating with the Congress leaders of Bogola and Darsana in the subdivisions of Ranaghat and Chuadanga. They worked together to provoke local cultivators into opposing Messars Carew and Company, who were trying to acquire lands for the cultivation of sugarcane for their recently established sugar mill. In the Sagore police station of 24 Parganas Congress workers agitated against the system of loans of paddy taken by the *Baghchasis* from the *Lotdars* at the interest rate of half a *maund* for every *maund* of loan. Shamsuddin Ahmed held Congress *Proja* meetings in the Khustia subdivision of the region.

The no-rent campaigns initiated by the Congress came under criticism from those who believed that the tactic was no longer effective. They thought that by directing no-rent campaigns against the government the Congress was actually challenging the KPP–Muslim League ministry and not the British Raj.[31] However, in 1937–38, the nature of the state was essentially imperialist. Any struggle against its apparatus, even a provincial coalition government of the KPP and the League, was a struggle against imperialism. One can therefore argue that the no-rent campaign of the Congress organization against the government (an apparatus of the British state) was essentially an anti-imperialist struggle.

Congress leaders only encouraged peasant agitation up to a certain point. In Midnapur, for example, the *Krishak* movement was spreading in *thanas* like Mahisadal and Nandigram where the landlords were non-Congressites. The *zamindar* of Narajole, faced with peasant resistance, stopped financing the Congress for the local board elections. Yet meetings and demonstrations continued to be held throughout his *zamindari* with support from the Congress leaders of the locality.[32] In Nandigram, Janardan Samanta of Manuchak and Kunja Giri of Behari Bera, both peasants themselves, led and organized other peasants against paying a certain quota to the landlords while harvesting paddy. The Congress leaders of the area, Govinda Bhowmik, Ajoy Mukherji and Satish Sahoo, supported the protest although they were cautious about stirring up too much confrontation with the small landlords, tenants and *Bhagchasis*.

The movement was the strongest in Manuchak in the *zamindari* of

Prabhat Chandra Dubey. The SDO of Sadar (North) reported that 'a curious thing happened at a *Krishak* meeting at *Chak* Shyampur in Union No IV Debra police station. The meeting was addressed by Debendra Nath Das of Kharagpur, Sripati Kanda of Sherpur in Debra, Khudi Pal and Bibhuti Bakshi. It resolved for seeing that *zamindars* did not get any part of the arrears rent. Attacks were made at the meeting against the Congress workers. Mohini Pati and his followers attempted to disperse the meeting. This shows the real attitude of the Congress workers as regards *Krishak Sabhas*. Most of the Congress workers held land and cannot view with pleasure any movement that will cripple their resources. The tenants are organizing themselves and moving against the interest of those workers.'[33]

In the Muslim majority districts, especially in Tippera, the Congress campaign was geared towards coalescing KPP and Congress organization. But very little was achieved in this area except in Tippera, where the *Krishak* movement completely merged with the Congress movement and regular meetings of the combined leadership were held. On 2 May, a Congress–*Krishak* meeting was held at Chandina that attracted an audience of 4,000. Meetings were also held in Bramanberia where the speakers were Congress MLA Dhirendra Nath Datta and Abdul Malek. The latter urged the Muslims to join the Congress and also appealed for donations to help the jute strikers.

These meetings often shared a common agenda which centred around three programmes; condemnation of the new constitution, attacks on debt settlement boards and appeals for Muslims to join the Congress. The government felt that 'they are a part of an organized campaign which may have a considerable effect on the attitude of the cultivating class'.[34] As for Muslim support of the Congress in Tippera, Kamini Datta had a great role to play. An appeal was sent to Subhas Bose from the various primary Congress committees in Tippera requesting the approval of Kamini Datta's candidature and several of its signatories were Muslims.[35]

There was much Congress activity in the Munshiganj subdivision of Dacca, where the subdivisional Congress committees decided to form local village committees to enlist Muslim support. In Kishoreganj the Congress committees tried to establish contact with the Muslim farmers. In Chittagong, the *Anushilan Samiti* dominated the Congress committees. The revolutionaries formed Communist groups within the local Congress camp in Chittagong. With the exception of Tippera, in most of the East Bengal districts Congress activities were either ignored or resisted with defiance.[36] Within the party itself there was a lurking fear among the Conservatives that the new policy might result in too much concession to the Muslims.

The other issue which preoccupied the Bengal Congress was the elections for various local boards. In Birbhum district the Communist Party of India (CPI) workers decided to organize a joint labour and peasant organization. They formed themselves into Bengal Party as a wing of the CPI under Amar Sarkar as secretary, and supported Jitendralal Banerjee for the post of chairman in the district board elections. In the local board elections Congress succeeded in capturing 10 of the 24 seats in the Sonamukhi circle. In Burdwan, local Congress workers tried to capture seats on the local boards. In Jalpaiguri the ex-detenus were prominent supporters of Congress in union board electioneering.

The centre of Congress activity was in Midnapur so it is unsurprising that the party swept all the seats in the local board elections there. Congress activities gained momentum in Midnapur after the general elections. Led by Debendra Lal Khan of Narajole the Congress leaders and the *externees* (returned exiles) of the district had formed two associations in Calcutta, the Midnapur Worker's Association or the Midnapur *Karmi Sangha* and the Midnapur Local Bodies Election Subcommittee. They had two main objectives. Firstly, they intended to contest the elections of the newly formed union boards and control those that already existed. Secondly, they wanted to bring about the withdrawal of curfew and the lifting of the ban on the Congress. In official circles it was rumoured 'if the ban on the Congress is lifted the Congress Committees which had lain dormant during the last few years will immediately spring into life. The result will be that the way will be open to the formation of *Krishak Samitis* and attempts made to re-establish the old national schools.'[37] The lifting of the curfew in Tamluk led immediately to a reorganization of the Congress Committees and the elections provided the necessary stimulus.

Despite careful moves to broaden the Congress organization, the party was not free from internal squabbles. In Mymensingh, problems were created by a conflict between the president and the secretary who was supported by the majority of members. The secretary was a follower of Subhas Bose, at whose insistence the BPCC often interfered in the work of the district Congress Committee, especially in election matters. Moreover, Mymensingh enjoyed a comparatively large quota of delegates to be sent to the AICC, as a result the BPCC was out to undermine the district Congress committee.

The Rajsahi District Congress Committee had two parallel Congress committees. The old committee was led by its secretary, Saradindu Chakrabarty, while the new committee was formed by Provash Chandra Lahiri. The Bengal Provincial Election Tribunal, however, decided that the old committee was to continue.[38] The Burdwan District Congress Committee was also facing a split. Jitendra Nath Mitra, president of the Burdwan District Congress Committee, belonged to Subhas Bose's group. On the other hand Sris Kumar Mitra, an ardent Congress worker since 1920, cut off his contact with the Congress in 1937 and started a Hindu Sabha in Burdwan. He stirred up communal excitement in the district and was joined by P Sarkar, the chief whip of the Congress Municipal Party. According to the report of the district Congress committee 'the hold of the Congress on the masses is gradually waning in Burdwan'.[39] In Barisal the vice-president, Nagendra Bijay Bhattacharjee with Amiya Kumar Roy Chowdhury and Tarapada Ghosh, formed an obstructionist clique against the secretary, Hiralal Dasgupta. The Darjeeling District Congress Committee, formed in June 1938, faced trouble from its inception in the form of opposition by the officials and their supporters, different associations and finally the European planters.[40] In Bengal the BPCC report showed that no primary members were enrolled in 1939. There were 35,321 female members and 33,082 Muslim members in this year.[41]

Meanwhile the BPCC was suspended by the Congress Working Committee in 1940 and all powers of the Bengal Provincial Congress was vested in an ad hoc committee with Maulana Azad as president. The Congress Rightists had put forward two proposals; that no individual Congress could adopt *satyagraha* without the consent of the provincial Congress committee and that any disputes between a Congress committee and the Congress parliamentary party should be referred to the parliamentary subcommittee.[42] Subhas Bose protested against the decision. Moreover the provincial Congress committee in Bengal, led by Bose, was supporting the fasting prisoners in Alipur Central Jail and Dumdum Jail, which Gandhi opposed.[43] The BPCC also disagreed with the Congress Working Committee that *khadi*, hand spinning and *harijan* work should be made essential for Hindus adopting non-violent *satyagraha*. They protested against the usage of the term *harijan* which gave a specific identity to the depressed classes and separated them from the general populace.[44] In July 1939 Bose organized a demonstration against the decision of the AICC to establish greater control over the provincial committees. The Congress Working Committee called for

new election to the BPCC, which Bose refused. He was dismissed from
the post of president of the BPCC.[45] As a result the Bengal Congress was
divided into two groups, one working as the official Congress Committee
and the other in a parallel committee set up by the followers of Bose.

Such division within the BPCC affected the functioning of the district
Congress committees. The Kalna Barakar Congress Committee and the
Vikrampur Dacca Congress Committees were among those that
welcomed the decision of the Congress Working Committee.[46] But the
Mymensingh, Hooghly and Jessore district Congress committees did
not accept the resolution, and they were disaffiliated. Among the
Congress workers the Ghandhians, known as the *Khadi* group, were
cooperating with the legally constituted BPCC.[47] On the other hand the
members of the Forward Bloc, vocal in four or five districts, were
propagating against individual *satyagraha* and demanded mass struggle.
In the Tippera District Congress Committee, Ashrufuddin Choudhury
was an avowed Forward Bloc supporter. In Noakhali District Congress
Committee, the executive had a majority of Forward Bloc supporters
while the President Haran Chandra Ghosh Choudhury belonged to the
Khadi group. The AICC suspended the district Congress committee
and the village Congress committees and replaced them with one or
two members entrusted with the work of the Congress. Thus by the
1940s, the organizational edifice of the BPCC was reduced to single
committees manned by an individual.[48]

Meanwhile the world was being drawn into the whirlpool of another
war and Britain's involvement once again impacted on the political events
of its colonies. In the background of the international situation, after
the Munich Pact in 1938, it was evident that 'in Europe as well as in
Asia, British and French Imperialism had received a considerable setback in the matter of strength and prestige'.[49] Even as early as March
1939 in his Tripuri address, Bose advocated a mass action:

> If no reply is received we should resort to such sanctions that we
> possess in order to enforce our national demand. The sanctions
> that we possess today are mass civil disobedience or *satyagraha*.
> And the British Government today are not in a position to face a
> major conflict like an All-India *Satyagraha* for a long period.[49]

He criticized the right-wing leaders for their pessimistic belief that the
time was not ripe for anti-British agitation. He felt that 'with the
Congress in power in eight provinces, the strength and prestige of our

national organization had gone up. The mass movement had made considerable headway throughout British India'.[50] He was also planning a united action by 'all anti-imperialist organizations in the country; all radical elements in the country must work in close harmony and co-operation and the efforts of all anti-imperialist organizations must converge in the direction of a final assault on British imperialism'.[51]

But it was not until 1942 that, embittered by the failure of the Cripps Mission and goaded by the Congress Socialists, Congress finally resorted to mass action through the Quit India Movement. In place of simple non-cooperation, *satyagraha* and the courting of imprisonment, more revolutionary methods were adopted to make the British quit India. The slogan now was to 'do or die'. The penultimate chapter in the story of the Indian freedom movement was beginning and Bengal emerged as one of the storm centres of the Quit India Movement of 1942.

Conclusion

This study has thus gone beyond the two received paradigms: (a) that organized politics of the Congress retained its elitist character throughout the period of nationalist struggle and (b) the idea that the politics of the people ran parallel to and was relatively autonomous of institutional politics. Both of these stereotypes have ignored the areas of interaction and interdependence of the two realms of political activities, especially during the phase of Gandhian nationalism. This work demonstrates that from 1919 the Congress tried to maintain its link with the people, which to a large extent contributed to an interaction between organized and unorganized politics. Gandhi's strategy of *satyagraha* and non-cooperation on specific issues sustained this process. However, Gandhi laid down specific conditions and boundaries within which the people were expected to act. Popular upsurges were withdrawn whenever they reached a certain momentum and began to cross this Gandhian barrier. In analysing the nature of this interaction, this book has concentrated primarily on the non-cooperation and civil disobedience movements and the periods immediately thereafter.

During the days of the non-cooperation movement, the institutional programme of the Congress was one of boycott and non-cooperation with the British educational, judicial and administrative systems. It also involved economic boycott of British commodities. To involve the masses in a year-long movement, it was necessary to resuscitate the Congress organization in Bengal and create a network through which it could reach the grass roots. The Congress organization was extended down to the village level so that the local people could be mobilized by Congress propaganda.

Institutional politics as represented by the Congress thus was able to mobilize the masses in the 1920s in accordance with its plans and programmes. But as the spirit of non-cooperation began to motivate the people, spontaneous attempts at self-organization began. The efforts of local people, rather than organizational imposition from above, became the driving force of political mobilization at local level. Local Congress committees were formed at several places at the initiative of the inhabitants. Very often the actual task of mobilization was shouldered not by established leaders but by local people connected with the Congress. A result of these combined efforts was the emergence of well-defined Congress strongholds in the districts, especially those of West Bengal, like Midnapur, Bankura, Hooghly, Birbhum and 24 Parganas. In building up the structural edifice needed for launching the movement the organizational effort of the political elite was thus as important as popular efforts.

A unique feature of this period was the beginning of Muslim participation in nationalist politics, especially during the non-cooperation movement. The joint efforts of the *Khilafat* and the Congress committees largely ensured this. Muslim organizations and newspapers accepted the Congress as a medium representing all sections through which the work of *Swaraj* could progress satisfactorily. Nevertheless the importance of Islam in Muslim life was never lost sight of.

The civil disobedience movement occurred at a time when Bengal was hit by international economic depression. The Bengal Congress during this period had lost much of its earlier centralized structure of command. The leadership was divided. In the districts most of the Congress committees ceased to exist or were in a moribund state. The Bengal situation was different from Uttar Pradesh or Bihar, which witnessed a more consolidated and strengthened position of the Congress organization by the 1930s. Consequently the civil disobedience movement in these areas was characterized by Gandhian restraint.[1] But in Bengal no such ideological or organizational imposition was noticeable. The movement relied on the initiative of the local leadership who worked for Congress rather than on metropolitan leaders. Unlike the non-cooperation movement, which spread from the urban to the rural sector, the salt *satyagraha* activated the rural coastal areas from the very beginning.

Analysing the nature of two Gandhian mass movements during the period under consideration it can be said that in Bengal, the structure of the Congress organization did not at all determine the nature of interaction between institutional and popular politics. Popular support of the Congress-led nationalist mass uprisings did not correspond to the strength of its central organization. Even when the organizational coordination of the provincial Congress tended to be weak, those at local level working within or outside the Congress helped to sustain the movements. During both the non-cooperation and the civil disobedience movements, it was the intermediate tier of leadership emerging from the local levels, represented by Congress workers, which actually helped the interaction between organized and unorganized politics.

While working within the programme of an institutionally sanctioned non-violent mass movement, these local leaders often found it difficult to match the decisions of their elite leaders with the hopes of the masses. As a result, interaction between the Congress organization and the people did not always take place exclusively according to the Congress creed. In creating the conditions for insurrection, mobilization by the elite leaders on a premeditated programme of action was as important as conscious acceptance of the nationalist message by the people. Even between the non-cooperation movement and the civil disobedience movement the involvement of different social and functional groups with nationalist politics varied in intensity. While non-cooperation saw extensive participation of labour, this was not the case during the civil disobedience movement. But at the same time people accepted the timing of Congress when they began and abruptly terminated both these movements. Thus, popular politics did not necessarily always exist parallel to the politics of their leaders.

Significantly enough, as this book shows, even during the years of peace the two streams of politics interacted with one another. Constructive social work was one of the most important means through which this connection was maintained. Electoral politics also required that contact with the electorate be maintained to influence the voters, although voting rights were limited. The present study also demonstrates that once nationalist fervour and the consequent popular movement subsided, the leaders of institutional politics failed to keep up a united front. This clearly happened in the interlude between the non-cooperation movement and the beginning of the civil disobedience movement and also after the cessation of the civil disobedience movement. At the end of both movements, while a sector of the Bengal Congress leadership followed the Gandhian ideal of constructive social work, others favoured council entry. Yet for each group the earlier movement provided the base for future politics.

Under the reformed constitution of 1935, the collective strength of mass politics became the instrument with which institutional leaders fought elections to the council and other local bodies. Although in Bengal the Congress did not form a ministry, it played an active role as the chief opposition group in the council. Outside the legislature, the Socialists within the Congress took the initiative to build up sustained contact with the masses especially through the formation of *Krishak Samitis*. By the end of the 1930s the official structure of the Congress in Bengal was crumbling, but Congress workers in the localities continued to remain active in mass politics. As the nation plunged into the last phase of the nationalist struggle, Bengal became a storm centre of the official Congress programme of the Quit India Movement of 1942.

Glossary

Abwab – Unauthorized cess levied in excess of rent.
Akhra – Gymnasium or sporting club.
Amin – Indian assistants in land survey duties.
Amla – Employee of a landlord.
Ashram – A place where the Hindu religious community lives in spiritual retreat.
Bargadar – Sharecroppers who paid a fixed proportion of the produce as rent.
Bastra – Cloth.
Belati – Foreign articles from Britain.
Bhadralok – Middle-class educated Bengalis.
Bhagchasi – Sharecropper.
Charka – Spinning wheel.
Chula – Oven.
Churi – Bangles.
Chowkidar/Chaukidar – Village watchman.
Daffadar – Village watchman.
Deshbandhu – A friend of the country.
Diwan – Chief native officer of a landlord.
Gurdwara – Religious place of the Sikhs.
Handi – Utensil.
Hat – Village market.
Hartal – Strike in protest.
Jatra – Folk theatre of Bengal.
Jehad – Revolt.
Jotdar – Intermediate tenure holders.
Katari – Sharp weapon.
Khadi – Hand-spun cloth.

Kirtan – Hindu devotional songs.
Krishak – Peasant.
Lathi – Rod.
Lotdar – Holder of a *lot* or a portion of a land with rights of intermediate tenure.
Madrassah – School for the Muslim students.
Mahakuma – Subdivision.
Mahalla – Locality.
Mandal – A committee of elders in a village.
Marawari – Inhabitants of Marwar in Rajasthan.
Mauja – Village as a unit.
Maulavi – A learned Muslim.
Moulavi – Man learned in Muslim law and literature.
Naib – Deputy.
Nagdi – Cash rent.
Nazar – A ceremonial present by an inferior to a superior.
Neel Kuthi – House of the indigo planters.
Panch – A village committee.
Praja – Subject.
Sadhu – Hindu religious man.
Samiti – Committee.
Sarbadhinayak – Captain.
Sardar – Head of the mill workers.
Satyagraha – The force of truth.
Satyagrahi – One who has taken the course of Satyagraha.
Suder/Sadar – District headquarter.
Swaraj – Home rule, or self rule.
Swadeshi – Goods produced in one's own country.
Taluka – An administrative sub-division of a district.
Zamindar – landlord.

Bibliography

Manuscript sources

All India Congress Committee Papers 1920–1940, Jawaharlal Nehru Memorial Library, New Delhi.

B C Roy Papers, Jawaharlal Nehru Memorial Library, New Delhi.

Government of India, 'Proceedings of the Home (Political) Department, 1919–1940', National Archives of India.

Government of Bengal, 'Home Political Confidential Reports 1919–1940', West Bengal State Archives.

Government Of Bengal, 'Report on the Native-Owned Newspapers in Bengal 1919–1940', West Bengal State Archives.

Government of Bengal, 'Proceedings of the Agriculture (Agriculture) Department, 1919–1930', West Bengal State Archives.

Government of Bengal, 'Proceedings of the Land Revenue (Land Revenue) Department, 1919–1934', West Bengal State Archives.

Reports and Files of the Intelligence Branch, 1919–1939.

Printed sources

Government publications and non-official reports

Bengal District Gazetteers, Dacca.
Bengal District Gazetteers, Jalpaiguri.
Bengal District Gazetteers, Mymensingh.
Bengal District Gazetteers, Malda.
Bengal District Gazetteers, Pabna.
Bengal District Gazetteers, Rajshahi.
Bengal District Gazetteers, Bogra.

Bengal District Gazetteers, Hooghly.
Bengal District Gazetteers, Bankura.
Bengal District Gazetteers, Midnapur.
F W Robertson, 'Final reports on the survey and settlement operations in the District of Bankura 1917–1924', Calcutta, 1926.
J M Pringle, A H Kamm, 'Final reports on the survey and settlement operations in the District of Nadia', Calcutta, 1928.
D Macpherson, 'Final reports on the survey and settlement operations in the Districts of Pabna and Bogra 1920–29', Calcutta, 1930.
Fortnightly Reports of the Government Of Bengal, 1919–1930.
Report of the Land Revenue Commission, 1940.
Report of the Committee of Industrial Unrest. Supplement to the *Calcutta Gazette* 22 June 1921.
Proceedings of the Bengal Legislative Council 1923–1939.
N N Mitra (ed.) 'Indian Annual Register', Calcutta.

Newspapers and Periodicals

Amrita Bazar Patrika.
Ananda Bazar Patrika.
Atmashakti.
Bengalee.
Bharatbarsha.
Prabasi.
Bengal Past and Present.
Forward.
Liberty.
The *Modern Review.*
The Musalman.
The *Statesman.*

Secondary   sources

Printed books

Ahmad, Abdul Mansur, 1970, *Amar Dekha Rajnitir Panchas Bachar,* Dacca.
Arnold, David, 1977, *The Congress in Tamil Nadu: Nationalist Politics in South India 1919–1937,* Manohar.

Azad, M A K, 1959 and 1988, *India Wins Freedom*, Calcutta.

Bagchi, A K, 1972, *Private Investment in India 1900–1939*, Cambridge.

Baker, C, Johnson, G, and Seal, A (eds.), 1981, *Power Profit and Politics: Essays on Imperialism, Nationalism and Change in Twentieth Century India*, Cambridge.

Bamford, P C, 1925, *History Of Non-Cooperation and Khilafat Movements*, Delhi.

Bandhopadhyaya, Gitasree, 1984, *Constraints in Bengal Politics 1921–1941: Gandhian Leadership*, Calcutta.

Bandyopadhyay, Sekhar, 1990, *Caste, Politics and the Raj: Bengal 1872–1939*, Calcutta.

Bannerjee, Nripendra Chandra, 1950, *At the Crossroads*, Calcutta.

Bannerjee, S N, 1925, *A Nation in Making*, London.

Birla, G D, 1953, *In the Shadow of the Mahatma: A Personal Memoir*, Calcutta.

Bhaduri, Satinath, 1973, *Satinath Granthabali Vol II*, Calcutta.

Bhattacharjee, Buddhadev, 1977, *Satyagrahas In Bengal*, Calcutta.

Bose, N K, 1943, *My Days With Gandhi*, Bombay.

Bose, Subhas Chandra, 1948, *The Indian Struggle, 1920–1942*.

Bose, Subhas Chandra, 1967, *Correspondence 1924–1932*, Calcutta, Netaji Research Bureau.

Bose, Subhas Chandra, 1995, *Netaji Collected Works: Vol 9*.

Bose, Sugata, 1986, *Agrarian Bengal Economy Social Structure and Politics 1919–1947*, Cambridge.

Bose, Sisir Kumar and Bose Sugata (ed.), *Congress President, Speeches, Articles and Letters, January 1938–May 1939*.

Brass, Paul and Robinson, Francis (ed.), 1987, *The Indian National Congress and Indian Society, 1885–1985*, Delhi.

Broomfield J H, 1968, *Elite Conflict in a Plural Society Twentieth Century Bengal*, Berkeley and Los Angeles.

Brown, Judith, 1972, *Gandhi's Rise To Power: Indian Politics 1915–1922*, Cambridge.

Brown, Judith, 1977, *Gandhi and Civil Disobedience: The Mahatma in Indian Politics 1928–34*, Cambridge.

Brown, Judith, 1984, *Modern India: The Origins of an Asian Democracy*, Delhi.

Chakrabarty, Bidyut, 1990, *Subhas Chandra Bose and Middle Class Radicalism: A Study in Indian Nationalism 1928–40*, Delhi.

Chakrabarty, Bidyut, 1997, *Local Politics and Indian Nationalism, Midnapur 1919–1944*, Delhi.

Chakrabarty, Dipesh, 1989, *Rethinking Working Class History Bengal 1890–1940*, Delhi.

Chandra, Bipan, 1986, *The Rise and Growth of Economic Nationalism in India*.

Chandra, Bipan, 1979, *Imperialism and Nationalism in India*, Delhi.

Chandra, Bipan, 1984, *Communalism in Modern India*, New Delhi.
    Chatterji, Bhola, 1969, *Aspects of Bengal Politics in Early 1930s*, Calcutta.

Chatterjee, Joya, 1995, *Bengal Divided, Hindu Communalism and Partition 1932–1947*, New Delhi.

Chatterjee, Partha, 1984, *Bengal 1920–1947: The Land Question*, Calcutta.

Chatterjee, Partha, 1986, *Nationalist Thought and the Colonial World*, Delhi.

Damodaran, Vinita, 1993, *Broken Promise Popular Protest: Indian Nationalism and the Congress Party in Bihar 1935–1946*.

Das, Suranjan, 1991, *Communal Riots in Bengal 1905–1947*, New Delhi.

Dasgupta, Hemendranath, *Deshbandhu Smriti. (Calcutta 1333B.S).*

Dasgupta, Purnanananda, *Biplaber Pathe*, Calcutta.

Dastidar, Purnendu, *Swadhinata Sangrame Chattogram (Chattogram 1374 BS).*

Dasgupta, Ranajit, 1992, *Economy, Society and Politics in Bengal: Jalpaiguri, 1869–1947*, Delhi.

Datta, Bhupendra Kumar, 1973, *Biplaber Padachinha*, Calcutta.

Datta Bhupendra Nath, *Aprakasita Rajnaitik Itihas (Calcutta 1333, B.S.).*

Dey, Amalendu, *Pakistan Prastab O Fazl ul Huq (Calcutta 1379).*

Desai, A R, 1948, *Social Background of Indian Nationalism*.

Dhanagare, D N, 1983, *Peasant Movements in India 1920–1950*, Oxford.

Gandhi M K, 1958, *The Collected Works Of Mahatma Gandhi*, Delhi.

Gallagher J, Johnson G, and Seal A (eds.), 1973, *Locality, Province and Nation: Essays in Indian Politics 1870–1940*, Cambridge.

Ghosh Atulya, 1980, *Kastakalpita Vol 1* and 1984, *Vol 2*, Calcutta.

Ghosh, Hemendra Prasad, 1921–22, *Congress*, Calcutta.

Gordon, Leonard, 1974, *Bengal: The Nationalist Movement 1876–1940*, Columbia.

Guha Ranajit (ed.), 1982–89, *Subaltern Studies: Writings on South Asian History and Society*, Vols I – VI.

Guha, Ranajit and Spivak, Chakravarti Gayatri (ed.), 1988, *Selected Subaltern Studies*, Delhi.

Hardiman, David, 1992, *Peasant Resistance in India 1858–1914*.

Johnson, Gordon, 1973, *Provincial Politics and Indian Nationalism: Bombay and the Indian National Congress 1880–1915*, Cambridge.

Kabir, Humayun, 1943, *Muslim Politics in Bengal 1906–1942*, Calcutta.

Kumar, Kapil (ed.), 1988, *Congress and Classes*, Delhi.

Kumar, Ravinder (ed.), 1971, *Essays on Gandhian Politics*, Oxford.

Low, D, 1968, *Soundings in Modern Asian History*, California.

Low, D, 1942, *Congress and the Raj: Facets of Indian Struggle 1917–1947*, London.

Minault, Gail, 1982, *The Khilafat Movement: Religious Symbolism and Political Mobilisation in India*, Oxford.

Misra, B B, 1961, *The Indian Middle Classes*, London.

Mukhopadhyay, Saroj, 1985, *Bharater Communist Party O Amra*, Volumes 1 and 2, Calcutta.

Niemejer, A C, 1972, *The Khilafat Movement in India 1919–1924*, Leiden.

Pal, Bipin Chandra, 1957, *Character Sketches*, Calcutta.

Pal, Bipin Chandra, 1932, *Memoirs of My Life and Times*, 2 volumes, Calcutta.

Pandey, B N (ed.), 1985, *A Centenary History of the Indian National Congress*, 4 volumes, New Delhi.

Pandey, B N, 1977, *Leadership in South Asia*, Delhi.

Pandey, B N, 1979, *The Indian Nationalist Movement 1885–1947*, Select Documents, London.

Pandey, Gyanendra, 1978, *The Ascendancy of the Congress in Uttar Pradesh 1926–34*, Delhi.

Ray, Rajat Kanta, 1979, *Urban Roots in Indian Nationalism: Pressure Groups and Conflict of Interest in Calcutta City Politics 1875–1939*, New Delhi.

Ray, Rajat Kanta, 1984, *Social Conflict and Political Unrest in Bengal 1875–1927*, Delhi.

Ray, Prithwis Chandra, 1927, *Life and Times of C R Das: The Story of Bengal's Self Expression*, London.

Sanyal, Hitesh Ranjan, 1994, *Swarajer Pathe*, Calcutta.

Roy, Chowdhuri Someswar Prasad, 1972, *Nilkar Bidraha*, Calcutta.

Roy, Tirthankar, 2000, *The Economic History of India 1857–1947*, Mumbai.

Sarkar, C P, 1991, *The Bengali Muslims: A Study in Their Politicization 1912–1929*, Calcutta.

Sarkar, Hemanta Kumar, 1939, *Deshbandhu Smriti*, Calcutta.

Sarkar, Tanika, 1987, *Bengal 1928–34: The Politics of Protest*, Delhi.

Sarkar, Sumit, *The Swadeshi Movement in Bengal*, Delhi.

Sarkar, Sumit, 1983, *Modern India*, Delhi.

Sarkar, Sumit, 1983, *Popular Movements and Middle Class Leadership in Late Colonial India: Perspectives and Problems of a History from Below*, Calcutta.

Sarkar, Sumit, 1985, *A Critique of Colonial Reason*, Calcutta.

Sarkar, Sumit, 1998, *Writing Social History*, Delhi.

Sasmal, Bimalanand, *Swadhinatar Phanki*, Calcutta, *(Calcutta 1374 B.S.).*

Sasmal, Bimalanand, 1981, *Bharat Ki Kore Bhag Holo*, Calcutta.

Sasmal, Birendranath, 1922, *Sroter Trina.*

Seal, Anil, 1968, *The Emergence of Indian Nationalism: Competition and Collaboration in the Later Nineteenth Century*, Cambridge.

Sen, S P (ed.), 1972–74, *Dictionary of National Biography*, Calcutta.

Sengupta, Padmini, 1968, *Deshapriya Jatindra Mohan*, Delhi.

Singha, Ananta, 1968, *Agnigarbha Chattogram*, Calcutta.

Sisson, R and Wolpert, S (ed.), 1988, *Congress and the Indian Nationalism: The Pre-Independence Phase*, Delhi.

Sitaramayya, B P, 1935, *History of the Indian National Congress 1885–1935*, Madras.

Tagore, Rabindranath, Rabindra Rachanabali Vol 12 (Biswabharati 1397).

Tomlinson, B R, 1976, *The Indian National Congress and the Raj 1929–42: The Penultimate Phase*, London.

Tomlinson, B R, 1979, The Political Economy of the Raj 1914–47: The Economics of Decolonization in India, *Cambridge.*

Tripathi, Amalesh, *Swadhinata Sangrame Bharater Jatiya Congress* (Calcutta 1397 B.S.).

Washbrook D A, 1976, *The Emergence of Provincial Politics: The Madras Presidency 1870–1920*, Cambridge.

Articles

Sanyal, Hitesh Ranjan. *Dakshin Paschim Banglay Jatiatabadi Andolan. Anya Artha and Chaturanga (Kartik-Poush 1383).*

Unpublished   PhD   Theses

De, Jatindranath, 'History of the Krishak Praja Party of Bengal 1929–1947: A Study of Change in Class and Intercommunity Relations in the Agrarian Sector of Bengal' (PhD thesis, University of Delhi, October 1977).

Ray, Ranjit Kumar, 'Bengal's Response to Civil Disobedience: A Study in the Forms of Protest Movements amongst Women and Students 1930–34' (PhD thesis, University Of Calcutta, April 1991).

Oral Interview

Bijay Singh Nahar.

Appendix

Rules of the Bengal Provincial Congress Committee

(Adopted at meetings of the Committee held on 12 February 1921, 15 February 1921 and 16 February 1921.)

1. The Bengal Provincial Congress Committee shall represent the Indian National Congress in the Province of *Bengal and Surma Valley* and shall act as for the Province in all Congress matters and take such steps as it may think proper to organize provincial, district and local Conferences and make rules for the conduct of their business and otherwise carry on the work of the Congress.

2. The Bengal Provincial Congress Committee shall be composed of members elected in manner hereinafter laid down.

3. The Bengal Provincial Congress Committee shall organize a District Congress Committee in each District (in accordance with the new Constitution of the Congress), which shall carry out the work of the Congress in the districts under its guidance and control. Such Committees shall abide by all the Rules framed and instructions issued by the Bengal Provincial Congress Committee.

Note: The city of Calcutta including the area within its Municipal Jurisdiction, shall for the purpose of these rules be treated as a District.

4. The District Congress Committees shall organize and establish local Congress Committees in such urban and rural areas as they consider necessary and such local committees shall abide by the rules and act under the guidance of the District Congress Committees subject to the control of the Provincial Congress Committees. The members of such

local committees shall be deemed to be members of the District Congress Committees of their respective districts.

5. Any person above the age of 21 who expresses in writings his or her acceptance of the objects and methods as laid down in Article 1 of the Constitution and Rules of the Indian National Congress and pays a subscription of four annas per year shall be entitled to be a member of any Congress Committee controlled by the Provincial Congress Committee and no person who does not satisfy the above qualifications shall be a member of such Committee.

6. The Council of the Bengal Provincial Congress Committee shall prepare a set of model rules for the District and other Congress Committees under its control and the district and other Congress Committees shall adopt such model rule or rules similar to them and not inconsistent with any rules made by the Provincial Congress Committee.

7. The district and local Congress Committees shall supply such information and submit such returns as may from time to time be required by the Bengal Provincial Congress Committee.

8. The Bengal Provincial Congress Committee shall have power for sufficient cause to disaffiliate any District Congress Committee and establish another at its place.

9. Each District shall be a constituency for the purpose of returning members to the Bengal Provincial Congress Committee and the number of members elected by each constituency shall be based mainly on population and shall for the present be as follows:

1.	Burdwan	8	15.	Jalpaiguri	4
2.	Birbhum	5	16.	Darjeeling	2
3.	Bankura	6	17.	Rungpore	12
4.	Midnapore	14	18.	Bogra	5
5.	Hooghly	6	19.	Pabna	7
6.	Howrah	5	20.	Maldah	5
7.	24-Pergs	12	21.	Dacca	16
8.	Calcutta	25	22.	Mymensingh	23
9.	Nadia	8	23.	Faridpore	11
10.	Murshidabad	7	24.	Backergunge	12
11.	Jessore	9	25.	Tippera	12
12.	Khulna	7	26.	Noakhali	7
13.	Rajsahi	8	27.	Chittagong	8
14.	Dinajpore	9	28.	Sylhet	12

Total   268

10. The Bengal Provincial Congress Committee Shall have power by the votes of a majority in general meeting to alter the allotments made above and to create new constituencies if they consider necessary.

11. Every person who is a member of a District Congress Committee and who has within the 31st May preceding paid his subscription for the current year to such committee or to any of the local committees controlled by it shall be qualified and entitled to have his name registered in the Electoral Roll of the Constituency in which the District Congress Committee is situated, provided that no person shall be entitled to have his name registered in the Electoral Roll of more than one constituency.

12. Every person whose name is registered in the Electoral Roll of any constituency shall be qualified and entitled to seek election to the Bengal Provincial Congress Committee from any constituency in the Province.

13. The election of members of the Bengal provincial Congress Committees shall be held every year as far as possible in the month of *August* and the method of election shall be as follows.

a) The Secretaries of the District Congress Committees shall in each year prepare a Roll of all members of such committees (including the local Congress Committees controlled by them) with their addresses, as have within the 12th June cause a copy of such Roll to be hung up in the principal office of the Committee and such portions of the Roll as relate to the local Committees to be hung up in the principal office of the respective local committees.

b) Any member of the District and local Congress Committees may prefer any application for or objection to the inclusion of any name in the Electoral Roll of the district to the council of the District or local Congress Committees concerned within the 20th June and the Council shall after due consideration decide the matter and such decision shall be arrived at within the 30th June and shall be final.

c) Any alteration of the Electoral Roll shall be published by the council of the District Congress Committees and in the office of the local Congress Committees within the 10th July.

d) The council of the Bengal Provincial Congress Committee shall within the 15th June in each year appoint a returning officer for the conduct of the elections in each constituency and forthwith send the name of such returning officer and the address of his office to the District Congress Committee concerned who shall publish such name and address in its principal office and the offices of the local Congress Committees within the 10th July.

e) The office of the Returning Officer shall be situated within the district for which he is appointed.

f) Any person intending to seek election from any constituency shall be nominated in writing by at least 5 electors of the constituency in the form appendix 'A' and the candidate shall signify his intention of seeking election in the same form which shall be forwarded duly filled up by the candidate to the Returning Officer on or before 20th July.

g) The Returning Officer shall on such days within the 25th July as he fixes, by notice published in his office at least 2 days before such date, scrutinize the nomination papers and the candidate or an agent of each appointed in writing by the candidate shall be entitled to be present at the scrutiny.

h) The Returning Officer shall within 10th August send to all persons whose names are entered in the Electoral Roll, Ballot papers with the names of all the duly nominated candidates, mentioning a date not later than the 25th August within which the Ballot papers shall have to be sent to his office duly filled up and signed. He shall also state in the Ballot paper the date and time (which must not be later than the 31st August) when the scrutiny shall take place. The method of voting in all cases be the single transferable vote.

i) The Council of the Bengal Provincial Congress Committee shall issue an instruction in the vernacular explaining the method of voting to be adopted and shall supply the Returning Officer with sufficient copies of such instructions and the Returning Officer shall send a copy of the same to all electors with the Ballot paper.

j) The candidates or one agent of each shall be entitled to be present at the scrutiny of the Ballot papers and the result of the scrutiny shall be communicated by the Returning Officers within the 10th September to the Secretary of the Bengal Provincial Congress Committee who shall send intimation to the successful candidates and to the Secretaries of the District Congress Committees.

k) No candidate shall withdraw his candidature after the scrutiny of nomination papers is over.

l) The Council of the Bengal Provincial Congress Committee shall have power if they think necessary in any year to alter the dates mentioned in the foregoing clauses by previous notification. They shall also have power to dismiss a Returning Officer and appoint another in his place and also to appoint a Returning Officer in case of any vacancy in the office for any cause.

m) The Returning Officer shall be competent to delegate, on his own responsibility, his powers and functions to such persons as he thinks fit, and to adjourn the holding of any scrutiny from time to time.

14. Notwithstanding the foregoing rules the first elections under these rules shall be held before the 31st May 1921 and the existing members shall remain in office till the said election, and there shall be no further election before August 1922.

15. There shall be no election in cases where the number of candidates duly nominated is equal to or less than the seats fixed by clause 9. In such cases all the candidates shall be declared to be duly elected.

16. If any person be elected by more than one constituency he shall within two weeks of the receipt of intimation of his election inform the Secretary, Provincial Congress Committee as to which constituency he shall serve and if he does not so inform his elections shall be void.

17. The members elected under the foregoing clauses hold office for one year from the first of November next and the old office-bearers shall continue in office till new office-bearers are elected. The members elected in the first election in 1921 shall hold office from the 1st June till the next election in 1922.

18. Any vacancies in the Bengal Provincial Congress Committee due to paucity of candidates or to any other causes shall be filled up by the Council of the District Congress Committee within such dates as the Council of the Bengal Provincial Congress Committee shall fix. The members so elected to fill to up the vacancy shall hold office till the next election.

19. Until otherwise decided by the Provincial Congress Committee every District Congress Committee shall pay to the fund of the Bengal Provincial Congress Committee an annual subscription of Rs. 5/- for every member returnable by it to the Provincial Congress Committee and such subscription shall be due and payable on or before the 31st May in each year and the members of such District Congress Committees as are in default shall not exercise the rights of electing members to the Bengal Provincial Congress Committee or delegates to the Congress.

20. Every member of the Bengal Provincial Congress Committee shall

pay an annual subscription of Rs 5/- to the Provincial Congress Committee shall pay an annual subscription of Rs. 5/- to the Provincial Congress Committee and no member shall exercise the rights of membership until he has paid his subscription for the current year.

21. The Bengal Provincial Congress Committee shall have the following office-bearers: one President, two Vice-Presidents, one Secretary, three Assistant Secretaries, one Treasurer and two Auditors.

22. The business of the Provincial Congress Committee shall be managed by a Council of 60 members besides the office bearers, provided that at least 20 of the elected members shall be ordinary residents of Calcutta or the suburbs.

23. The office bearers and the members of the Council shall be elected annually at the first meeting of the Bengal Provincial Congress Committee to be held in the month of November and so soon thereafter as possible provided that in case of any vacancy occurring during the year the Council may fill up.

24. The Bengal Provincial Congress Committee shall ordinarily meet three times a year; as far as possible, once in November to elect members of the Council and office bearers, once in June to suggest to the Reception Committee names of persons who are in their opinion eligible for the presidentship of the Congress of that year, once in August for the final recommendation for the presidentship of the Congress. At such meetings any other business may also be transacted.

25. The Secretary may at any time of their own motion and shall within 15 days of the receipt of a requisition stating the business to be transacted and signed by not less than 20 members call a meeting of the Provincial Congress Committee. If the Secretary fails to call the meeting required by the requisition, the requisitionists may themselves call the meeting.

26. For all meetings of the Provincial Congress Committee, except emergent meetings, at least 7 days previous notice shall be given and at such meetings 20 members shall form a quorum.

27. Three days' previous notice will be required to convene a meeting of the council. A meeting of the council may be called by the Secretaries at any time and shall be called on the requisition of 5 members of the council. Five members other than the office-bearers shall form a quorum.

28. The council may appoint sub-committees for special purposes and assign to them such duties and delegate to them such powers and functions as they may think fit. Members of such sub-committees need not necessarily be members of the committee.

29. The council shall have power to frame Bye-Laws to give effect to these rules.

30. The Provincial Congress Committee shall organize such funds as may be thought necessary.

31. No change or amendment of these rules shall be made except at a meeting of the Provincial Congress Committee specially convened for the purpose and at which at least 50 members are present, and unless passed by a majority for at least two-thirds of the members present at the meeting. No proposal for a change or amendment of the rules shall be considered unless notice of such proposal is given with the notice of the meeting.

Provided that the First Provincial Congress Committee constituted in accordance with these rules shall be competent to alter or amend the rules by a bare majority.

Notes

Introduction

1. Seal, Anil, 1968, *The Emergence of Indian Nationalism, Competition and Collaboration in the late Nineteenth Century*, Cambridge.
2. Traditional nationalist historiography has tended to view the movement as an idealist venture in which the indigenous elite led the people to freedom. The notion of a unified national movement characterized much of the earlier historical writings. Contrary to this, the Cambridge School emphasized regional and local variations within the nationalist movement. Bengal occupied a prime place in their writings. In the study of this particular province and its relation with the nation in the field of nationalist politics, the Cambridge School has concentrated mainly on factionalism and cliques among the elite and the consequent decline of the Congress in Bengal. It has been argued that the Congress in Bengal, which was based on the great city, was facing a crisis within 20 years of the First World War. By 1929 the extension of franchise and the communal award spelt ruin for the Bengal Congress. Its breach with the central leadership forced the Bengal Congress to accept decisions which affected its organizational strength. Bengal no longer played the role of trendsetter in the nationalist movement. In recent times contributions by scholars belonging to the subaltern studies group have shifted attention from the elite to the subaltern classes in their analysis of the dynamics of nationalist politics. They pointed out that throughout the colonial period the domain of subaltern politics existed parallel to the domain of elite politics. This was an autonomous area that did not depend on the elite for their origin or existence. The two domains merged only with the efforts of the bourgeoisie and in an atmosphere of strong and clearly defined anti-imperialist objective.
3. Jibanananda Das, *Rupasi Bangla; Deshbandhu 1326–1332 smarane rachanakal 1932* (published 1957). The poem describes the coming of C R Das to Bengal as its leader and also the expectations that he would free the country from all crisis.
4. First Annual Report of the Bombay Presidency Association, 1885; also cited in Seal, *The Emergence of Indian Nationalism, op. cit.*
5. It had no permanent organization, no officials other than a general secretary, no central office, no funds and no paying members. The members gathered every year in an annual conference in a particular city. Here the reception committee recruited and financed and collected funds locally, hired lodgings and made general preparations for the conference. After the session, this committee worked for a few

more weeks to arrange for the printing and distribution of the Congress reports Then there was an interregnum for some months until another reception committee was organized in the city hosting the next Congress. Each session was a separate and independent undertaking, organizationally and financially. Cited in Seal, *The Emergence of Indian Nationalism, op. cit.*

6. *Liberty,* April 1930.
7. Ray, Rajat, 1984, *Social Conflict and Political Unrest in Bengal, 1875–1927,* Delhi.
8. *Ibid.*
9. Tripathi, Amalesh, 1967, *The Extremist Challenge. India Between 1890 and 1910,* Calcutta.
10. Bipin Chandra Pal, 'Swadeshi and Swaraj', quoted in Tripathi, *The Extremist Challenge, op. cit.*
11. Gokhale Papers, Satyananda Bose to Gokhale, 16 December 1906. Cited in Ray, *Social Conflict and Political Unrest in Bengal, op. cit.*
12. Ray, *Social Conflict and Political Unrest in Bengal, op. cit.*
13. *Bengalee,* 1917.
14. *Ibid.*
15. In the first case it was a revolt against the racial domination of the European planters, their use of coercive methods in the cultivation of indigo by the plantation system. Throughout the 1840s and the 1850s Muslim peasantry of the Faraidi sect led by Dudhu Miya clashed with the planters, *zamindars* and government officials. Between 1859 and 1862, a definite anti-planter movement developed first in Nadia and then across the entire delta region of Bengal. Incidentally, the movement developed when the Bengal government refused to support the planters and demanded that they should conform to the law. The uprising took a more radical turn to a no-rent campaign against the planters and the landlords. Even threats of eviction failed to break the solidarity of the peasants, who fought back on legal grounds against eviction. Peasant revolt against the coercion of the landlords crystallized in the districts of Pabna, Bogra, Dacca, Mymensingh, Tippera, Faridpur, Bakarganj, Rajshahi, Hooghly and Midnapur in the 1870s. The agitation occurred as a result of ever-increasing rent demand by the *zamindars* and was also due to attacks on the rights of occupancy granted to the tenants by the Rent Act of 1859 which the landlords refused to recognize. The peasants formed agrarian leagues in Dacca and Pabna and collected money to fight rent cases in the courts. The movement remained largely non-violent. The peasants demonstrated anti-*zamindar* feeling but there was no anti-British sentiment among them. They wanted to be made '*rayats* of Queen of England' so that they could enjoy a fixed land-tax settlement like the peasants of British India. Cited in Hardiman, David, 1992, *Peasant Resistance in India 1858–1914.*
16. Sumit Sarkar, 'The Condition and Nature of Subaltern Militancy' in Ranajit Guha (ed.), 1984, *Subaltern Studies Vol III.*
17. *Ibid.*
18. The *Amrita Bazar Patrika,* 1920.
19. Rajkumar, N V, 'The Development of the Congress Constitution'; also cited in Pandey, Gyan, 1978, *The Ascendancy of the Congress in Uttar Pradesh 1926–34,* Delhi.
20. 'Rules and Regulations Framed by Various Provincial Congress Committees 1921', All India Congress Committee Papers, File No 2.

Chapter I

1. 'Report on the Newspapers Published in Bengal during the Year 1920', Home Poll Conf File No 145, Sl No 1–4.
2. *Ibid*.
3. 'Census of India 1921' Vol V, Government of India, Bengal pt-2, tables, R H; Cassen 'India Population Economy and Society', quoted in Basu, Sugata, 'Peasant Labour And Colonial Capital: Rural Bengal Since 1770', in *The New Cambridge History Of India*, Cambridge 1993.
4. *Ibid*.
5. *Ibid*.
6. Evans, G, Director of Agriculture, 'Season and Crop Report', Government of Bengal Agriculture Department, Agriculture Branch, File No 7R–8, Sl No 1–2.
7. Government of Bengal Commerce Department, File No 3C–1, April 1930.
8. Curjel, Dagmar F, Womens' Medical Service, India, 'Women's Role in the Bengal Industries', Bulletin of the Indian Industries and Labour No 31.
9. 'The Journal of Indian Industries and Labour', The *Statesman*, March 1921.
10. 'Report on Strikes', Home Poll File No 264 Part B, November 1920.
11. *Ibid*.
12. Kumar, Ravinder, 1983, *Essays in the Social History of Modern India*, Delhi.
13. 'Fortnightly Report on the Political Situation in Bengal 1920', Home Poll Conf.
14. Bandyopadhyay, Sekhar, 1990, *Caste, Politics and the Raj: Bengal 1872–1939*, Calcutta.
15. Gordon, Leonard, 1979, *Bengal :The Nationalist Movement 1876–1940*, New Delhi.
16. Digindra Narayan Bhattacharya; *Jatibhed (Sirajganj, Jaistha* 1319) quoted in Bandhopadhyay, *Caste, Politics and the Raj, op. cit.*
17. 'Fortnightly Report on the Internal Political Situation for the Second Half of December 1920', Government of India Political Deposit No 77, February 1921.
18. Sekhar, *Caste, Politics and the Raj, op. cit.*
19. Gandhi, M K, 1958, *Collected Works* Vol 15, Delhi.
20. *Ibid*.
21. 'Calcutta Disturbances', Home Poll File No 223 Sl No 1–15.
22. An Appeal To The Public. Mahatma Gandhi arrested. Printed at the *Biswamitra Karjyalaya*. Banerji Press, Burrabazar, Calcutta:
Friends wake up,
   This is not the time to sit idle. The Black Bill has been set in motion. The leader of the Satyagraha and a great man of action, Mahatma Gandhi had been arrested. What wonder if the people of India are excited at this. There is no need for this Act to the innocent Indians. Now is the time to show how much inherent power the Indians possess. When man has got the power to avert his own calamity, then what difficulty can there be in abrogating the Black Bill. thirty-three crores of Indian souls are like gods. If all the Indians take the vow of Satyagraha and unite themselves to act, the Government will be compelled to give up their brute force. So long as Mahatma Gandhi is not ordered to return all Indians (Hindus, Musalmaans and other sects) should observe this (vow) by agitating. There will be plenty of time to earn money. But we won't have such evil days as have fallen upon us. Consequently so long as the Rowlatt Bill no-12 is not repealed, every Indian should take the vow of Satyagraha. It is hoped every Hindu and Musalmaan will give up their luxuries, be ready to devote themselves for the welfare of the country and will act up peacefully to the bidding of Mahatma Gandhi.
   An Indian.

'Calcutta Disturbances', Home Poll Conf File No 223 Sl No 1–15.

23. 'Calcutta Disturbances', Home Poll Conf File No 223, Sl No 1–15.
24. *Ibid*.
25. *Ibid*.
26. *Ibid*.
27. *Ibid*.
28. *Ibid*.
29. 'Fortnightly Report on the Political Situation in Bengal 1920', Home Poll Conf.
30. Brown, Judith, 1972, *Gandhi's Rise to Power in Indian Politics 1915–1922*, Cambridge.
31. *Ibid*.
32. '*Khilafat* Agitation', Home Poll Conf File No 106/20 (51–61).
33. 'Mohammedan Agitation in Connection with the Allies Settlement with Turkey', Home Poll Conf File No 106/20 (1–36).
34. *Ibid*.
35. *Ibid*.
36. '*Khilafat* Agitation', Home Poll Conf File No 106/20 (51–61).
37. *Amrita Bazar Patrika*, February 1920.
38. The other resolutions of the conference were as follows: Muslims engaged in the British forces should sever connections with the government and if they failed to do so, they would be ostracized; the conference expected Hindu brethren to cooperate with the Muslims in this matter.
39. *Amrita Bazar Patrika*, February 1920.
40. '*Khilafat* Agitation', Home Poll Conf File No 106/20 (51–61).
41. *Ibid*.
42. *Ibid*.
43. 'The Non-Cooperation Movement in Bengal', Home Poll Conf File No 39.
44. *Ibid*.
45. *Ibid*.
46. 1920 saw two historic sessions of the National Congress which virtually changed the character and creed of the Indian National Congress. After much deliberation, the Calcutta special session in September and then the Nagpur session of the Congress in December agreed to experiment with the new technique of non-cooperation, which would carry institutional politics to the people.

Chapter 2

1. Congress constitution adopted at Nagpur CW Vol 19. Information about the appointment of the committee is in a letter drafted by Gandhi from the committee to the AICC, 25 September 1920; also cited in Judith Brown, 1972, *Gandhi's Rise to Power, Indian Politics 1915–22*, Cambridge.
2. Khaparde Papers; also cited in Brown, *Gandhi's Rise to Power, op. cit.*
3. Rajkumar, N V, *The Development of the Congress Constitution*; also cited in Pandey, *The Ascendancy of the Congress in Uttar Pradesh, op. cit.*
4. Brown, *Gandhi's Rise To Power, op. cit.*
5. *Ibid*.
6. 'Rules and Regulations Framed by Various PCCS, 1921', AICC Papers, File No 2.T.L.24.
7. *Ibid*.

8. *Ibid.*
9. *Ibid.*
10. *Ibid.*
11. *Ibid.*
12. Hemendranath Dasgupta, B S, 1333, *Deshbandhu Smriti*, Calcutta.
13. *Ibid.*
14. *Ibid.*
15. *The Musalman*, 18 April 1921.
16. *Ibid.*
17. *The Musalman*, May 1921.
18. 'Fortnightly Report of the Political Situation in Bengal, 1921'.
19. 'Rules and Regulations Framed by Various PCCS, 1921', AICC Papers *op. cit.*
20. Bandyopadhyay, Gitashree, 'Impact of Gandhi on Bengal Politics 1921–41', (PhD Thesis, Calcutta University, 1978).
21. *The Musalman*, 1921.
22. *Ibid.*
23. *Amrita Bazar Patrika*, 14 May 1921.
24. In principle every village with a maximum of five Congress members could set up a village Congress committee. Each town with a population of 50,000 was to have a town Congress committee and a town circle committee.
25. *The Musalman*, 1921.
26. Sarkar, Chandi Prasad, 1991, *The Bengali Muslims: A Study in Their Politicization, 1912–1929*, Calcutta.
27. GBIB Conf File No 121/22, Part II, week ending 26 November 1921.
28. 'Report on the Non-Cooperation and *Khilafat* Activities for the Months of January–March 1922', GBIB Conf File.
29. 'Report on the Non-Cooperation and Labour for the Week Ending 26th February 1921', IB File No 121/21.
30. 'Statement of Tilak Swaraj Fund Collection Compiled from Civil Disobedience Report', Home Poll File No 741, 1922.
31. Dasgupta, *Deshbandhu Smriti, op. cit.*
32. *Ibid.*
33. *Ibid.*
34. *Ibid.*
35. 'Propaganda Arrangements in East Bengal', Home Poll Conf File No 209/192 SL No 1–9.
36. Dasgupta, *Deshbandhu Smriti, op. cit.*
37. *Ibid.*
38. *Ibid.*
39. *Ibid.*
40. Interview with Vijay Singh Nahar, March 1992.
41. Ray, Rajat, 1984, *Social Conflict and Political Unrest in Bengal, 1875–1927*, Delhi.
42. Birla, G D, 1953, *In the Shadow of the Mahatma; A Personal Memoir*, Calcutta.
43. Hitesh Ranjan Sanyal, *Dakshin Paschim Banglay Jatiatabadi Andolan* published in *Anya Artha* and *Chaturanga* in *Kartik Poush*, 1383.
44. *Ibid.*
45. *Ibid.*
46. 'The Situation as regards Non-Cooperation in Rangpur', Home Poll Conf File No 333 SL No 30–46.
47. *Ibid.*
48. 'Proclaiming of Swaraj Ashram as an Unlawful Association Under Act XIV of 1908', Home Poll Conf File No 333 SL No 55–9.

49. *Ibid.*
50. *The Musalman*, April 1921.
51. Ray, *Social Conflict and Political Unrest in Bengal, op. cit.*
52. *Ibid.*
53. *Ibid.*
54. *The Musalman*, April 1921.
55. *Ibid.*
56. Gordon, Leonard, 1974, *Bengal: The Nationalist Movement 1876–1940.*
57. Dasgupta, *Deshbandhu Smriti, op. cit.*
58. *Ibid.*
59. Roy, Prithwis Chandra, 1927, *Life and Times of C R Das*, London.
60. *Ibid.*
61. Gordon, *Bengal: The Nationalist Movement, op. cit.*
62. Roy, *Life and Times of C R Das, op. cit.*
63. *Ibid.*
64. *Ibid.*
65. Gordon, *Bengal: The Nationalist Movement, op. cit.*
66. Roy, *Life and Times of C R Das, op. cit.*
67. *Ibid.*
68. Gordon, *Bengal: The Nationalist Movement, op. cit.*; Dasgupta, *Deshbandhu Smriti, op. cit.*
69. Roy, *Life and Times of C R Das, op. cit.*
70. *Ibid.*
71. *Ibid.*
72. Ray, *Social Conflict and Political Unrest in Bengal, op. cit.*
73. 'Proclaiming of Swaraj Ashram as an Unlawful Association under the Act XIV of 1908', Home Poll Conf File No 333.
74. Padmini Sengupta, 1968, *Deshapriya Jatindra Mohan*, Delhi.
75. *Ibid.*
76. *Ibid.*
77. *Ibid.*
78. Hitesh Ranjan Sanyal, *Dakshin Paschim Banglay Jatiatabadi Andolan, op. cit.*
79. *Ibid.*
80. *Ibid.*
81. *Ibid.*
82. *Ibid.*
83. *Ibid.*
84. *Ibid.*
85. *Ibid.*
86. Gordon, *Bengal: The Nationalist Movement 1876–1940, op. cit.*
87. Banerjee, Nripendra Chandra, 1950, *At the Cross Roads*, Calcutta.
88. *Ibid.*
89. Ghosh, Atulya, 1984, *Kastakalpita* Vol 1, Calcutta.
90. Subhas Chandra Bose, 1981, *The Indian Struggle 1920–42, Netaji Collected Works Volume II*, Calcutta.
91. *Ibid.*
92. Gordon, *Bengal: The Nationalist Movement 1876–1940, op. cit.*
93. Ray, *Social Conflict and Political Unrest in Bengal, op. cit.*
94. Datta, Bhupendra Kumar, 1973, *Viplaber Padachinha*, Calcutta. Also in Purnananda Dasgupta, 1954, *Viplaber Pathe*, Calcutta.
95. *Ibid.*
96. *Ibid.*

97. *Ibid.*
98. *Ibid.*
99. 'Measures for Dealing with Revolutionary Activities in Bengal', HP 1924 KW File No 379/I.
100. Datta, *Viplaber Padachinha, op. cit.*
101. Sen, S P, (ed.), 1972–74, *Dictionary of National Biography*, Calcutta.
102. *Ibid.*
103. *Ibid.*
104. *Ibid.*
105. Datta, *Viplaber Padachinha, op. cit.*
106. Sen (ed.), *Dictionary of National Biography, op. cit.*
107. Datta, *Viplaber Padachinha, op. cit.*
108. *Sansad Bangali Charit Abhidhan, Vol 1, Sahitya Sansad*, third edition, July 1994.
109. *Ibid.*
110. 'Revolutionary Movement in Bengal', Home Poll 1924 File No 379/II.
111. Ray, *Social Conflict and Political Unrest in Bengal, op. cit.*
112. 'Non-Cooperation Movement in Bengal', IB File No 121/21.
113. *Sansad Bangali Charitabhidhan, op. cit.*
114. *Dictionary of National Biography, op. cit.*
115. 'Measures for Coping with Revolutionary Activities in Bengal', Home Poll KW 1924, File No 379/I.
116. *Sansad Bangali Charitabhidhan, op. cit.*
117. *Dictionary of National Biography, op. cit.*
118. *Ibid.*
119. Sanyal, *Dakshin Paschim Banglay Jatiatabadi Andolan, op. cit.*
120. *Ibid.*
121. 'Fortnightly Report of the Political Situation in Bengal, 1921'.
122. 'Search of Hooghly *Vidya Mandir*', IB File No 244/23.
123. Menault, Gail, 1982, *The Khilafat Movement: Religious Symbolism and Political Mobilisation in India*, Oxford.
124. *Ibid.*
125. *Ibid.*
126. Sarkar, *The Bengali Muslims, op. cit.*
127. *Ibid.*
128. *Ibid.*
129. *Ibid.*
130. *Ibid.*
131. Sarkar, *The Bengali Muslims, op. cit.*
132. *Ibid.*
133. *Ibid.*
134. 'Fortnightly Report for the 1st half of October 1920', GI Secret Home (Poll) Deposit Progs December 1920, No 59.
135. *Ibid.*
136. 'History of the Non-Cooperation and *Khilafat* Movement in Bengal', Home Poll Conf File No 395, 1921.
137. *The Musalman*, 12 March 1920.
138. *The Musalman*, 1920.
139. *Ibid.*
140. 'Fortnightly Report for the 1st half of October 1920', GI Secret Home (Poll) Deposit Progs December 1920, No 59.
141. Hardy, Peter, 1972, *The Muslims of India*, Cambridge.
142. Report of The Native Newspapers, 1921.

143. Report on The Native Newspapers of Bengal, 1921.
144. *The Musalman*, 1921; *The Muhammadi*, 1921.
145. *The Musalman*, October 1919.
146. '*Khilafat* Agitation', Home Poll Conf File No 106 Sl No 62/75, 1920.
147. 'Non-Cooperation Movement and *Khilafat* Agitation', Home Poll Conf File No 46/21.
148. Kabir, Humayun, 1944, *Moslem Rajniti*, Calcutta.
149. Notes by Intelligence Branch, CID Bengal.
150. *Ibid.*
151. *Ibid.*
152. 'Question of Introduction of Special Legislation to Deal with the Volunteer Movement', Home Poll Conf File No 333 Sl No 14.
153. *Ibid.*
154. *Ibid.*
155. *Ibid.*
156. *Ibid.*
157. *Ibid.*
158. *Ibid.*
159. *Ibid.*
160. *Ibid.*
161. *Ibid.*
162. *Ibid.*
163. *Ibid.*
164. *Ibid.*
165. *Ibid.*
166. 'The Situation as Regards Non-Cooperation in Rangpur', Home Poll Conf File No 333 Sl No 30–46.
167. *Ibid.*
168. *Ibid.*
169. *Ibid.*
170. *Ibid.*
171. *Ibid.*
172. *Ibid.*
173. *Ibid.*
174. 'Question of Introduction of Special Legislation to Deal with the Volunteer Movement', Home Poll Conf File No 298 Sl No 1–8, 1921.
175. *Ibid.*
176. 'Proclaiming of Certain Objectionable Volunteer Corps Under Acts XIV of 1908', Home Poll Conf File No 333.
177. *Ibid.*
178. *Ibid.*
179. 'Proclaiming of the *Swaraj Ashram* as an Unlawful Association under Act XIV of 1908', Home Poll Conf File No 333.
180. 'Report on the National Schools in Bengal in the Year 1919', Home Poll Conf File No 145, Sl No 1–3, 1921.
181. 'Report of the National Schools in Bengal for the Year 1920', Home Poll Conf File No 210, Sl No 1–3, 1921.
182. *Ibid.*
183. 'National Schools Opened as a Result of Non-Cooperation Movement', Home Poll Conf File No 401/20.
184. *Ibid.*
185. *Ibid.*

186. Ghosh, *Kastakalpita*, Vol 1, *op. cit.*
187. Banerjee, *At the Cross Roads, op. cit.*
188. The *Forward*, 1926.
189. Fortnightly Report on the Political Situation in Bengal, 1921.
190. 'The Bangiya Swaraj Sevak Sangha', IB File No 91/1921 Sl No 108, 1921.
191. *Ibid.*
192. Ghosh, *Kastakalpita*, Vol I, *op. cit.*
193. Datta, *Viplaber Padachinha, op. cit.*
194. 'Anushilan Activity', IB File No 258, 1923.

Chapter 3

1. 'History of the Non-Cooperation and Khilafat Movement in Bengal', Home Poll Conf File No 395/24.
2. *Ibid.*
3. *Ibid.*
4. *Ibid.*
5. *The Musalman*, Report on Native Newspapers 1921, WBSA.
6. *The Musalman*, January 1921.
7. *Amrita Bazar Patrika*, 1921.
8. *Ibid.*
9. 'History of the Non-Cooperation and Khilafat Movement in Bengal', *op. cit.*
10. *Ibid.*
11. Ray, Rajat, 1984, *Social Conflict and Political Unrest in Bengal, 1875–1927*, Delhi.
12. *Ibid.*
13. Home Poll, March 1921, 53 Deposit Collection of Information Regarding Non-Cooperation.
14. 'Strike at Ichapur Rifle Factory', IB File No 75, 1921.
15. 'Non-Cooperation Movement in Bengal', IB File No 267 (IV)/20.
16. 'The Present Political Situation', Home Poll Conf File No 14/21 Sl Nos 1–20.
17. The *Amrita Bazar Patrika*, 1920.
18. Report on Native Newspapers, 1921.
19. *Ibid.*
20. RNP List of Papers and Periodicals, 1921.
21. *Ibid.*
22. *Ibid.*
23. RNP 1921.
24. Ray, *Social Conflict and Political Unrest in Bengal, op. cit.*
25. Hitesh Ranjan Sanyal, *Dakshin Paschim Banglay Jatiotabadi Andolan*, in *Anya Artha* and *Chaturanga, Kartik-Poush, 1383*.
26. RNP 1921.
27. *Ibid.*
28. *The Musalman*, 1921.
29. RNP 1921.
30. *Ibid.*
31. 'List of Common Bengali Songs on Record in the political Branch of CID', Home Poll Conf File No 72/21, 1921.
32. 'Fortnightly Report on the Political Situation in Bengal', 1921.

33. Ray, *Social Conflict and Political Unrest in Bengal, op. cit.*
34. Sanyal, *Dakshin Paschim Banglay Jatiotabadi Andolan, op. cit.*
35. 'Report on Non Cooperation and Labour', IB File No 121/21.
36. *Ibid.*
37. *Ibid.*
38. *Ibid.*
39. *Ibid.*
40. 'The Bangiya Swaraj Sevak Sangha', IB File No 91, Sl No 108, 1921.
41. 'Report on the Non-Cooperation Movement in Bengal During February 1921', IB File No 267 (IV)/20.
42. *Ibid.*
43. 'Report on Non-Cooperation and Labour', IB File No 121/21.
44. 'History of the Non-cooperation and Khilafat Movement in Bengal', Home Poll Conf File No 395, 1924.
45. Sanyal, *Dakshin Paschim Banglay Jatiotabadi Andolan Bankur, op. cit.*
46. 'Proclaiming of the *Swaraj Ashram* as an Unlawful Association Under Act XIV of 1908', Home Poll Conf File No 333/21 Sl. No 55–9.
47. *Ibid.*
48. Home Poll Deposit, No 90, July 1920. Also cited in Judith Brown, 1972, *Gandhi's Rise to Power, Indian Politics 1915–22*, Cambridge.
49. *Ibid.*
50. *The Musalman*, 1921.
51. 'History of the Non-Cooperation and Khilafat Movement in Bengal', Home Poll Conf File No 395, 1924.
52. *Ibid.*
53. Brown, *Gandhi's Rise To Power, op. cit.*
54. *The Musalman*, January 1921.
55. *Ibid.*
56. *Ibid.*
57. *Ibid.*
58. *Ibid.*
59. The *Indian Daily News*, 25 January 1921, RNP 1921.
60. Someswar Prasad Roy Chaudhuri, 1972, *Nilkar Bidroha*, Calcutta.
61. 'Non-Cooperation in Schools and Colleges in Bengal', Home Poll Conf File No 34/21.
62. 'The Non-Cooperation and Khilafat Movement in Bengal', IB File No 267 (IV)/20.
63. 'Non-Cooperation in Schools and Colleges in Bengal', Home Poll Conf File No 34/21.
64. *Ibid.*
65. 'Orders Prohibiting C R Das from Entering Mymensingh and the General Situation in Mymensingh', Home Poll Conf File No 93/21 SL No 1–2.
66. 'Report on the Non-Cooperation and Labour for the Week Ending 26th February 1921', IB File No 121/1921.
67. 'The Non-Cooperation Movement in Bengal', IB File No 267 (IV)/20.
68. Prabasi, Baishak-Chaitra, 1328.
69. *Ibid.*
70. 'Report of the Effect of the Visit of H.R.H The Duke of Connaught to Calcutta', Home Poll Conf File No 49 Sl No 1–6, 1921.
71. *Ibid.*
72. *Ibid.*
73. 'History of the Non-Cooperation and Khilafat Movement in Bengal', Home Poll Conf File No 395/24.
74. 'Proclaiming of the Swaraj Ashram as an Unlawful Association under Act XIV of 1908', Home Poll Conf File No 333/21 Sl No 55–59.

75. *Ibid.*
76. 'Report on the Non-Cooperation Movement in Bengal During February 1921', IB File No 267 (IV)/20.
77. 'Report on Non-Cooperation and Labour', IB File No 121/1921, Sl No 118/21.
78. *Ibid.*
79. *Ibid.*
80. 'History of the Non-Cooperation and Khilafat Movement in Bengal', Home Poll Conf File No 395/24.
81. *The Musalman*, 1921.
82. *Ibid.*
83. *Ibid.*
84. *Ibid.*
85. *Ibid.*
86. 'The Present Political Situation in Bengal', Home Poll File No 39/21, SL No 129–139.
87. 'The Present Political Situation', Home Poll Conf File No 14/22, SL No 24.
88. 'The Non-Cooperation Movement and the Attitude of the Government Towards That Movement', Home Poll Conf File No 39, SL No 1–2, 1921.
89. 'Extracts from Intelligence Branch Secret Reports for the Week Ending 12 March 1913', Home Poll File No 66/1913; cited in Sarkar, Sumit, 'The Conditions and Nature of Subaltern Militancy', in Guha, Ranajit (ed.), *Subaltern Studies III*, Delhi.
90. *Ibid.*
91. *The Statesman*, 12 March 1921.
92. *Ibid.*
93. *Ibid.*
94. *Ibid.*
95. *Ibid.*
96. 'Report on Non-Cooperation and Labour', IB File No 121, 1921.
97. President: J N Ray; Vice-Presidents: C R Das, C F Andrews, S N Haldar, Syed Irfan Ali, Padam Raj Jain; Secretary: Muhammad Mohsin; Assistant Secretaries: Nisith Chandra Sen, Bhola Nath Barman, office bearers of the different labour unions.
98. *Ibid.*
99. 'List of Labour Unions and Associations', IB File No 318, 1921.
100. *Ibid.*
101. *Ibid.*
102. 'Report on Non-Cooperation and Labour', IB File No 121, 1921.
103. *Ibid.*
104. *Ibid.*
105. *Ibid.*
106. *Ibid.*
107. *Ibid.*
108. *Ibid.*
109. *Ibid.*
110. *Ibid.*
111. 'Report on Non-Cooperation and Labour', IB File No 121, 1921.
112. *Ibid.*
113. 'Report of the Committee on Industrial Unrest'. Supplement to *The Calcutta Gazette*, 22 June 1921.
114. *Ibid.*
115. *Ibid.*
116. *Ibid.*
117. *Ibid.*
118. *Ibid.*

119. 'Volunteer Movement', Home Poll Conf File No 333, Sl No 14.
120. Ray, *Social Conflict and Political Unrest in Bengal, op. cit.*
121. 'Non-Cooperation Movement in Bengal', IB File No 267 (IV)/20.
122. *Ibid.*
123. 'Report on Non-Cooperation and Labour', IB File No 121, 1921.
124. *Ibid.*
125. Gourlay, S N, 'Nationalists, Outsiders, And Labour Movement in Bengal', in Kumar (ed.), *Congress and Class, op. cit.*
126. 'Report on Non-Cooperation and Labour', IB File No 121, 1921; Ray, *Social Conflict and Political Unrest in Bengal, op. cit.*
127. 'Production of Original Telegrams Exchanged between Non-Cooperators on the Chandpur and Chittagong Strikes', IB File No 248/21, Sl No 44, 1921.
128. Padmini Sengupta, 1968, *Deshapriya Jatindramohan*, Delhi.
129. 'Report on Non-Cooperation and Labour', IB File No 121, 1921.
130. *Ibid.*
131. 'Production of Original Telegrams Exchanged between the Non-Cooperators on the Chandpur and Chittagong Strikes', *op. cit.*
132. 'Report on Non-Cooperation and Labour', *op. cit.*
133. *Ibid.*
134. *Ibid.*
135. 'The Present Political Situation in Bengal and the Policy to be Adopted towards Non-Cooperation Movement', Home Poll Conf File No 39/21, Sl No 129–137.
136. Report of the 35th INC in Judith Brown, *Gandhis Rise To Power, op. cit.*
137. The *Amrita Bazar Patrika* 25 December 1921, RNP, 1921.
138. *The Collected Works of Gandhi* (WMG) Vol XIX. (Ahmedabad 1966).
139. *The Musalman*, 8 April 1921.
140. 'History of the Non-Cooperation and Khilafat Movement in Bengal', Home Political Conf File No 395/24.
141. 'Season and Crop Report', Agriculture Department, Agriculture Branch File No 7R-8, Sl No 1–2.
142. Sarkar, *The Condition and Nature of Subaltern Militancy, op. cit.*; Judith Brown, *Gandhi's Rise to power, op. cit.*
143. 'Season and Crop Report', Agriculture Department, *op. cit.*
144. Sanyal, *Dakshin Paschim Banglay Jatiyatabadi Andolan, op. cit.*
145. Bhaduri, Satinath, 1973, *Dhorai Charit Manas Satinath Granthabali*, Vol II.
146. Shahid Amin, 'Gandhi as *Mahatma*' in *Subaltern Studies III, op. cit.*
147. 'History of the Non-Cooperation and Khilafat Movement in Bengal', *op. cit.*
148. *Ibid.*
149. Bengal Legislative Council Proceedings, 1921.
150. 'History of the Non-Cooperation and Khilafat Movement in Bengal', Home Political Conf File No 395/24.
151. *The Musalman*, 16 February 1921.
152. *The Musalman* 11 March 1921.
153. 'History of the Non-Cooperation and Khilafat Movement in Bengal', *op. cit.*
154. *Ibid.*
155. *Ibid.*
156. Rabindra Nath Tagore, *Swaraj Sadhan, Kalantar, (Aswin 1332)* Rabindra Rachanabali Dwadash Khanda, *Biswabharati* 1397.
157. 'History of the Non-Cooperation Movement in Bengal', *op. cit.*
158. 'Final report on the Survey and Settlement Operations in the District of Rajsahi, August 1923', Land Revenue Department, Land Revenue Branch.
159. Chaudhuri, *Nilkar Bidroha, op. cit.*

160. *Ibid.*
161. *Ibid.*
162. *Ibid.*
163. *Ibid.*
164. *Ibid.*
165. *Ibid.*
166. *Ibid.*
167. 'The Present Political Situation', Home Poll Conf File No 14/22.
168. *Ibid.*
169. 'History of the Non-Cooperation and Khilafat Movement', *op. cit.*
170. *Ibid.*
171. Annual Report of Survey and Settlement Operations in Pabna, Bogra. Revenue Department Land Revenue Branch Proceeding Volume, June 1923.
172. *Ibid.*
173. *Ibid.*
174. *Ibid.*
175. 'Assault on M R Macpherson while on Visit to Dakumara *hat* Thana, Garbetta', Home Poll Conf File No 315, Sl No 1–11, 1921.
176. *Ibid.*
177. Survey and Settlement Report of Pabna and Bogra, Land Revenue Department, Land Revenue Branch.
178. 'Assault on M R Macpherson while on Visit to Dakumara *hat* Thana, Garbetta', *op. cit.*
179. *Ibid.*
180. *Ibid.*
181. 'Proposed Action Against Obstruction to Settlement Operations in the Birbhum District', Home Poll Conf File No 347, Sl No 1–5.
182. Eastern Midnapur was comprised of Ghatal Mahakuma, Sadar Mahakuma, Keshpur, Debra, Midnapur Sadar, Kharagpur, Pingla, Sabong, Narayanganj, Datan, and Mohanpur *thana*. The agricultural lands here were owned by influential *Jotedars* or *Chakdars*. They employed share croppers who cultivated their lands in return for a share of half the rice and straw. In eastern Midnapur the dominant caste group was the *Mahisya*. Since the eighteenth century the *Mahisyas* had been trying to raise their caste status and this social movement had spread considerably among the poorer section. Uniformity of caste enabled the rich *Mahisyas* to establish control over their less affluent brethren through this social movement. In political movements too, this link between the rich and poor *Mahisyas* helped to build up a united agitation. Birendra Nath Sasmal, who led the movement in Midnapur, came from an affluent family of Chandibheti village, which had a premier position in the earlier social movement.
183. Bhattacharjee, Buddhadev, 1977, *Satyagrahas in Bengal*, Calcutta.
184. *Ibid.*
185. This would also affect the permanently settled areas, as the tax increase was to take place in reference to the villagers agricultural income. Moreover, the villagers felt that the appointments and dismissals of the *chaukidars* by the district magistrate or his delegates contradicted the term 'local self-government'. It was entirely possible that in order for the Act to have any effect at all the maximum rate allowed had to be imposed, but the people maintained that they simply could not pay that rate. It was implied that the Act would increase party factions. The villagers also felt that such tax increases would directly impact health conditions in the villages, where most deaths occurred from malnutrition. Finally Sasmal pointed out that all the repressive measures (such as attachment of property by

Tahsildars appointed under section 54) undertaken in the name of the Act were illegal, including such official proceedings as the election of presidents after 15 April. The union boards could not make assessment of any kind even two and a half months before 15 April although the Union Boards were supposed to start functioning on 15 April based on these assessments, nor did old assessments of any kind exist after that date. So resentment was high as the authorities began to carry out the Act.

186. GB Local Self Government, Local Boards Branch L2U – 5(i)A 36–43, July 1923.
187. *Ibid.*
188. *Ibid.*
189. *Ibid.*
190. Bhattacharya, *Satyagrahas In Bengal op. cit.*
191. 'History of the Non-Cooperation and Khilafat Movement in Bengal', *op. cit.*
192. *Ibid.*
193. *Ibid.*
194. The Jungle Mahals comprised the *thanas* of Binpur Garbetta, Gopiballavpur, Jhargram and Salboni. This tract of land, a heavily forested and infertile area of about 1,827 square miles in the north and west of Midnapur district was mainly inhabited by *adivasis – Santal, Bhumij, Kurmi (Mahato)* and some low caste Hindus (*Bagdis, Goala* and *Sadgope*) mainly in the southern part of the area. At the end of the nineteenth century this tract of land was divided among several large landowners. They included the Midnapur Zamindari Company, managed by Andrew Yule and Company, with holdings scattered around Garbeta, Salboni and Silda Pargana, the Jhargram Raj over the major portions of Jhargram *thana* and estates belonging to the Raja of Mayurbhanj and the Nawab of Murshidabad in extensive tracts in Gopiballavpur.
195. 'Disturbances in Jamboni in the district of Midnapore', Home Poll Conf File No 181, 1923.
196. *Ibid.*
197. *Amrita Bazar Patrika*, 1921.
198. 'Disturbances In Jamboni in the District of Midnapore', Home Poll Conf File No 181, 1923.
199. *Ibid.*
200. *Ibid.*
201. 'Report of L Birley, 28 January 1922', Home Poll File No 87/22.
202. 'Disturbances in Jamboni in the District of Midnapore', Home Poll Conf File No 181, 1923.
203. Sanyal, *Dakshin Paschim Banglay Jatiatabadi Andolan, op. cit.*
204. *Ibid.*
205. 'Report on Non-Cooperation and Labour', IB File No 121, 1921.
206. *Ibid.*
207. The Lessons Of Assam, *Young India*, 1921, Also cited in 'Report on Non-Cooperation and Labour', IB File No 121, 1921.
208. Sanyal, *Dakshin Paschim Banglay Jatiotabadi Andolan, op. cit.*
209. *Ibid.*
210. *Ibid.*
211. Sumit Sarkar discusses the role of rumours and religion in peasant activity in *The Condition and Nature of Subaltern Militancy, op. cit.*

Chapter 4

1. A civil disobedience committee was formed which rejected civil disobedience, boycott of schools, colleges and law courts unanimously. Motilal Nehru and Chittaranjan Das recommended that Congress should contest the elections and capture the councils. This group also included Lala Lajpat Rai, M R Jayakar, Vithalbhai Patel, the Tilak group in Bombay and the politicians of South India. C Rajagopalachari and the Gandhites objected to the question of participation in the reformed councils.
2. 'Effect of the Bardoli Resolution of the Congress Working Committee', IB File No 73/22.
3. *Ibid.*
4. Ray, *Social Conflict and Political Unrest in Bengal, op. cit.*
5. *Ibid.*
6. 'The Constitution of the Swarajya Party', AICC Papers, File No 12–14.
7. *Ibid.*
8. *Ibid.*
9. On 30 November 1923 a meeting of the provincial Congress committee was held. The Gandhites were in the majority as several members of Das's group were absent. Chittaranjan was compelled to make a compromise and a tentative offer to them to form a coalition executive committee with 30 members from each party. The no-changers accepted the offer. Das gave no definite assurance and the meeting was adjourned at his persuasion as it was late in the evening. Urgent telegrams were sent to provincial members who would support Das. The meeting reassembled on 2 December, with the *Swarajist* members having a clear majority. The no-changers made an unsuccessful attempted to elect Jitendra Lal Banerjee. 'Proceedings of the Khilafat Swaraj Party', IB File No 47/23, 1923.
10. *Ibid.*
11. Nirmal Chandra Chunder was the treasurer of the BPCC. Tulsi Charan Goswami was the treasurer of the All-India *Swarajya* Party. Nalini Ranjan Sarkar who was elected to the council with the help of the *Swarajya* Party became a member after the election and later became the chief whip and the secretary of the party. Bidhan Chandra Roy, a newcomer to politics successfully contested the election as a *Swarajya* candidate against the veteran politician Surendranath Banerjee. He became a member of the council. Sarat Chandra Bose was an important member of the party and was elected alderman of the Calcutta Corporation in 1924.
12. 'Anushilan Activity', IB File No 258, 1923.
13. 'Note on the Connection between the Revolutionaries and the Swarajya Party', Home Poll File No 379/II, 1924.
14. Home Poll File No 61, cited in Gordon, *Bengal, The Nationalist Movement, op. cit.*
15. 'Note on the Connection between the Revolutionaries and the Swarajya Party', Home Poll File No 379/II.
16. *Ibid.*
17. *Ibid.*
18. 'Non-Cooperation Movement', IB File No 3/23.
19. 'The *Wahabis*', IB File No 34/22, 1922.
20. *Sansad Bangali Charitabhidhan*, third edition, *Sahitya Sansad*, 1994.
21. 'The *Wahabis*', IB File No 34/22, 1922.
22. *Ibid.*
23. *Ibid.*
24. Atulya Ghosh, *Kastaklpita, op. cit.*
25. *Sansad Bangali Charitabhidhan, op. cit.*

26. Sanyal, *Dakshin Paschim Banglay Jatiotabadi Andolan, op. cit.*
27. 'Non-Cooperation and Khilafat Agitation', IB File No 2/24, 1924.
28. *Ibid.*
29. *Ibid.*
30. *Ibid.*
31. *Ibid.*
32. *Ibid.*
33. 'Muhammadans in Government Service', Bengal Legislative Council Proceedings, Vol XIV, No 4, March 12–14, 1924.
34. *Ibid.*
35. *Ibid.*
36. *Ibid.*
37. *Ibid.*
38. 'Fortnightly Reports on the Political Situation in Bengal, 1924', Freedom Movement Papers, File No 32.
39. *Ibid.*
40. Chatterjee, *Bengal, The Land Question 1920–1947, op. cit.*
41. Kenneth Macpherson, 1974, *The Muslim Microcosm: Calcutta 1918–1935*, Wiesbaden.
42. 'The Hindu Mahasabha, Mymensingh', IB File No 279, 1925.
43. 'Mohammedan Affair', IB File No 41, 1925.
44. *Ibid.*
45. 'Fortnightly Report of the Political Situation in Bengal', Freedom Movement Papers, File No 32.
46. 'Instructions to the District Magistrates about Village Reorganization Scheme of Swaraj Party', Home Poll Conf File No 469/25 (1):
    Calcutta: Suresh Chandra Das, Jnananjan Neogy (inspector of villages), Prafulla Mukherjee of Kishoreganj, Mymensingh (lecturer).
    Faridpur: Rebati Bose (revolutionary).
    Rajbari: Pramatha Guha (revolutionary).
    Gopalganj: Bidhu Bhusan Majumdar (revolutionary).
    Madaripur: Sudhendu Majumdar (revolutionary).
    Goalundo: Nagendra Nath Ghose.
    Khulna: Ananta Chakrabarty (revolutionary), Ranada Kanta Roy Choudhury (Headmaster, Maghia High School).
    Jessore: Bandabilla: Bejoy Chandra Ray (revolutionary).
    Bongong: Nanda Lal Biswas.
    Barisal: Rakhal Chandra Das (revolutionary).
    Malda: Jyotirmoy Sarma.
    Dacca, Munshiganj: Surendra Majumdar (revolutionary), Surendra Chandra Das (revolutionary).
    Midnapur, Gidni: Sailajananda Sen.
    Tamluk: Ajoy Mukherjee, Satish Samanta.
    Noakhali: Akterozzaman.
    Hooghly: Ananta Ghatak (revolutionary).
    Rangpur: Anuj Kumar Sen (revolutionary).
    24 Parganas: Diamond Harbour: Rasiklal Das (revolutionary).
    Sonarpur: Kali Charan Ghosh (revolutionary).
    Chittagong: Abdul Karim, Nizam Puri, Jagat Chandra Das.
    Burdwan: Jitendra Nath Ghose.
    Howrah: Bijay Ratan Bakshi (revolutionary), Rajendra Nath Dey (revolutionary), Bibhuti Bhusan Ghose.
    Sylhet: Anil Kumar Roy.

47. 'Fortnightly Report on the Political Situation in Bengal, 1925', Freedom Movement Papers, File No 33.
48. 'The Congress Party', IB File No 40, 1925.
49. *Ibid.*
50. *The Musalman*, November 1927.
51. 'The Congress Party', IB File No 40, 1925.
52. 'Bengal Election Dispute', AICC Papers G 120.
53. 'Non-Cooperation Movement In Bengal', IB File No 3, 1923.
54. 'Bengal Election Dispute', *op. cit.*
55. 'The Congress Party', IB File No 40, 1925.
56. 'Anushilan Activity', IB File No 258, 1923.
57. 'Enquiries regarding the Bankura Revolutionary Organization', IB File No 281, 1925.
58. *Ibid.*
59. 'Mohammedan Secret Organization in Calcutta', IB File No 196, 1925.
60. 'Youth Movement', Home Poll Conf File No 441, 1929.
61. 'The All Bengal Youngmen's Association', IB File No 320/22.
62. *Ibid.*
63. *Ibid.*
64. *Forward*, 1926.
65. *Ibid.*
66. 'Abhoy Ashram, Dacca', IB File No 30/30.
67. 'Abhoy Ashram, Comilla', IB File No 30/30.
68. 'Abhoy Ashram, Midnapore', IB File No 30/30.
69. 'The Congress Party', IB File No 40/25, 1925.
70. '*Sabha Samitis* in Bengal', IB File No 46/24.
71. '*Anushilan* Activity', IB File No 258, 1923.
72. 'Search of *Hooghly Vidyamandir*', IB File No 244/23, 1923.
73. *Ibid.*
74. *Ibid.*
75. *Ibid.*
76. 'Question of Control of *Akhras*', IB File No 875/30.
77. *Ibid.*
78. *Ibid.*
79. *Forward*, 1926.
80. '*Bideshi Bastra Barjan*', AICC File.
81. 'Notes on the *Hindusthani Seva Dal*', IB File No 583/27, Sl No 45, 1927.
82. *Ibid.*
83. 'Fortnightly Report on the Political Situation, 1924', Freedom Movement Papers, 32.
84. *Sansad Bangali Charitabhidhan, pratham khanda, Sahitya Sansad, (kalikata 1988).*
85. 'Programme of the Bengal's Worker' and Peasants' Party', Meerut Conspiracy Case Papers.
86. *Ibid.*
87. 'Fortnightly Report on the Political Situation in Bengal, 1928'.
88. *Ibid.*
89. *Forward*, 1928.
90. *Forward*, 13 March 1928.
91. *Ibid.*
92. 'Programme of the Bengal's Worker and Peasants' Party', Meerut Conspiracy Case Papers.
93. *Ibid.*

94. *Forward*, 1928.
95. *Ibid.*
96. 'Communal Tension', Home Poll Conf File No 117/27.
97. 'Agitation against the Management of the Atia Forest', Home Poll Conf File No 482/28.

Chapter 5

1. 'Fortnightly Report of the Political Situation in Bengal, 1930'.
2. *Ibid.*
3. 'Civil Disobedience in Dacca', IB File No 105 N/30.
4. 'Bengal Satyagraha', AICC Papers File No G 86.
5. 'Programme of Work at Satyagraha Centres in the District of Midnapore', Home Poll Conf File No 436/30.
6. *Ibid.*
7. *Ibid.*
8. 'Civil Disobedience in Bogra', IB File No 105s/30.
9. *Ibid.*
10. *Liberty*, April 1930.
11. 'Tippera Civil Disobedience', IB File No 105 B 30; *Liberty*, 9 April 1930.
12. *Ibid.*
13. The Dictator was authorized to lead the movement in his locality and take all decisions regarding the organization of the movement.
14. *Ibid.*
15. *Ibid.*
16. 'Notes on Organization in Noakhali', IB File No 592/30.
17. *Liberty*, 1930.
18. *Liberty*, April 1930.
19. 'Civil disobedience movement in Birbhum', IB File No 105T–30.
20. 'Activities of the Tippera District Congress Committee', IB File No 245, 1931.
21. *Ibid.*
22. 'Bengal Satyagraha', AICC Papers File No G 86.
23. 'Civil Disobedience in Twenty-Four Parganas', IB File No 105–A–30.
24. Sanyal, Hitesh Ranjan, 1994, *Swarajer Pathe*, Calcutta.
25. 'All Bengal Volunteer Activities', IB File No 686/31.
26. *Ibid.*
27. *Ibid.*
28. 'Tippera Civil Disobedience', IB File No 105B/30.
29. 'Civil Disobedience in Bogra', IB File No 105s/30.
30. *Liberty*, 14 April 1930.
31. 'Civil Disobedience in Dacca', IB File No 105/N.
32. *Ibid.*
33. 'Fortnightly Reports', GOI Home Poll 18–5, 1930.
34. 'Civil Disobedience in Bogra', *op. cit.*
35. *Ibid.*
36. 'Fortnightly Report on the Political Situation in Bengal, 1931'.
37. 'Fortnightly Report on the Political Situation in Bengal, 1930'.
38. 'Extract from the Confidential Report on the Political Situation at Tamluk, District Midnapur', Home Poll Conf File No 771/30.

39. *Ibid*.
40. *Ibid*.
41. *Ibid*.
42. *Ibid*.
43. 'Bengal Satyagraha', AICC Papers, File No G 86.
44. *Ibid*.
45. 'Fortnightly Report on the Political Situation in Bengal, 1930'.
46. *Ibid*.
47. *Ibid*.
48. *Ibid*.
49. The *Statesman*, October 1930.
50. 'Report on the Native Newspapers, November 1930'.
51. *Liberty*, 1930.
52. *Ibid*.
53. RNP 1930.
54. *Ibid*.
55. *Ibid*.
56. *Ibid*.
57. Sanyal, *Swarajer Pathe, op. cit*.
58. 'Civil Disobedience in Twenty Four Parganas', IB File No 215/30.
59. *Liberty*, April 1930.
60. 'Disobedience at Noakhali in Connection With Manufacture of Salt', IB File No 213, 1930.
61. 'Weekly Progress Report of Satyagraha Movements from the Provinces', AICC Papers, File No G 80.
62. *Liberty*, April 1930.
63. 'Bengal Satyagrahas', AICC Papers, File No G 86, 1930.
64. *Ibid*.
65. 'Extract from the Confidential Report on Political Situation at Tamluk, District Midnapur', *op. cit*.
66. *Ibid*.
67. 'Tamluk', AICC Papers, File No G 86, 1930.
68. 'Programme of Work at the Satyagraha Centres in the District of Bengal', Home Poll Conf File No 436/30.
69. *Ibid*.
70. 'Civil Disobedience Reports in Bengal', Home Poll Conf File 248/30.
71. *Ibid*.
72. *Ibid*.
73. *Ibid*.
74. Tanika Sarkar, *Bengal 1928–34, op. cit*.
75. *Ibid*.
76. *Ibid*.
77. 'Civil Disobedience in Twenty Four Parganas', IB File No 215/30.
78. *Ibid*.
79. *Liberty*, April 1930.
80. 'Report of Civil Disobedience in Bengal', Home Poll Conf File No 248/30.
81. *Ibid*.
82. *Ibid*.
83. 'Civil Disobedience in Twenty Four Parganas', IB File No 215/30.
84. 'Fortnightly Report on the Political Situation in Bengal, 1930'.
85. *Liberty*, April 1930.
86. *Liberty*, July 1930.

87. *Liberty*, May 1930.
88. *Liberty*, 31 October 1930.
89. 'Civil Disobedience in Jalpaiguri', IB File No 105R/30, 1930.
90. *Liberty*, September 1931.
91. *Ibid.*
92. *Ibid.*
93. 'Bengal Satyagrahas', AICC Papers, File No G 86, 1930.
94. *Liberty*, 10 September 1931.
95. Confidential Letter No F/17 dated Calcutta 5 September 1932, from the Imperial Chemical Industries (India) Ltd to the Bengal Chamber Of Commerce. NAI.
96. 'Fortnightly Report of the Political Situation in Bengal, 1931'.
97. 'Civil Disobedience in Twenty Four Parganas', IB File No 215/30.
98. 'Civil Disobedience in Bengal', Home Poll File No 5/77/32.
99. *Ibid.*
100. *Ibid.*
101. *Ibid.*
102. Arnold, David, 'Famine In Peasant Action', in Guha, Ranajit (ed.), 1984, *Subaltern Studies III*, Delhi.
103. 'Fortnightly Report on the Political Situation in Bengal, 1931; Sanyal, *Swarajer Pathe, op. cit.*
104. Majumdar, R C, 1962–63, *History Of the Freedom Movement*, Calcutta.
105. 'Report on the Land Revenue Administration of the Presidency of Bengal for the Year 1931–32', GOB File No 11–R–40, 1932.
106. *Ananda Bazar Patrika*, 1931.
107. *Ibid.*
108. 'Report on the Land Revenue Administration of the Presidency of Bengal for the Year 1931–32', *op. cit.*
109. 'Report of Satyagraha in Bengal', AICC Papers, File No 4, 1932.
110. 'Fortnightly Report on the Political Situation in Bengal 1933', Home Poll Conf File No 14/33.
111. 'Fortnightly Report on the Political Situation in Bengal, 1932'.
112. *Ibid.*
113. *Ibid.*
114. 'Fortnightly Report on the Political Situation in Bengal, 1933'.
115. *Liberty*, 1930.
116. *Ibid.*
117. 'Bengal Satyagraha', AICC Papers, File No G 86.
118. *Ibid.*
119. AICC Papers G–120, 1931.
120. *Ibid.*
121. *Liberty*, 1930.
122. *Sansad Bangali Charitrabhidhan, op. cit.*
123. *Ibid.*
124. 'Fortnightly Report on the Political Situation in Bengal, 1931'.
125. *Liberty*, August 1930.
126. *Liberty*, 1 August 1930.
127. 'Reports from the Provinces', AICC Papers, File No 1, 1932.
128. 'Civil Disobedience in Dacca', IB File No 105/30.
129. *Laban Satyagraha*, cited in Sarkar, *Bengal 1928–1934, op. cit.*
130. Sarkar, *Bengal 1928–34, op. cit.*
131. Sanyal, *Swarajer Pathe, op. cit.*

132. 'Civil Disobedience Movement: Treatment of Women', Home Poll Conf File No 599, SI No 1–14.
133. *The Musalman*, April 1930.
134. *Ibid*.
135. *Ibid*.
136. 'Notes on Organization in Noakhali', IB File No 592/30.
137. 'Fortnightly Report on the Political Situation in Bengal, 1930'.
138. 'Civil Disobedience in Bogra', IB File No 105/30.
139. *Ibid*.
140. *Ibid*.
141. 'Fortnightly Report on the Political Situation in Bengal, 1930'.
142. 'Fortnightly Report on the Political Situation in Bengal, 1931'.
143. *Ibid*.
144. GOI File No Home Poll 39/11/33, cited in Sarkar, *Bengal 1928–34*, *op. cit.*
145. 'Jute Mill Strikes', Home Poll Conf File, 1929.
146. IB File No 187, 1940.
147. Sarkar, *Bengal 1928–1934*, *op. cit.*
148. *Ibid*.
149. *Ibid*.

Chapter 6

1. Roy, B C, 'M S Aney to B C Roy', Dr B C Roy Papers, NMML Library, Delhi.
2. According to the Government of India Act 1935 (Provisions as to Franchise, Sixth Schedule, Part IV, Bengal), the following were the main qualifications for inclusion in the electoral roll for the 1937 elections:
   a) Qualifications dependent on taxation: 'In respect of the previous year municipal or cantonment taxes or fees of not less than eight annas or road or public work cesses under the Cess Act, 1880, of not less than eight annas or Chaukidari tax under the Village Chaukidari Act, 1870, of not less than six annas or Union rate under the Bengal Village Self Government Act, 1919, of not less than six annas.'
   b) Qualifications dependent on property: 'A person shall also be qualified to be included in the Electoral Roll of any territorial constituency if at any time during the previous financial or Bengali year he has occupied by virtue of his employment a house in the province, the annual valuation (annual rental of the house) of which is not less than forty-two rupees.'
   c) Educational qualifications: 'A person shall also be qualified to be included in the electoral roll for any territorial constituency if he is proved in the prescribed manner to have passed the matriculation examination of any prescribed University or an examination prescribed as at least equivalent to any such examination.'
   d) Qualifications by reason of services in His Majesty's forces.
3. 'Fortnightly Report on the Political Situation in Bengal, 1936'. Home Poll Conf.
4. *Ibid*.
5. De, Jatindra Nath, 'History of the Krishak Praja Party of Bengal 1929–1947: A Study of Change in Class and Intercommunity Relations in the Agrarian Sector of Bengal' (PhD Thesis, University of Delhi, October 1977).
6. *Ibid*.

7. *Ibid.*
8. 'Fortnightly Report on the Political Situation in Bengal 1937', Home Poll Conf File No 10/37.
9. 'Results of Elections to the Provincial Legislatures', Home Poll File No R 3E–27 (1), Election and Constitution Branch.
10. *Ibid.*
11. *Ibid.*
12. *Ibid.*
13. Chatterjee, Joya, 1995, *Bengal Divided Hindu Communalism and Partition 1932–1947*, New Delhi.
14. Bose, Sugata, 1986, *Agrarian Bengal Economy, Social Structure and Politics 1919–1947* Cambridge; Chatterjee, Partha, 1984, *Bengal, The Land Question 1920–1947*, Calcutta.
15. Chatterjee, *Bengal Divided, op. cit.*
16. *Ibid.*
17. Unemployment among the educated Hindus increased significantly in the post 1937 period, largely as a result of the Muslim League ministry's rigid enforcement of the communal ratio in public offices, cited in Das, Suranjan, 1991, *Communal Riots in Bengal 1905–1947*, New Delhi.
18. 'A Brief Summary of the Political Condition in Bengal 1938', Home Poll Conf.
19. 'Report of the Constitution Committee', AICC Papers, G 28, 32, 35 and 36, 1937.
20. *Ibid.*
21. *Ibid.*
22. *Ibid.*
23. 'Fortnightly Reports on the Political Situation in Bengal, 1936', *op. cit.*
24. 'Fortnightly Reports on the Political Situation in Bengal', Home Poll Conf File No 10/37.
25. 'Krishak Samitis at Rajsahi, Howrah', Home Poll Conf File No 228/38.
26. *Ibid.*
27. 'Reports regarding Krishak Samitis and No Rent', Home Poll Conf File No 264/38.
28. *Ibid.*
29. *Ibid.*
30. *Ibid.*
31. Chatterjee, *Bengal Divided, op. cit.*
32. 'Fortnightly Report on the Political Situation in Bengal, 1938'.
33. Chatterjee, *Bengal Divided, op. cit.*
34. 'Fortnightly Report on the Political Situation in Bengal, 1938', *op. cit.*
35. 'Report of the Constitution Committees', AICC Papers.
36. Chatterjee, *Bengal Divided, op. cit.*
37. 'Fortnightly Report on the Political Situation in Bengal, 1938', *op. cit.*
38. *Ibid.*
39. *Ibid.*
40. 'Report Of the Constitution Committee', AICC Papers, File No G 28, 32, 35 and 36, 1937.
41. AICC Papers, File No G 54, 1939.
42. Tripathi, Amales, 1397, *Swadhinata Andolane Bharater Jatiya Congress 1885–1947*, Calcutta.
43. *Ibid.*
44. 'Inspection Report of Bengal PCC', AICC Papers, File No G 28, 1940.
45. Mitra, N N, Indian Annual Register, 1939.
46. 'Inspection Report of Bengal PCC', AICC Papers, File No G 28, 1940.
47. *Ibid.*

48. 'Removal Of the Congress Committees', AICC File:
    Chittagong: Barada Prasad Nandy (president)
    Noakhali: Haran Chandra Ghosh Choudhury
    Tippera: Dr Nripendra Nath Bose (secretary)
    Sylhet: Prabodhananda Kar (secretary)
    Cachar: Achintya Kumar Bhattacharya (secretary)
    Dacca: Birendra Mohan Poddar (secretary)
    Mymensingh: Benode Chandra Chakrabarty (secretary)
    Faridpur: Durga Shankar Bose (secretary)
    Backarganj: Nirmal Chandra Ghose (secretary)
    Murshidabad: Shyamapada Bhattacharjee.
    Nadia: Amiya Kumar Roy (secretary)
    Jessore: Bijay Chandra Roy (secretary)
    Khulna: Jnanendra Nath Bhowmick
    24 Parganas: Prabhas Chandra Roy (secretary)
    Rajsahi: Saradindu Chakrabarty
    Pabna: Amulya Lahiri (secretary)
    Bogra: Anil Banerjee (secretary)
    Rangpur: Mani Krishna Sen (secretary)
    Jalpaiguri: Aghore Nath Sarkar
    Darjeeling: R P Singh
    Dinajpur: Jamini Kanta Goswami (secretary)
    Malda: Satish Chandra Agarwal
    Burdwan DCC: Sib Shankar Chaudhury (secretary)
    Birbhum: Lal Behari Singh (secretary)
    Bankura: Sushil Chandra Palit (secretary)
    Midnapur: Charu Chandra Mahanty (secretary)
    Hooghly: Atulya Ghosh
    Howrah: Arun Kumar Banerjee
    North Calcutta DCC: Sudhir Kumar Ghosh
    Barabazzar DCC: Satya Narain Mishra
    South Calcutta DCC: Bina Das
    Central Calcutta: Narendra Mohan Sen
49. Bose, Sisir Kumar and Bose, Sugata, 1995, *Congress President: Speeches, Articles and Letters, January 1938–May 1939, Subhas Chandra Bose*, Delhi.
50. *Ibid.*
51. *Ibid.*
52. *Ibid.*

Conclusion

1. Pandey, Gyan, 1978, *The Ascendancy of the Congress in UP, 1926–1934*, Delhi; Damodaran, Vinita, 1993, *Broken Promises: Popular Protest, Indian Nationalism and the Congress Party in Bihar 1935–1946*.

Index